Andrew Marvell Revisited

Twayne's English Authors Series

Arthur Kinney, Editor

University of Massachusetts, Amherst

TEAS 531

ANDREW MARVELL. PORTRAIT BY AN UNKNOWN ARTIST.
By courtesy of the National Portrait Gallery, London.

Andrew Marvell Revisited

Thomas Wheeler

University of Tennessee

Twayne Publishers
An Imprint of Simon & Schuster Macmillan
New York

Prentice Hall International
London • Mexico City • New Delhi • Singapore • Sydney • Toronto

Twayne's English Author Series No. 531

Andrew Marvell Revisited
Thomas Wheeler

Twayne Publishers
An Imprint of Simon & Schuster Macmillan
1633 Broadway
New York, New York 10019

Library of Congress Cataloging-in-Publication Data

Wheeler, Thomas, 1926–
    Andrew Marvell revisited / Thomas Wheeler.
        p.   cm. — (Twayne's English authors series ; TEAS 531)
    Includes bibliographical references (p.) and index.
    ISBN 0-8057-7033-X (cloth)
    1. Marvell, Andrew, 1621–1678—Criticism and interpretation.
    I. Title.   II. Series.
    PR3546.W4   1996
    821'.4—dc20   96-36040
                                                                CIP

The paper used in this publication meets the minimum requirements of American National Standard for Information Sciences—Permanence of Paper for Printed Library Materials. ANSI Z39.48-1984. ∞ ™

10 9 8 7 6 5 4 3 2 1

Printed in the United States of America

Contents

Preface

The twentieth century has seen two Marvell tercentenaries: in 1921, that of his birth, and in 1978, that of his death. In 1921 he was still primarily the nature poet and the member of Parliament for Hull, which staged a rather quaint civic celebration featuring tramcars decorated with historic designs and a lament that his political career deprived English literature of a great poet. But in that year T. S. Eliot published an essay that led to an enormous change in the way the world thought of Andrew Marvell. For Eliot, Marvell represented a European culture that flourished in England for only a few decades during the sixteenth and seventeenth centuries, a complex culture that allowed a fusion of seriousness and levity, a sophisticated wit, "something precious and needed and apparently extinct." By the tercentenary in 1978 Marvell was the subject of an academic industry that had produced dozens of books and hundreds of scholarly articles in an attempt to recover that vanished culture. For the most part, these studies took themselves and Marvell's writing quite seriously. As Muriel Bradbrook remarked in 1979, "the notion of wit disappeared under a load of learning."

Learning served the worthy purpose of placing Andrew Marvell in the context of his time. But in doing so, it tended to miss the levity and overemphasize the seriousness that Eliot found fused in Marvell's work and to suppose that Marvell's speakers *were* Andrew Marvell, that they enunciated his beliefs and reflected his life. Most unfortunately, in emphasizing the intellectual and cultural background of Marvell's writing, it overlooked the wonderfully polished surface of his lyrics. Chapters two through six of this volume encourage a reading of Marvell's verse that responds to his evident joy in creating speakers and situations that allow a free play of his wit. Rather than developing a portrait of the "real" Andrew Marvell, these chapters take each work as the product of a mind that reveled in the possibilities of composition; they assume that the speakers are fictitious, as are the situations in which they find themselves.

Marvell himself encourages such an approach. No doubt he was a learned man, but his speakers wear their learning lightly, and they are usually more interesting than their ideas. They may be serious, but the works in which they speak are hardly ever sober. A good reading of "The Garden" must see how much sheer fun it offers simply by allowing its speaker to make outrageous assertions. To take "A Dialogue between the Soul and Body" as a sober meditation on the human predicament is to miss the pleasure offered by the comic exchanges between the two speakers. The element of play is central to Marvell's work, and while play can be serious, it cannot be sober. It celebrates freedom and a release from limitations.

Marvell's famous wit is the most obvious aspect of his playfulness. It expresses the mind's power to shape or reshape the world, to play games with reality and the reader's expectations. Nearly everything that Marvell wrote is touched by his wit. "The Coronet," which seems to be a straightforward statement of the Christian doctrine of mankind's sinful nature, is complicated by the fact that even as he declares that his art debases heaven's diadem, the speaker affirms his pride in his art and gives us an example of his skill in weaving poetic lines. Logically, he ought not to be writing a poem at all. So in the "Epitaph Upon—" the speaker first declares that the only way to honor the lady is to utter her name, then steadfastly refuses to name her. Marvell's speakers may give themselves over to a simple view of the world, but the work in which they speak does not. Each poem is a game. To enjoy it, the reader must be prepared to discover and to play by its rules.

To read Marvell's works this way is an exhilarating experience. There is something dispiriting about the search for consistency in a writer whose mind is so original and entertaining. Even in *The Rehearsal Transpros'd*, when he is most seriously engaged in controversy, he allows his speaker to rail at his opponent for railing and imagines conversations in which the speaker actually argues on behalf of his opponent. In his best-known poem, "To his Coy Mistress," his speaker develops an obviously fallacious argument in lines of compelling passion. If, as so many have noted, Marvell is elusive, the best response is not to find him out but to find out and admire the skill with which he hides himself while giving us a variety of engaging speakers.

But there *was* an Andrew Marvell, a seventeenth-century Englishman who lived in a real world. While the speakers of his poems may be fictitious, he was not. The people and events he satirized, the opponents he attacked in his prose works, belonged to that real world. These works, satirical and political, are the subjects of chapters seven and eight. The speakers show the same kind of wit that characterizes everything Marvell wrote, but the playfulness of the lyrics gives way to the need for a serious treatment of religious freedom and political corruption.

Marvell was only one of many seventeenth-century English writers. He wrote the kind of verse and prose that seventeenth-century readers expected. His individuality stands out best against that background. Scholars have been able to place Marvell in relation to his audience, his fellow writers, and the traditions of poetry from the ancients to the Renaissance. I have used the notes to refer to scholarship of this sort, especially when it seemed to me to help the reader to appreciate Marvell's originality or to provide a different way of looking at his work. In addition, I have devoted a good part of the second chapter to a study of Marvell's skill in handling the verse form which he and many other seventeenth-century poets favored: the couplet.

In the three centuries since his death, Marvell's reputation has undergone some striking changes. Perhaps there is nothing more revealing about a writer's achievement than the contrasts between the ways in which he has been appreciated over the years. Chapter Nine, devoted to a survey of Marvell's reputation, records these changes and attempts to put modern responses to his works in perspective.

Many learned and perceptive accounts of Marvell's writings have been published since 1921. My aim has been to simplify for the benefit of readers who want to get at the essence of Marvell's accomplishment, to make available to them the same kind of pleasure that I found in reading Marvell: an encounter with a writer whose works liberate the reader's imagination and are more likely to offer questions than answers, all in an atmosphere of gaiety and civility.

I have been aided in this work by my colleagues Norman Sanders and Allan Carroll. Financial assistance and released time were provided by the John C. Hodges Better English Fund. Most of all, I was encouraged and assisted by my wife, Sarah.

Chronology

1656   At Saumur with Dutton in 1656 from January to
        August.

1657   Appointed an assistant to John Thurloe, Secretary of
        State, at £200 per annum. Writes two songs for the
        wedding of Cromwell's daughter.

1658   Composes "A Poem upon the Death of O. C.," first
        published in full in 1776.

1659   Elected a member of Parliament for Hull; reelected in
        1660 and 1661; served until his death.

1660   Acts vigorously in Parliament to defend Milton from
        suffering as a regicide (according to Milton's nephew
        Edward Phillips).

1663–1665   Travels to Holland and later to Russia, Sweden, and
            Denmark as secretary to the Earl of Carlisle's embassy.

1667   Composes "The last Instructions to a Painter."

1672–1673   Publishes, anonymously, *The Rehearsal Transpros'd* and,
            under his own name, *The Rehearsal Transpros'd: The Second Part*, in favor of toleration for Nonconformists.

1674   Composes commendatory verses for the second edition
        of *Paradise Lost*.

1676   Publishes anonymously another prose satire, *Mr.
        Smirke; Or, The Divine in Mode.*

1677   Publishes anonymously *An Account of the Growth of Popery, and Arbitrary Government in England.*

1678   Publishes anonymously *Remarks upon a late Disingenuous
        Discourse*. On 16 August dies of a fever in London, and
        on 18 August is buried in the Church of St. Giles-in-
        the-Fields.

1681 (or at the end of 1680)

        His *Miscellaneous Poems*, containing all his lyric poetry,
        published by Mary Palmer, who claimed to be his
        widow.

Chapter One
Marvell's Life

It would be difficult to write a substantial biography of Andrew Marvell. The reliable sources of information about him are scarce. His own recollections of his life as a young man provide only a few details. The brief biographical sketches written by his contemporaries leave most of his life unaccounted for, while the biographies of the following century introduce material that cannot be relied upon. Some very simple questions about him are impossible to answer. When did he write the verse for which he is famous today? How did he earn a living? Was he ever in love? Did he ever marry? What did his contemporaries think of him? Not until the last two decades of his life is it possible to find a plentiful supply of facts. But by that time he had probably written all the compositions for which he is known today. And he was so deeply embroiled in partisan politics that one must be cautious about accepting the truth of any statements made by his enemies or his friends.

For more than a century after his death, he had a well-defined public reputation as a defender of English liberty and an incorruptible patriot. His career as a member of Parliament and a writer of controversial pamphlets in prose helped to establish that reputation. But for anyone familiar with his lyric verse, his status as the ardent champion of political liberty is so at odds with the retiring lover of privacy that it creates a special problem: can both versions of Andrew Marvell be true?

Very little is known of Marvell's early years. He was born on 31 March 1621 at Winestead rectory in Holderness, Yorkshire, the third child of Andrew Marvell and Anne Pease. In 1624 his father became Master of the Charterhouse in Hull and lecturer at Holy Trinity Church. It is likely that the young Andrew attended Hull Grammar School. He entered Trinity College, Cambridge, in 1633. Marvell's matriculation in his thirteenth year was unusual but not unprecedented. Evidently his grammar school education had already given him a command of Latin and Greek (John Aubrey, in his brief life of Marvell, noted that "[f]or Latin verses there was no man could come into competition with him"). In 1637 he contributed verses in Latin and Greek to a volume celebrating the birth of Princess Anne.

In 1639 Marvell took his B.A. and began his studies for an M.A. He may have intended to become a clergyman.[1] The death of his mother the preceding year apparently had no effect on his academic career. But the death of his father in January 1641 ended his connection with Cambridge and began a period of 10 years during which his whereabouts and his activities can only be conjectured. Judging by his satirical poem "Fleckno, an English Priest at Rome," he encountered Richard Flecknoe in Rome in 1645 or 1646 (Flecknoe is known to have been in Rome in those years). But there is no indication of what Marvell was doing there. Since he later tutored the daughter of Thomas Fairfax and the ward of Oliver Cromwell, it would be logical to suppose that he was serving in the same capacity, perhaps escorting a recent graduate on the Grand Tour. Several years later, John Milton noted that Marvell had spent four years in Holland, France, Italy, and Spain. But that still leaves six years unaccounted for, and it does not make clear what Marvell was doing on the Continent. He must have been in England in 1647, for his signature appears on a deed drawn up in that year. His contribution to Richard Lovelace's volume of poems, *Lucasta*, and his poem on the death of Lord Hastings make it likely that he was in England in 1649. "An Horatian Ode upon Cromwel's Return from Ireland" must have been composed in 1650. Finally, in 1650 or 1651, Marvell took up residence at Nun Appleton as tutor to Mary Fairfax.

During this ten-year period England went through an enormous upheaval—a civil war that changed a centuries-old monarchy into a republic, destroyed the episcopal organization of the state church, and released a torrent of radical thought and opinion. Wherever Marvell was while his country was being turned upside down, his poetry is scarcely touched by the revolution. Among the poems that are indisputably his, only "An Horatian Ode" comments directly on events that "ruin[ed] the great work of Time." In view of his willingness to use his verse to make political statements in the 1650s and 1660s, one might guess that Marvell was simply out of touch with what was happening in England while he was abroad.

It is, therefore, all the more striking that at the end of this decade in the shadows, Marvell should emerge as an employee of one of the most famous men in England. Thomas Fairfax had been commander in chief of the Parliamentary armies from 1645 until his retirement in 1650. He relinquished his command because he opposed a projected invasion of Scotland, the same campaign that Marvell anticipated enthusiastically in his "Horatian Ode." It is not known who recommended Marvell to the general. The position of tutor to the general's daughter was certainly not an exalted one, but it made Marvell a part of the household of a powerful and influential man. Either there was a personal connection of which nothing is now known or Marvell had distinguished himself in some way, perhaps as a tutor for the child of an important person. At any rate, none of the known facts of Marvell's life point toward his becoming Mary Fairfax's tutor "in the languages," as John Milton phrased it.

Fairfax had a choice of four houses, all in Yorkshire. Certainly he must have resided for some time at Nun Appleton, the subject of Marvell's longest lyric. Appleton House, Denton, and Billborow were all located in the countryside. In his poems that celebrate these houses, Marvell concentrates on the natural surroundings, not the buildings. To a great extent his nineteenth-century reputation as a poet of nature depends on these poems. Scholars have made the reasonable assumption that they were composed during the two years he spent as Mary Fairfax's tutor. But the further assumption—that all of the lyrics having to do with nature, with gardens, and with love are the products of Marvell's two years in the country—is questionable. The poem about Flecknoe, for example, emphasizes Flecknoe's desire to inflict his miserable verse upon the speaker. Although much of the poem is fictitious, it seems likely that Flecknoe wanted the opinion of someone he recognized as a fellow poet. Many of Marvell's lyrics may have been written in the 1640s. "An Horatian Ode," as polished and sophisticated as any of his poems, must have been composed before he took up residence with Fairfax.

If there were a reason to be concerned with Andrew Marvell other than his poems, the issue of when they were composed might not merit discussion. But the chief events in a poet's life *are* his or her poems, and it would be desirable to find in them some chronological progression, some sense of a developing mastery. One cannot suppose that a man who obviously loved verse and wrote it with enormous skill produced in a two-year period nearly all of the poems that now give readers so much pleasure and then simply stopped writing lyric poetry. The first stanzas of "The Garden," with their strong emphasis on a yearning for quiet and repose, are much more logically associated with Marvell's career in the House of Commons than with a peaceful sojourn in the country.[2] Unfortunately, the kind of discussion that might establish an order of composition would require far more space than is available here.[3] But it should be made clear that, among all the gaps in Marvell's life, the largest is the lack of connection between the events that can be narrated in a biography and the poems that make his life significant.

However satisfying or productive his tenure as tutor to Mary Fairfax may have been, by February 1653 Marvell was looking for other employment. In a letter to the President of the Council of State, John Milton recommended him for the position of Assistant Secretary for Foreign Tongues in the Commonwealth government. Marvell did not get the appointment, but by July 1653 he had become tutor to William Dutton, whose guardian was the most powerful man in England, Oliver Cromwell. How he got this post is not clear; his praise of Cromwell in "An Horatian Ode" may have weighed heavily in his favor. In 1654 he was residing with Dutton at Eton, and in 1656 he escorted Dutton to Saumur, a center of French Protestantism. Finally, in 1657, he was appointed Assistant Secretary for Foreign Tongues and so became a part of Cromwell's government.

Marvell's admiration of Cromwell seems to have been genuine. Other poets, among them Edmund Waller and John Dryden, wrote in praise of the Lord Protector and, shortly after his death, wrote in praise of the restored King Charles II. Judging by his "First Anniversary of the Government under O. C." (1655) and his "Poem upon the Death of O. C." (1658), Marvell was impressed by Cromwell's energy and authority, and was saddened by his death. He was one of those who walked beside Cromwell's coffin at his state funeral. In 1657 he wrote two songs for the wedding of Cromwell's daughter Mary, and he attributed Cromwell's death to sadness over the loss of his daughter Elizabeth. Probably he had some personal acquaintance with Cromwell and his family. Unlike many other poets, Marvell did not write a poem to celebrate the restoration of Charles II in 1660.

In 1659, while still serving as Assistant Secretary for Foreign Tongues, Marvell was elected to the House of Commons as one of the members for Hull. When the government of Richard Cromwell was ousted and Parliament dissolved, Marvell was elected to the new Parliament in 1660. With the restoration of Charles II, Marvell lost his secretaryship, although his connection with Cromwell's government did not put him in any danger. Finally, in January 1661, Charles's first Parliament included, as junior member for Hull, Andrew Marvell. This Cavalier Parliament was in session on and off until 1679, a year after Marvell's death. So, for the last two decades of his life, he held a responsible position at or near the center of English politics.

That being the case, it would be useful to know about Marvell's politics. Modern politics are largely a matter of political parties that have a history, a tradition, a party discipline. Though the word *party* in Marvell's time could refer to a body of partisans or a side in a dispute, it had no specifically political connotations. The names *Whig* and *Tory*, denoting political parties, came into use in 1689, 11 years after Marvell's death. During his time in Parliament there were sides in regard to particular issues, but they tended to be informal and not tightly organized. Despite the contemporary references to the court party and the country party, on any given issue a member of the House of Commons who had previously supported the King might vote against him. For over a century after his death Marvell was thought of as a Whig, but in his lifetime the word referred to a country bumpkin or a Scot who adhered to the Presbyterian form of church government.[4]

Still, it is possible to know something about Marvell's politics. As a member for Hull he wrote 294 letters to the mayors of Hull, the last one written within six weeks of his death, and 69 letters to Trinity House (the Hull Seaman's Guild). These make it clear that he took his duties seriously and was especially concerned with any development that might affect that city and its commerce. The letters are so completely devoted to Parliamentary business that they give few personal insights into the man who wrote them. But in their single-minded attention to the details of business and their concentration on day-to-day occurrences they do not in any way resemble the polished and elusive lyrics of the poet who celebrated quiet and repose.

And they are strangely colorless. On 10 May 1675 something like a brawl erupted in the House. Apparently feelings ran very high, and each member was required to stand and promise that he would not harbor any resentment after the House had adjourned. Marvell's letter of 11 May simply refers to "a misunderstanding." The debates in October 1666 over a revenue bill, which in "The last Instructions to a Painter" are vividly presented as a comic epic battle, are soberly reported in the letters. References to individuals are scarce. Arguments for and against proposed legislation are seldom mentioned, and even though Marvell frequently reports the numbers of votes for and against a particular bill, he scrupulously avoids any reference to the persons who spoke for either side. Nor does he disclose which side he voted on. His letters might well serve a historian who wanted to know what was being debated and decided in the House, but they give no clue as to who took part in the arguments.[5]

Neither do these letters give an indication of Marvell's opinions. The man who had written poems celebrating the greatness of Oliver Cromwell noted, without comment, the order to dig up Cromwell's body, to draw it on a sledge to Tyburn (the treatment given to a com-

mon criminal), to hang it there for some time, and then to bury it under
the gallows. But from other sources[6] it is clear that Marvell had opinions and was willing to voice them. In Milward's diary (September
1666 to May 1668) Marvell is mentioned six times. On 15 February
1668, "Mr. Marvell made a most sharp speech against some of the
Council, and especially hinted at the Lord Arlington as that he had got
£1000 and a barony" (185). Marvell's letter of 15 February to Mayor
Lambert says nothing of this. Again, according to Milward (225), Marvell spoke against renewing the act against conventicles (meeting places
of Protestant congregations not associated with the Anglican Church).
Although his letter of the next day to Mayor Lambert alludes to this
issue, he does not refer to his speech. According to Milton's nephew
Edward Phillips, one of Marvell's concerns in 1660 was to defend Milton from suffering penalties and imprisonment for supporting the
beheading of Charles I, but there is no mention of Milton in the letters
to Hull.

Fortunately Marvell also wrote other letters in which he was often
willing to declare his opinions. His letters to his nephew William Popple
are full of the kinds of detail lacking in the reports to Hull. In regard to
the brawl on 15 May 1675, Marvell writes, "both Parties grew so hot,
that all Order was lost; Men came running confusedly up to the Table,
grievously affronted one by another; every Man's Hand on his Hilt; qui-
eted tho' at last by the present Prudence of the Speaker; and every Man,
in his Place, was obliged to stand up, and engage his Honour, not to
resent any thing of that Day's Proceeding."[7] His first surviving letter to
Popple, dated 21 March 1670 (Margoliouth, 2:314), states quite memo-
rably his opinion of the act against conventicles: "the Quintessence of
arbitrary Malice." His opposition to the King's policies is clearly implied
by the following:

> It is also my Opinion that the King was never since his coming in, nay,
> all Things considered, no King since the Conquest, so absolutely power-
> ful at Home, as he is at present. Nor any Parliament, or Places, so cer-
> tainly and constantly supplyed with Men of the same Temper. In such a
> Conjuncture, dear *Will*, what Probability is there of my doing any Thing
> to the Purpose? (Margoliouth, 2:315)

His next letter, dated 14 April 1670, is just as frank:

> In this Session the Lords sent down to Us a Proviso for the King, that
> would have restored Him to all civil or ecclesiastical Prerogatives which

his Ancestors had enjoyed at any Time since the Conquest. There was never so compendious a Piece of absolute universal Tyranny. (Margoliouth, 2:317)

Sometimes his opinion is presented with quiet irony: "The *Prince of Orange* here is made much of. The King owes Him a great deal of Mony" (Margoliouth, 2:318). He sums up the contemporary state of affairs by observing, "The Court is at the highest Pitch of Want and Luxury, and the People full of Discontent" (Margoliouth, 2:322) and "never had poor Nation so many complicated, mortal, incurable, Diseases" (Margoliouth, 2:323). There is little to be hoped of Parliament: "We are all venal Cowards, except some few" (Margoliouth, 2:317).

These letters to his nephew show exactly what one might deduce from a reading of Marvell's verse satires: that he strongly distrusted the King and the court. That is, they indicate his *attitude* toward Charles II. But they do not provide the grounds for determining Marvell's political philosophy. For example, did Marvell distrust monarchy? Cromwell had greater power than Charles, but Marvell apparently trusted and admired the Lord Protector, even though he never found a Parliament he could work with. Was Marvell a republican—that is, a believer in a form of government that vested supreme power in a representative body like Parliament? His criticisms of the House of Lords and of venal members of Commons suggest that he was not ideologically committed to a republic. Undoubtedly he had strong feelings about particular political issues, but these do not constitute a political philosophy.

Recently scholars have taken a strong interest in Marvell's politics and have attempted to interpret his lyric poems in the light of his political beliefs. The difficulty they face is twofold. First, it is hard to know what his beliefs were. When Marvell and six other members, according to Milward (86), spoke against a vote of thanks to the King for dismissing Clarendon as Lord Chancellor, it is not to be inferred that these members represented a party position. In fact, Marvell's attitude toward Clarendon in "The last Instructions" is hostile. Other evidence (Milward, 328) suggests that Marvell's speech reflected not his attitude toward Clarendon but his disgust with the court, a feeling that is amply illustrated in "The last Instructions." The second difficulty arises from the fact that most of Marvell's lyrics cannot be dated with any confidence. Christopher Hill's attempt to read a political significance into individual poems illustrates both difficulties. He associates "The Garden" with "the years before [Marvell] plunged into public life."[8] But it is at least as likely that the poem reflects Marvell's *experience* of public life. Hill's frequent use of the term *Puritan* begs the question of Marvell's religious loyalties. His conclusion that Marvell's poems reflect "the problems of an individual in an age of revolutionary change" (363) rests on highly selective quotations from poems (like "Upon Appleton House") that, when read entire, are far more interesting than Hill's formula suggests.[9] Just as biographers are tempted to deduce Marvell's personality from his lyrics, some scholars read his lyrics as political statements.

While it is possible to know something about Marvell's politics, it is more difficult to ascertain his loyalties in regard to religion. He was, without any doubt, opposed to Roman Catholicism, as his *Account of the Growth of Popery, and Arbitrary Government in England* (1677) makes clear. His other prose treatises show a strong animosity toward the hierarchy of the Church of England and an equally strong sympathy for Nonconformists (persons who refused to accept the ceremonies and rituals of the Church of England). At no point in his life did he ever challenge the doctrines of that Church, but his opponents in almost all his controversial treatises were its spokesmen. He must have remained in communion with the Church of England, for he was buried in St. Giles-in-the-Fields, which would have been his parish church. His most authoritative modern biographer finds it impossible to define Marvell's religious beliefs,[10] and the editors of a recent edition of his verse conclude that "the exact nature of his own religion is characteristically ambiguous and obscure."[11]

Although the Cavalier Parliament lasted from 1661 to 1679, it was frequently prorogued by the King, and when it was not in session Marvell received no pay. Since he was not, as far as is known, possessed of independent means, it is not surprising that he found other occupations. His 12 March 1663 letter to the mayor and alderman was posted from Holland. It does not make clear what he was doing there, but he apparently had not received permission to absent himself and got into some trouble for missing a Parliamentary session. His letter of 20 June 1663 asks permission to accompany the Earl of Carlisle as his secretary on a mission to Russia, Sweden, and Denmark that was supposed to take about a year. Marvell was reluctant, or wanted to appear reluctant, in regard to this journey. He writes that Carlisle had "used his power which ought to be very great with me to make me goe along with him" and notes, "It is no new thing for members of our house to be dispens'd with for the service of the King and the Nation in forain parts" (Margoliouth, 2:37, 38). This embassy kept Marvell out of England for nearly two years, during which time there were several sessions of Parliament. Without pressing the evidence too hard, it appears that he was not so dedicated to his Parliamentary duties as to pass up an opportunity to travel and perhaps to enjoy a regular income.

Because there are so many gaps in our knowledge of Marvell's life, scholars are tempted to fill them with conjectures.[12] One of these, not widely accepted, is that between 1674 and 1678 he was involved in some way with Peter Du Moulin's organization, working to supply the Dutch with information to counter the alliance between England and France.[13] Because this was necessarily a secret organization, the evidence is slight and not particularly convincing. Another conjecture has much more to commend it: that Marvell was at various times and in various ways employed in trade (Empson, 37–38, and Kenyon, in Brett, 8, 28). Hull was a trading city, and some of Marvell's in-laws and his nephew William Popple were merchants. His letters to the mayors of Hull frequently discuss the effect of proposed legislation on the commercial health of the city. In the present state of scholarship, however, these conjectures cannot be verified.

In 1672 Marvell issued the work he was best known for in his lifetime. *The Rehearsal Transpros'd*, published anonymously, was so well received and provoked so many replies that he composed a second part, which appeared in 1673 under his name. Both works argued the case for toleration of religious dissent, as did his *Mr. Smirke; Or, The Divine in Mode* (1676). *An Account of the Growth of Popery, and Arbitrary Government in England*, published anonymously in 1677, attempts to show that certain members of the government were conspiring against the liberties of Englishmen. Marvell's last treatise, *Remarks upon a late Disingenuous Discourse*, was published in April 1678. The subject of all these treatises is freedom, religious or political. Because of their topical nature and because their style is so unfamiliar to moderns, they are read today only by scholars, but *The Rehearsal Transpros'd* was still well known in the eighteenth century.

On 10 June 1678 Marvell wrote to William Popple about the publication of *The Growth of Popery, and Arbitrary Government*. With characteristic elusiveness and sarcastic wit (here justified by the fact that rewards had been offered for any information about the author or the printer) he refers to books that described "the Man being a Member of Parliament, Mr. *Marvell* to have been the Author; but if he had, surely he should not have escaped being questioned in Parliament, or some other Place" (Margoliouth, 2:357). On 6 July he wrote his final letter to the Corporation of Hull. The same month he visited Hull and, while returning to London, was seized by an attack of malaria and on 16 August 1678 died at his house in Great Russell Street.

It was the custom of poets in the seventeenth century to write tributes to the dead. Marvell himself wrote several such poems. But his own death passed without notice. His fame, such as it was, rested almost entirely on the two parts of *The Rehearsal Transpros'd*. Three years after his death, a small folio volume entitled *Miscellaneous Poems by Andrew Marvell* was published in London. The poems were preceded by a short statement, "To the Reader":

> These are to Certifie every Ingenious Reader, that all these Poems, as also the other things in this Book contained, are Printed according to the exact Copies of my late dear Husband, under his own Hand-Writing, being found since his Death among his other Papers, Witness my Hand this *15th* day of *October*, 1680.
>
> *Mary Marvell*

"Mary Marvell" was, or had been, Mary Palmer, Marvell's housekeeper. There is no evidence that Marvell ever married her or anyone else. She was involved in complicated litigation over money that had been deposited in Marvell's name by some of his friends from Hull who had gone bankrupt. Apparently she hoped to establish her right to the money by representing herself as Marvell's widow. By these somewhat sordid circumstances, the best part of one of the most original poets in English literature came to be preserved. Although it is fruitless to ask whether Marvell himself would have published these poems with these titles and in this order, it is well to remember that he had nothing to do with their publication.

The 1681 folio contains 37 poems in English and 15 in Latin. Three poems on Cromwell were set up and printed, then canceled (removed) from all but two copies. The standard modern edition (Margoliouth's), based on the 1681 folio, also includes 14 satires that have been attributed to Marvell.[14] In 1945 the *Bodleian Library Record* announced that the library had acquired a manuscript (MS. Eng. poet. d. 49), referred to as the Popple manuscript because of its presumed connection with Marvell's nephew William Popple. It contains a copy of the poems in the 1681 folio (with deletions and corrections), the Cromwell poems that had been canceled, and a number of satirical verses. It is apparently the "manuscript volume of poems" that Edward Thompson, in the preface to his edition of 1776, claimed to have received from Marvell's grand-nephew.[15]

The poems for which Marvell is famous today present very few textual problems. The satirical verses, however, have become a battleground. As Annabel Patterson points out, "Andrew Marvell" is a cultural construct, a product of the critics' expectations and their concept of what a poet should be and do.[16] For a large part of the twentieth century, Marvell was the urbane, elusive, sophisticated writer of polished lyric verse. The satires—combative, partisan, nasty—could not be accommodated to the image of the uncommitted lyricist. Thus there was a natural desire to overlook them. This inclination was reinforced by the fact that it was, and probably always will be, impossible to know exactly which satires were actually written by Marvell. The latest edition of Marvell's verse (Kermode and Walker, 1990) includes, under the heading "Satires of the Reign of Charles 2," only "The last Instructions to a Painter," "Clarindon's House-Warming," and "The Loyall Scot." Remarkably, there has been no complete edition of Marvell's prose works since Alexander B. Grosart's of 1872–1875.

There are several portrait images of Marvell, but they tell nothing of what sort of person he was.[17] The wit and imagination that animate his poetry may not have been evident in his conversation. John Aubrey provides the only contemporary description. As is usual with Aubrey, everything he says is both gossipy and fascinating:

> He was of a middling stature, pretty strong sett, roundish faced, cherry cheek't, hazell eie, browne haire [the portraits confirm these details]. He was in his conversation very modest, and of very few words: and though he loved wine he would never drinke hard in company, and was wont to say that, *he would not play the good-fellow in any man's company in whose hands he would not trust his life.*
>
> He kept bottles of wine at his lodgeing, and many times he would drinke liberally by himselfe to refresh his spirits, and exalt his muse.[18]

Everything in Aubrey's first paragraph he could have learned from conversing with Marvell or his acquaintances. It all points to a prudent, guarded, even secretive personality. Perhaps the real Andrew Marvell was as elusive as the speakers of many of his poems are. But how could Aubrey know that Marvell drank by himself unless this taciturn person told him of it? It may be a mistake to put much faith in Aubrey's comments or to make them the basis for a construction of Marvell's personality.

There is evidence to support another view of Marvell's elusiveness. He may, in fact, have guarded his feelings so cautiously because they were dangerously powerful. In 1661 he reports to Mayor Richardson that "[t]he bonds of civility" between himself and the senior member for Hull have "unhappily snappd in pieces, and in such manner that I can not see how it is possible ever to knit them again" (Margoliouth, 2:27). During his journey with the Earl of Carlisle, he was reported to have become so exasperated with a wagon driver that he put a pistol to the man's head and nearly started a battle (Bradbrook and Thomas, 154). On at least two occasions he was in trouble in Parliament when he crossed the line of acceptable behavior. In 1662 he quarreled with Thomas Clifford in the House of Commons. The Speaker reported that Marvell had provoked the quarrel, and he was made to apologize to the whole House. In 1677 he got involved in some kind of physical altercation with Sir Philip Harcourt. The Speaker called it to the attention of the House. Marvell's "apology" was so insulting to the Speaker that he had to apologize again in more acceptable terms to avoid being sent to the Tower. At least a dozen members spoke in the debate over this contretemps.[19] Behind the mask of irony and wit, Marvell may have been hiding a combative anger that demanded rigid control.

Those who preserved Marvell's name in the following century thought of him as an incorruptible patriot, a champion of liberty. They either did not know or did not respond to the speakers of his lyrics. Marvell spoke through so many different masks and adopted so many different voices that it is hardly possible to determine which, if any, conveys the truth about him. His greatest achievement seems to have been to hide himself or, like Clora in "The Gallery," to appear in "[t]hese Pictures and a thousand more." His wit, the one trait to be found in all his poetry and most of his prose, baffles every attempt to isolate the "real" Andrew Marvell. But it also provides the best reason for reading and studying this elusive shadow.

Chapter Two
A Seventeenth-Century Poet

When Andrew Marvell was born, Shakespeare had been dead for five years. Among the poets of seventeenth-century England whose work is still widely read, only Henry Vaughan was his exact contemporary. John Milton was 13. Ben Jonson, chief speaker in one of Marvell's satiric poems, was over 50. Richard Lovelace, for whose volume *Lucasta* Marvell wrote a commendatory poem, was three years his senior, as was Abraham Cowley. The most popular poet of the mid–seventeenth century, John Cleveland, was eight. Five of the great poets of the English Renaissance died long before Marvell's birth—Sir Thomas Wyatt, Henry Howard Surrey, Christopher Marlowe, Edmund Spenser, and Sir Philip Sidney. The first editions of John Donne's poetry and George Herbert's *The Temple* were published when Marvell was 12 years old, Robert Herrick's *Hesperides* when he was 27.

Why are these figures significant? Because Marvell, like any other poet, wrote poetry as his age defined it. His own style, individual as it is, belongs in the mainstream of seventeenth-century poetry. His concepts of what poetry could do and the forms it could take depended on his awareness of what poetry had done and the forms it had taken. Although he found his own voice and his own particular themes, he does not stand out as a rebel against the traditions of English poetry. To understand and appreciate the accomplishments of Marvell's poetry, it is useful to look at English poetry as he encountered it.

To do so does not require a history of English verse. Nothing in Marvell's work suggests a debt to Old or Middle English poetry. Even in regard to the great poets of the sixteenth century, none of Marvell's poems are imitative or derivative. His engagement with English poetry has to be seen not as a direct imitation but as a choice among various possibilities.

Marvell did not often mention other English poets in his verse. In fact, almost all references cluster in a single poem—"Tom May's Death" (discussed in chapter seven). The chief speaker in the poem is the shade of Ben Jonson, who rejects the attempt by May to enter the poets' Elysium. Ben refers to "reverend Chaucer," to Spenser, and to "surviving

Davenant." Marvell also mentions Richard Lovelace in the poem he wrote for the publication in 1649 of Lovelace's *Lucasta*. In his dedicatory poem for the second edition of *Paradise Lost* (1674), he does not use Milton's name, although it does appear in the title. In this same poem there is also a coded reference to John Dryden. Nowhere in his verse does Marvell mention Shakespeare, Michael Drayton, Donne, Herbert, Herrick, or other accomplished seventeenth-century English poets.[1]

There is one other English poet who figures in Marvell's verse— Richard Flecknoe, whom John Dryden promoted to rule over the kingdom of dullness. One could argue that Marvell covered the field from the best to the worst of seventeenth-century poetry. He praised Lovelace and Milton, scorned Flecknoe and May. But Marvell could praise a writer without imitating him. In his treatment of Milton, he acknowledges the fact that his own poetic medium—rhyming couplets—is not the sublime verse that Milton created. He praises Lovelace in such general terms that anyone ignorant of Lovelace's poetry would not be able to guess what sort of verse Marvell admires. In short, the associations between Marvell's poetry and seventeenth-century poets cannot be determined from his references to them.

Perhaps the most convenient way to place Marvell in relation to the poetry of his time is to begin with the poem Marvell wrote for Lovelace's *Lucasta* (1649).[2]

To His Noble Friend Mr. Richard Lovelace, *upon his Poems*

Sir,
Our times are much degenerate from those
Which your sweet Muse which your fair Fortune chose,
And as complexions alter with the Climes,
Our wits have drawne th'infection of our times.
That candid Age no other way could tell   5
To be ingenious, but by speaking well.
Who best could prayse, had then the greatest prayse,
Twas more esteemd to give, then weare the Bayes:
Modest ambition studi'd only then,
To honour not her selfe, but worthy men.   10
These vertues now are banisht out of Towne,
Our Civill Wars have lost the Civicke crowne.

He highest builds, who with most Art destroys,
And against others Fame his owne employs.
I see the envious Caterpillar sit   15
On the faire blossome of each growing wit.
The Ayre's already tainted with the swarms
Of Insects which against you rise in arms.
Word-peckers, Paper-rats, Book-scorpions,
Of wit corrupted, the unfashion'd Sons.   20
The barbed Censurers begin to looke
Like the grim consistory on thy Booke;
And on each line cast a reforming eye,
Severer then the yong Presbytery.
Till when in vaine they have thee all perus'd,   25
You shall for being faultlesse be accus'd.
Some reading your *Lucasta*, will alledge
You wrong'd in her the Houses Priviledge.
Some that you under sequestration are,
Because you write when going to the Warre,   30
And one the Book prohibits, because *Kent*
Their first Petition by the Authour sent.
But when the beauteous Ladies came to know
That their deare *Lovelace* was endanger'd so:
Lovelace that thaw'd the most congealed brest,   35
He who lov'd best and them defended best.
Whose hand so rudely grasps the steely brand,
Whose hand so gently melts the Ladies hand.
They all in mutiny though yet undrest
Sally'd, and would in his defence contest.   40
And one the loveliest that was yet e're seen,
Thinking that I too of the rout had been,
Mine eyes invaded with a female spight,
(She knew what pain 'twould be to lose that sight.)
O no, mistake not, I reply'd, for I   45
In your defence, or in his cause would dy.

> But he secure of glory and of time
> Above their envy, or mine aid doth clime.
> Him, valianst men, and fairest Nymphs approve,
> His Booke in them finds Judgement, with you Love.   50

One aspect of this poem that places it in the mainstream of mid-seventeenth-century verse is the fact that it is composed in iambic pentameter couplets. From the time of Chaucer, English poets had written couplets, usually consisting of two ten-syllable lines with end rhyme. But by the end of the sixteenth century there were many competing verse forms: rime royal, ballad stanza, six–line stanzas, and longer, more complicated stanzas such as ottava rima, the Spenserian stanza, and the sonnet. In Marvell's time most of these were seldom used, while couplets had become the accepted medium for lyric, narrative, and dramatic poetry.

A couplet that is constructed so that the reader can pause at the end of the second line is closed or end-stopped. If a poet chooses to do so, he can write run-on couplets. That is, he can make the second line lead directly into the first line of the following couplet. Here is an example of run-on couplets from Christopher Marlowe's *Hero and Leander*:

> I could tell ye
> How smooth his breast was, and how white his belly,
> And whose immortal fingers did imprint
> That heavenly path, with many a curious dint,
> That runs along his back; but my rude pen
> Can hardly blazon forth the loves of men,
> Much less of powerful gods; let it suffice
> That my slack muse sings of Leander's eyes,
> Those orient cheeks and lips, exceeding his
> That leapt into the water for a kiss
> Of his own shadow, and despising many,
> Died ere he could enjoy the love of any.

For Marvell, as for his contemporaries, this construction is unusual. They willingly accepted the discipline of the closed couplet. The poem to Lovelace is made up entirely of such couplets: every even-numbered line concludes with a mark of punctuation, usually a period.

The couplet could be used as one long syntactical unit (see lines five and six of the poem to Lovelace). In a couplet so constructed, the reader cannot pause at the end of the first line; he or she has to read on because the first line does not make sense by itself. The technical term for this procedure is *enjambment*. An enjambed couplet cannot be read as two independent lines. But the trend in the seventeenth century was to make each line a grammatically independent statement (see lines 35–38), even though it might need the preceding or following line to complete its meaning. This kind of couplet allowed the second line to echo the antithesis and parallelism of the first line (see the last two lines of the Lovelace poem).

Since each line of an iambic pentameter couplet is composed of 10 syllables, the poet is faced with the necessity of producing a complete unit of sense in no more than 20 syllables. The preceding sentence contains 53 syllables, enough to furnish two complete couplets and more than half of a third. But it would be misleading to exaggerate the difficulties imposed by the couplet form. Its popularity in the seventeenth century and, indeed, throughout the history of English poetry, indicates that poets have not regarded it as unduly restrictive. Moreover, it has the advantage of concentrating the effect of rhyme. It is no easier to find a rhyming word at a distance of two or three lines (as in the pattern *abab* or *abcabc*) than it is to make contiguous lines rhyme. In the couplet, rhyme and grammatical structure are closely associated. The phonological closure brought about by rhyme falls at the same point as the syntactical closure indicated by a full-stop punctuation (e.g., a period or a semi-colon). The effect can be quite satisfying. In lines 45–46 of the Lovelace poem, for example, the climax of the speaker's declaration occurs in the last foot of the second line: "would dy." The ordinary syntax of English prose would dictate the following structure: "for I would die in your defence, or in his cause." Marvell's couplet allows "for I" and "would dy" to occupy the privileged position of climax at the end of the line.

When the couplet works best, it involves fewer words than a prose paraphrase. But the requirement of rhyme may result in awkward constructions ("Some that you under sequestration are") or unneeded compounds ("Thinking that I too of the rout had been"). Frequently the sign of a poet's need to find a rhyme is some form of the verb *do* (*did*, *does*, *doth*) followed by an infinitive. For example, in his poem written for the 1674 edition of *Paradise Lost*, Marvell wrote,

> That Majesty which through thy Work doth Reign
> Draws the Devout, deterring the Profane.

The first line distorts ordinary English syntax ("That majesty which reigns through thy work") but in doing so emphasizes the verb *reign* by putting it in the privileged position. The real problem comes in the second line. "Profanes" (which would rhyme with "reigns") has to be a verb; Marvell chooses to use an adjectival noun because he needs an antithesis to "Devout" (used as a noun). His habit of making the two parts of a line stand in an antithetical relationship clashes with his need for a rhyme. "Profane" can be a verb as well as an adjective; "Devout" cannot. It is impossible to establish the order of the choices that led to the final form of this couplet. Was the first line the first in order of composition? Or did Marvell begin with the antithesis of the second line and work back to the first? In other words, did he see the possibility of the "reigns"-"profanes" rhyme, or did he begin with the "Devout"-"Profane" antithesis? Clearly, at some point Marvell made a choice that put the control of this couplet in the second line and required the compound "doth reign."

It should be understood that the couplet is no more artificial than any other verse form. All poetry differs from prose, even when the restrictions it imposes are less narrow than those of the closed couplet. It could be argued that the couplet, by limiting the possibilities open to the poet, makes it easier to write verse. Certainly the poets of the seventeenth century were attracted to it. Ben Jonson is reported to have called couplets "the bravest sort of verses."

Most of Marvell's poems are in couplets. In fact, Marvell's best-known poems are composed in an even more restrictive form: the octosyllabic (or tetrameter) couplet, which allows the poet only 16 syllables in two lines. Here is an example:

> An Epitaph upon————
>
> Enough: and leave the rest to Fame.
> 'Tis to commend her but to name.
> Courtship, which living she declin'd,
> When dead to offer were unkind.
> Where never any could speak ill,   5
> Who would officious Praises spill?
> Nor can the truest Wit or Friend,
> Without Detracting, her commend.
> To say she liv'd a *Virgin* chast,

In the Age loose and all unlac't;   10
Nor was, when Vice is so allow'd,
Of *Virtue*, or asham'd, or proud;
That her Soul was on *Heaven* so bent
No Minute but it came and went;
That ready her last Debt to pay   15
She summ'd her Life up ev'ry day;
Modest as Morn; as Mid-day bright;
Gentle as Ev'ning; cool as Night;
Tis true: but all so weakly said;
'Twere more Significant, *She's Dead*.   20

These are all closed couplets. Even within the short line, Marvell is able to achieve balance and parallelism (e.g., lines 17 and 18). He plays off one line against another (e.g., lines five and six). The wit of this poem is best seen in lines seven and eight: a poem written to commend the dead lady will not avoid detracting from her virtue because it will not find terms powerful enough to express her perfection. Marvell's wit involves a comparison and contrast: the power of the lady's virtue is set against the power of the verse that tries to commend her, and the act of commending is set against the lady's modesty. It would be unkind to offer her praise that she rejected when alive, but that is what the poem does. The best way to commend her is simply to speak her name (which the poem does not do). Nothing the poet can say is as significant as the acknowledgment: "*She's Dead.*" This playful approach to the composition of an epitaph may seem frivolous, but it is typical of seventeenth-century poetry.

There is a greater need for compression in these short lines than in the longer pentameters. For example, lines three and four, rendered in prose, would read something like this: It would be unkind, now that she is dead, to offer courtship that she declined when she was alive. The paraphrase requires 24 syllables; the couplet uses 16. But compression in an epitaph is conventional. Although the first line of each couplet is less able to stand by itself as an independent unit than the first line of a pentameter couplet, in no instance does the first line compel the reader to go directly into the second line without a break.

The important fact about Marvell's tetrameter couplets in this poem is that they are not essentially different from his pentameter couplets in other poems. He can do the same things in the shorter line that he does in the longer. Sometimes Marvell wrote couplet lines of unequal length. His "Horatian Ode upon Cromwel's Return from Ireland," for example, utilizes a tetrameter couplet followed by a trimeter (six-syllable) couplet, a most unusual form. "A Dialogue between Thyrsis and Dorinda" and "A Dialogue between The Resolved Soul, and Created Pleasure" mix a few pentameter lines in with the predominating tetrameters. "Two Songs at the Marriage of the Lord Fauconberg and the Lady Mary Cromwell" mix trimeter and pentameter couplets with tetrameters. But Marvell's usual method is to stick to one meter, either tetrameter or pentameter, for the whole poem.

Marvell also wrote couplet stanzas. "Upon Appleton House," for example, is composed of 97 eight-line stanzas. But each stanza consists of four iambic tetrameter couplets. If the poem were read aloud, the hearer might not be able to tell that it is divided into stanzas. Similarly, "The Garden" is made up of nine stanzas of iambic tetrameter couplets. Marvell wrote 11 poems in couplet stanzas.

One of the outstanding features of several great seventeenth-century poets—Donne, Herbert, Cowley, Vaughan—was their ingenuity in developing stanzaic forms. Of the 167 poems in Herbert's *The Temple*, 116 are in unique stanzaic forms. The poems in Donne's *Songs and Sonets* use many nontraditional stanzas. By the middle of the seventeenth century, however, such variety was seldom found. Marvell wrote only 10 poems in stanzas not made up of couplets. Eight of these are in four-line stanzas rhyming *abab*, the commonest alternative to couplets. This lack of metrical ingenuity, as much as anything else, distinguishes his poetry from that of the poets usually regarded as "metaphysical."

Solely on the basis of verse form, Marvell may be fairly characterized as a poet who, in most of his poems, reflects the taste of his time for witty compositions in the neatest imaginable form—the closed couplet. Like his contemporaries, he used the couplet with ease. All of his verse is in rhyme. Even when he wrote in praise of Milton's blank verse, Marvell stuck to rhyming couplets. Some of the political satires (see Chapter Seven) make use of multisyllabic feet. But the uniqueness of Marvell's poetry is not to be found in the verse forms he uses.

His topics, however, tend to be less conventional. It is hard to know what a seventeenth-century reader would have made of "The Nymph complaining for the death of Her Faun." It has no place among the types of poems regularly composed by both Marvell and his contemporaries: love lyrics, poems celebrating important events or famous people, pastoral poems, devotional or meditative poems, patriotic poems. "The Nymph" does not resemble any other poem in English literature. The same can be said for "The unfortunate Lover," a mysterious tale of shipwreck and despair. Many an unfortunate lover had complained in what Donne called "whining poetry" before Marvell imagined his poor lover, but these lovers always spoke in person. Marvell's poem is *about* an unfortunate lover who is involved with a shipwreck. Not a word in the poem tells us who he is in love with or why he is unfortunate in love or what he is doing at sea. And, having cast his lover into a stormy sea where he is holding on to a rock and defying the tempest, Marvell simply leaves him there at the end of the poem. Scholars struggle to find some category for this strange unfinished narrative: emblem, impresa, Petrarchan lover's complaint, allegory, masque, disguised political comment. But they are not close to reaching a consensus.

Even when Marvell is writing a poem that does fit into a conventional category, his treatment is usually unconventional. The Mower poems, for example, are pastoral poems of a sort. They present a person who in real life would almost surely be an illiterate rustic. He bears the unlikely name of Damon and is devastated by the power of his love for Juliana. Lovesick shepherds are the stock-in-trade of pastoral poetry. They often have classical names, and for shepherds they are remarkably articulate. But they tend to appear in company, not alone as Damon always is. They do not converse with glowworms. They do not actually work at all, but Damon is cutting grass so energetically that he wounds himself in the ankle. And, above all, he is not a shepherd.

Marvell's best-known poem, "To his Coy Mistress," is a fairly conventional example of *carpe diem*, a theme that derives from classical Latin verse. Nearly every writer of amatory verse wrote at least one carpe diem poem. John Donne wrote several, ranging from the outrageous "The Flea" to the exalted "The Ecstasie." Although Marvell's poem is probably the best of its type in the English language, it is distinguished by its detailed, grim view of the inevitable future the lovers face and in its portrayal of the violent struggle that is their only means of combating the unstoppable force of time.

The poem on Lovelace offers another example of a conventional kind of poem that Marvell treats in an unusual way. Clearly Lovelace was in difficult circumstances. He had supported the losing side in a civil war; his estate had been sequestered; and the publication of his volume of poems was being held up. In the first 16 lines Marvell's speaker associates Lovelace's lyrics with a kind of golden age, uninfected by envy and ambition. The next 16 lines portray an iron age of censors and accusers. In contrast to these allusions to fairly grim realities, the last 18 lines, devoted to the imagined picture of a mutinous band of ladies sallying forth ("though yet undrest") to defend their champion, can hardly be taken as anything but playful. And the playfulness is emphasized when the innocent speaker finds himself in the unfair position of being glared at by one of the ladies, "the loveliest that was yet e'er seen," who has mistaken him for one of Lovelace's enemies. The power of her eyes could cost him his own sight, and she knows how painful that loss would be. In the context of this hyperbole, it is impossible to take seriously the speaker's declaration that he would die in her or Lovelace's defense.

How serious, then, is anything in this poem? This same question will apply to most of Marvell's work and will haunt any study of his prose and poetry. The quality of playfulness that predominates in much of his verse is foreign to the modern concept of a poet, based as it is on stereotypes that developed during the period of romanticism. Even the seventeenth-century word for this playfulness—*wit*—has a different meaning now, suggesting jokes or banter.

More than anything else in Marvell's poetry, this witty playfulness identifies him as a seventeenth-century poet. The same quality is to be found in Donne, Herbert, Thomas Carew, Jonson, Herrick, Lovelace, Sir John Suckling, Richard Crashaw, Cowley, Cleveland, and even, in a ponderous way, in Milton. Among prose writers, Sir Thomas Browne, Robert Burton, Izaak Walton, John Earle, and even Francis Bacon have it. It was as common in Donne's sermons as in his seduction poems. But by the middle of the eighteenth century, tastes had changed considerably, and in his *Life of Cowley* (1779) Samuel Johnson, using a term that had developed late in the seventeenth century, criticized a group of writers that he called "metaphysical poets" and described almost entirely in terms of their wit. The name "metaphysical poets" caught on and is now firmly established in English literary history.

Although Dr. Johnson did not include Marvell among the metaphysical poets, modern scholars generally do. Unfortunately the term *metaphysical* has proven to be more of a stumbling block than an aid to understanding. It has led to exaggerated claims of profundity for metaphysical writers and strange associations between poetic excellence and chills along the spine. Supposedly there was some special kind of wit that distinguished the metaphysical poets from those who weren't. This study of Marvell will not use the term *metaphysical* to describe Marvell's verse or to link his poetry with that of any other writer. It will, however, illustrate and discuss Marvell's wit and playfulness on the grounds that they are the most important aspects of his art.

Marvell's wit is most often seen in the comparisons, stated or implied, that he draws. Two of these are basic to the poem on Lovelace. The first 16 lines compare "Our times" and "That candid Age" (not clearly specified) with which Lovelace's poetry is associated. Since Lovelace was just 31 in 1649, only a playful stretching could make his poems the product of another age. The second comparison involves a "let's pretend" view of Lovelace's situation—he is menaced by "Word-peckers, Paper-rats, Book-scorpions" and about to be defended by a band of undressed women. The poem dramatizes and heightens the really difficult situation that Lovelace, who may have been in prison when these lines were written, in fact had to face: a change in poetic taste brought on by the English civil war and an unsympathetic audience of censors. Like all comparisons, these involve both likeness and difference: without a certain degree of likeness things cannot be compared, without a certain degree of difference there is no point in comparing. By seventeenth-century standards Marvell's comparisons are original enough to be witty, but not so original as to be far-fetched.

These basic comparisons are developed more specifically in individual lines. For example, the difference between "Our times" and "That candid Age" is expressed succinctly in these two lines:

> Who best could prayse, had then the greatest prayse,
> Twas more esteemd to give, then weare the Bayes.

Early in his poetic career, Marvell was already cultivating a stylistic device that grew consistently more pervasive in English poetry until it reached its highest development in the poetry of Dryden and Alexander Pope: antithesis (the rhetorical contrast of ideas by means of parallel arrangements of words). In the lines just quoted, it is seen most clearly in the contrast of "to give" and "weare," both infinitive forms of verbs with the second "to" (*to wear*) understood. (In the second line, "then" is a standard seventeenth-century spelling of "than"). Because of the grammatical parallelism, "Bayes"—the object of both infinitives—appears only once, and the second "to" is omitted, saving two syllables in the line. In prose, such a saving would have little effect, but poetry is more concentrated. To save another syllable, Marvell uses "Twas" instead of "It was." In other poems Marvell uses antithesis with greater skill. It is not the most important aspect of his art, nor is it the only expression of his wit. But it marks him as a poet of the middle and later seventeenth century, taking advantage of a rhetorical strategy that was becoming increasingly popular during his lifetime.

Since wit involves the perception of a relationship between two separate beings or areas of experience, a relationship on which comparison or contrast can be founded, it frequently takes the form of simile or metaphor. For example, in "Upon Appleton House" Marvell compares the haystacks in a meadow to rocks surrounded by the sea:

> When after this 'tis pil'd in Cocks,
> Like a calm Sea it shews the Rocks.

This simile is signaled by the word *like*. The reader might have had some trouble with the reference of "it" in the second line if Marvell had not already compared the meadow to a sea in a previous stanza. The comparison of haystacks in a meadow to rocks in a sea is not a part of the stock imagery available to seventeenth-century poets. But the comparison of a meadow to the sea (as in "a sea of grass") seems so natural that the simile does not appear farfetched.

Marvell's similes usually spread over both lines of the couplet so that the comparison develops at a leisurely pace. The same is true of the similes signaled by the word *as*. One of the best-known of these (from "An Horatian Ode") concerns the demeanor of Charles I at his execution:

> But bow'd his comely Head,
> Down as upon a Bed.

This simile does show a more subtle wit. Charles laid his head on a chopping block, not a pillow ("Down," which completes the verb "bow'd," will make the reader think of the soft filling in a pillow, especially in a line that concludes with "Bed"). But the King was certainly going to his rest. And his behavior as he faced death helps to support one of the implications of the poem: the King was giving a marvelously successful performance. In this simile, contrast greatly outweighs comparison. Charles's action may be compared to that of a man going to bed, but in his circumstances very few men could have shown his dignity and courage.

Marvell's wit is more striking in the metaphors he uses. In the lines preceding the simile just discussed, Marvell plays on the multiple meanings of *scaffold* (as he had with *down*) in a metaphor that implies a certain ambiguity about the King's behavior:

> That thence the *Royal Actor* born
> The *Tragick Scaffold* might adorn:
> While round the armed Bands
> Did clap their bloody hands.

The scaffold erected for the King's beheading resembles a stage on which a play might be performed. Standing on that scaffold surrounded by applauding soldiers, the King is identified as an actor in a tragedy accepting the applause of an attentive audience. But this audience claps with bloody hands and the tragedy is no play; this actor will take no curtain calls. Marvell's stage metaphor is intriguing because, unlike his similes, it is complex and open-ended. How are we to understand a metaphor that makes the King an actor? Is he only playing the role of a king (because he does not know how to be a king in fact)? Is his apparent courage only a piece of stagecraft? Are the soldiers clapping in triumph or in admiration of a performance?

In a manner that is found in the work of many other seventeenth-century poets, Marvell's metaphors enrich and complicate his verse. If we disregard the stage metaphor and read for the general sense of the quoted lines, they say that the King acted like a king. But the stage metaphor suggests another response to the King's beheading: he is putting on a performance and doing it convincingly. Perhaps the soldiers are applauding the King's skill in impersonation. Still, the implication is that his behavior is an act. If he really is the King of England, how should he act if not like a king? Is there not some irony in implying praise for a king simply for behaving like a king?

Irony is an important aspect of Marvell's wit. Like similes and metaphors, it involves comparison and contrast. Specifically, there is a contrast between what we expect and what we get. In the preceding paragraph, the basis for Marvell's irony is the phrase *"Royal Actor."* We expect a king to act like a king, but we do not expect his behavior to be an act (i.e., a deliberate attempt to create an effect). The most famous of Marvell's couplets (from "To his Coy Mistress") involves the irony of understatement:

> The Grave's a fine and private place,
> But none I think do there embrace.

It is the "I think" that gives this couplet its force. The speaker has been urging his beloved to seize the day. He has spoken of "Times winged

Charriot" and of the "Desarts of vast Eternity" that lie before them. He has asked her to see her body entombed and turning to dust. So, when the reader reaches the couplet quoted above, he or she cannot be prepared for the speaker's modest "I think." The couplet would lose its force if for "I think" Marvell had written "I vow" or "I'm sure" or "I know." The tremendous impact of "I think" derives in part from its contrast with the vivid detail in which the speaker has described what certainly lies ahead for the lovers. But even more important is the fact that what the speaker is saying in the couplet is totally obvious. It is not a matter of judgment or opinion. The speaker's modesty is grimly comic. His tone is playful and, in its context, quite unexpected.

Marvell's wit often shows itself in his habit of playing with words. In his "Dialogue Between The Resolved Soul, and Created Pleasure," Pleasure offers many enticements designed to make the Soul forget its heavenly destination. Among these is music:

> Heark how Musick then prepares
> For thy Stay these charming Aires;
> Which the posting Winds recall,
> And suspend the Rivers Fall.

The Soul replies,

> Had I but any time to lose,
> On this I would it all dispose.
> Cease Tempter. None can chain a mind
> Whom this sweet Chordage cannot bind.

In no other poem does Marvell use "Chordage." The word *cordage* appears in his "Last Instructions to a Painter," where it refers to ropes used in the rigging of a ship. In the "Dialogue," the "Chordage" that the Soul rejects is made up of musical chords, but like the ropes in a ship's cordage it has the power to tie down, to bind, to cause the Soul to stay, caught in the charms of music. The fact that a Chorus breaks into a hymn of praise immediately following the Soul's rejection of "sweet Chordage" may strike the reader as another example of Marvell's sense of irony.

But wit cannot be fully defined.[3] Like play, wit expresses itself best when it is not confined by rules. One more specific example will illustrate the complexity and subtlety of Marvell's wit. It follows the simile already quoted in which Charles, at his execution, " . . . bow'd his comely Head, / Down as upon a Bed." Marvell concludes his treatment of the King's execution with these lines:

> This was that memorable Hour
> Which first assur'd the forced Pow'r.
>   So when they did design
>   The *Capitols* first Line,
> A bleeding Head where they begun,
> Did fright the Architects to run;
>   And yet in that the *State*
>   Foresaw it's happy Fate.

A comparison is involved, this time between an event in recent English history and one in ancient Rome. As in any comparison, there is an element of contrast. According to accounts by three ancient Roman writers, the builders, digging the foundation for the temple to Jupiter on the Capitoline hill, discovered a human head (not a skull—a head with its features intact). But these writers make no mention of bleeding or of fright or of running.[4] Marvell's comparison, introduced by the word *so*, links the English Commonwealth with ancient Rome. Perhaps Marvell wants his reader to remember that when the head was discovered Rome was under the rule of a king who was soon to be driven out. Why, in the poem, is the head described as bleeding? Charles's severed head was certainly bleeding, even though the only reference the poem makes to Charles's head does not involve bleeding. Why are the frightened architects brought into the comparison? Perhaps because many English "architects" of the Commonwealth were frightened by what Parliament had done to the King. The ancient Romans interpreted the severed head to mean that Rome was to be the head of the world, a "happy Fate" indeed. But was the execution of Charles I an omen of a happy fate for England? Does Marvell say it was?

This comparison is built on a very narrow foundation. Nothing in the events in English history that Marvell alludes to truly compares with the strange event in Roman history. Only the importance of a head is common to both. What, then, is the purpose of this unlikely comparison? Perhaps there is an answer in the two lines that introduce this comparison:

> This was that memorable Hour
> Which first assur'd the forced Pow'r.

What does it mean to assure the forced power? And why "first"? Does Marvell mean that the King's execution made it clear for the first time that Parliament was the sole power in England ("assured" in the sense of "established securely")? Or does he mean that, in case there had been any doubt, the execution assured (in the sense of "made certain") for the first time that Parliament had achieved its power by force, not by legitimate means? Is it possible that he meant both? And, regardless of what he means, how does he feel about the King's execution?

This mystifying comparison shows how subtle Marvell's wit can be. We must recall that he is writing about a dangerous subject: the execution of the legitimate King of England. (Marvell, of course, would have seen the pun in "dangerous subject"; he would have regarded Cromwell, the ostensible subject of his poem, as a subject of the King who clearly had proved how dangerous he could be). In writing about such men and such events, any poet would realize the need for tact. But in this poem Marvell goes beyond tactfulness: he becomes enigmatic. The term used over and over to describe Marvell's special quality in his best-known poems is *elusive*. He cannot be pinned down. We don't know where he stands. If there is a conflict, he sees both sides and will not declare himself for either. He plays with both but gives himself to neither. The man who seldom declared his views in Parliament is just as reluctant in many of his poems.

There are exceptions to this cool, uncommitted attitude: Marvell's political satires and his prose treatises are certainly not elusive. But his esteem among modern readers does not depend on these works. While it is useful to discuss the political satires in one chapter and the prose works in another, it would be confusing to lump all the other poems together; they differ considerably in subject matter and in tone. If it were possible to establish the order in which the poems were composed, one could divide them into early, middle, and late. But that kind of treatment is ruled out by the fact that most of them were first published after Marvell's death. What is needed is a principle of organization that will allow for an orderly discussion of poems that, unfortunately, do not in the 1681 volume reveal any such principle.[5]

Any principle of organization is apt to create certain distortions. For example, if one were to divide Marvell's poems into such categories as amatory, religious, and political, many poems would either be neglected or forced into an inappropriate category. "The Nymph complaining for the death of her Faun" might fit into any one of the three categories, but only at the cost of overlooking the aspects of the poem that would allow it to be discussed in one of the other categories. If one looks for apocalyptic themes in Marvell's verse, many of his poems have little to offer. The same is true for studies that center on pastoral elements or allegorical techniques or political messages. A volume aiming to include as much of Marvell's work as possible needs to be organized on a principle that is inclusive. For this study, the principle is rhetorical.

Regardless of their subject matter, all of Marvell's works, whether in poetry or in prose, are discourses in which the reader hears a speaking voice. Marvell's imagination, not the reader's, has created this voice. It may have only a slight resemblance to Marvell's own voice. In his poems, for example, the speaker may be a young woman, a rural laborer, a passionate lover, a garden enthusiast, or simply a person who overhears and repeats someone else's words. Compared to the poems of his contemporaries, Marvell's lyrics exhibit an impressive variety of speakers and attitudes. By listening carefully to the speaker and not assuming that he *is* Andrew Marvell, this study will attempt to recognize the playfulness of Marvell's compositions and the pleasure he took in adopting various poses and attitudes. It will ask the same question of all of Marvell's poems: what sort of person is the speaker and where does he stand? That is to say, in what relationship to his material and his audience does he place himself?

In some poems it is clear that the speaker stands in a public place and speaks on public events and issues, presumably to influence his readers.[6] The political and satirical poems are public in this sense. So is the poem to Lovelace, prompted as it is by the publication of Lovelace's volume. A few of these poems were published in Marvell's lifetime; many were not. "An Horatian Ode," undoubtedly a public poem, was struck from all but two copies of the 1681 volume and not published in anything like its original form until 1776. What distinguishes the public poems is that the speaker is concerned with events and issues that impinge on the lives of his readers.

Poems that are not public may be called private. This is not to imply that Marvell did not want them to be published, for no one can know that. Rather, the private poems deal with the inner life—hopes and fears, love and desire, the sense of self and the self's relations with others—expressed either as the speaker's own experiences or the experiences of others (perhaps imagined). A private poem may present the experiences of someone other than the speaker (for example, "The unfortunate Lover" or "Bermudas"). It may even impinge on public issues, as "Bermudas" certainly does. The principle involved here is rhetorical: the speaker does not present himself as addressing public events and issues. Neither does he present himself as deeply involved personally. In fact, in some poems in this category the speaker or speakers are imagined characters or abstractions.

But some of the poems seem to be highly personal. About a dozen, including three of Marvell's greatest lyrics—"To his Coy Mistress," "The Garden," and "Upon Appleton House"—are both private and personal. The speaker directly addresses his own experiences. In these poems the reader is most likely to identify the speaker with Andrew Marvell. For the purposes of this study it makes no difference whether the "I" of the poem is Marvell or an imagined character. What is important is that the speaker stands in a direct relation to the experience he confronts; it is his or, in one poem, hers, not someone else's.

The advantage of this principle of organization is that it allows each poem to be treated as a unique composition, a contribution to the striking variety of Marvell's works. It need not illustrate some thesis about Marvell's personality or beliefs; it can be discussed and evaluated solely on the basis of its individual merits.[7] But the method entails at least two disadvantages. For one, it makes it difficult to draw general conclusions based on similar themes treated in several poems. The Mower poems, for example, cannot be analyzed as a group, and poems about love appear in three different chapters. Three famous poems are discussed in chapter six because putting them together brings out the fact that they have little in common beside the enormous skill that went into their composition. An even greater disadvantage is that, in the multiplicity of speakers, "Andrew Marvell" tends to disappear; the poems seem to have written themselves. Consequently, this study will point out frequently that the speakers are Marvell's inventions. They do not necessarily speak *for* him, but their words are ultimately his.

Because most of the political and satirical poems were composed late in Marvell's career, this study will consider them after the private and personal poems. But it will be necessary to make one departure from what is otherwise a useful principle of organization. "Upon Appleton House" is by far the longest of Marvell's nonpolitical poems. Its length and complexity put it in a category by itself. It treats many of Marvell's favorite themes and exhibits important characteristics of his verse. Because it is virtually an anthology, it provides a useful introduction to Marvell's poetry and, for this reason, will be the subject of the next chapter.

Chapter Three

"Upon Appleton House"

In 1650 or 1651 Andrew Marvell became the tutor of Mary Fairfax, the daughter of the great Parliamentary general Thomas Fairfax, who had recently resigned his position and gone into retirement. Marvell remained at Nun Appleton, one of Fairfax's country estates, for about two years. It is likely that "Upon Appleton House" was composed during this period.[1]

The poem belongs to a subgenre that arose early in the seventeenth century with Ben Jonson's "To Penshurst," a 102-line lyric addressed to the country estate of the Sidney family. Celebrations of the simplicity of country life go back to Horace, but poems concerned with the country estates of noble families were a new development in English literature. Among Marvell's contemporaries, Jonson and Carew made notable contributions.[2] Besides proclaiming the sweet contentedness of country life, these poems also emphasize the plain, unprepossessing architecture of the house and its openness and hospitality to its neighbors. The house is viewed as an extension of its owners, displaying their virtues and values. Although it is certainly man-made, it is completely in harmony with its natural setting. The tone of these poems is wholeheartedly positive; there is never a hint of criticism.

Characteristically, Marvell makes his country house poem different from its predecessors in several ways. To begin with, it is far longer than any other poem in the genre. The usual length of such poems is about 100 lines; Marvell's poem is over seven times as long. He entitles it "Upon," not "To," "Appleton House," indicating a perspective different from Jonson's and Carew's. It is not addressed to the house or to some named person for whom the house is being described. The speaker of "Upon Appleton House" directs his comments to a number of auditors, many of whom are *in* the poem. He is self-conscious and self-concerned: he, not the house, often becomes the subject of the poem. And, given its length, it is not surprising that "Upon Appleton House" develops its themes in more complex and ambiguous ways than any other poem in the genre.

"Upon Appleton House" might best be described as a tour of the Fairfax estate, and, as one critic has noted, the speaker of the poem

resembles a tour guide.³ It is tempting to refer to him as Andrew Marvell, but at no point does he identify himself either by name or by occupation. For the most part, his audience is also unidentified. By not
assuming that he is the historical Andrew Marvell, we free ourselves to
respond imaginatively to the intriguing mind that is revealed in these
776 lines, for everything in the poem comes to us from the mind of this
speaker.

Looked at as a whole, the poem is striking in its orderliness. It is precisely the order of a tour.⁴ We begin in front of the house, hear something about its history, move to the gardens, then to the meadow, then
to the wood, back to the meadow, and finally back to the garden where
we encounter Mary (called Maria) Fairfax. This tour requires some time.
It begins at dawn and concludes with the coming of darkness. During
the tour we observe the mowers working and, when they have finished,
celebrating. We are chased from the meadow when the River Denton is
allowed to inundate it. We return from the wood to observe the meadow
after the water has subsided. By the end we are at the entrance to the
house. The orderliness of the poem's structure is clearly seen in its two
most rigidly structured stanzas:

'Tis *She* [Maria] that to these Gardens gave
That wondrous Beauty which they have;
She streightness on the Woods bestows;
To Her the Meadow sweetness owes;
Nothing could make the River be
So Chrystal-pure but only *She*;
She yet more Pure, Sweet, Streight, and Fair,
Then Gardens, Woods, Meads, Rivers are.

Therefore what first *She* on them spent,
They gratefully again present.
The Meadow Carpets where to tread;
The Garden Flow'rs to Crown *Her* Head;
And for a Glass the limpid Brook,
Where *She* may all *her* Beautyes look;
But, since *She* would not have them seen,
The Wood about *her* draws a Skreen. (stanzas 87 and 88)

But this orderly structure contains a surprising variety. Indeed, the variety of "Upon Appleton House" will strike even a casual reader. At different points the speaker is describing a scene, telling a story (with several characters and many stanzas of dialogue), meditating on a theme, expressing his own enraptured condition, or moralizing. He speaks to us, of course, but he also addresses flowers, birds, characters in his narrative, woodbines and briars, the whole female sex, England itself, and Mary Fairfax. His is not the only voice we hear. 100 lines are spoken by a "suttle" nun, 22 by an ancestor of the present owner. These words originate in the guide's imagination. In one stanza (61) a woman in the meadow has actually overheard him and calls out to her companions. At no point does the speaker address the house, though that is what we would expect him to be doing throughout the poem. No other seventeenth-century country house poem begins to approach the variety in "Upon Appleton House." A clearly delineated order is a necessity, especially in a poem of 776 lines that offers so many different topics and approaches.

Orderly as he is, the speaker constantly surprises us by his habit of metamorphosing and animating nearly every aspect of the estate. Jonson and Carew had both done this in a limited way, but Marvell's speaker seldom sees any part of the estate in a naturalistic fashion. The house itself swells and sweats in its attempts to contain its great owner. The flowers in the garden are soldiers on parade; they fire volleys of sweetness to salute their governor. Grasshoppers, seated atop tall blades of grass, become giants who look down and laugh when men are swallowed up by the meadow as by a sea. Mowers cutting a swath across the meadow are like Israelites walking through the divided waters of the Red Sea. Cattle seen from afar remind the speaker of fleas viewed in a magnifying glass. When the nightingale sings in the wood, oaks bend down to hear her and the thorn bush "draws / Within the Skin its shrunken claws." Again and again we encounter not the estate itself but the pictures and associations it creates in the speaker's mind. Whatever his purpose is, it is not to describe with photographic clarity.

In fact, the speaker is not primarily concerned with describing anything. He seems to be viewing the estate as if *it* were a work of art that demands to be interpreted by someone adept at reading signs. This impression comes across most powerfully in the stanzas dealing with the wood:

> Already I begin to call
> In their most learned Original:

And where I Language want, my Signs
The Bird upon the Bough divines;
And more attentive there doth sit
Then if She were with Lime-twigs knit.
No Leaf does tremble in the Wind
Which I returning cannot find.

Out of these scatter'd *Sibyls* Leaves
Strange *Prophecies* my Phancy weaves:
And in one History consumes,
Like *Mexique Paintings*, all the *Plumes*.
What *Rome, Greece, Palestine*, ere said
I in this light *Mosaick* read.
Thrice happy he who, not mistook,
Hath read in *Natures mystick Book*. (stanzas 72 and 73)

Throughout the poem the speaker appears to be reading nature as
hieroglyph—that is, as sign language. If he is a kind of tour guide, he
evidently wants us to see more than meets the eye of a casual observer.
He has, by his own claim, gained access to a mystic book. However we
understand these words, it is apparent that he is intrigued less by what
is around him than by what his mind makes of it.

Although all of the country house poems utilize a first-person
speaker, none of the others makes him as self-conscious as "Upon Appleton House." His enraptured experience in the wood (stanzas 61–78) has
no parallel in this genre. Marvell's speaker is frequently concerned with
his own personal reactions to what he sees. We are never in doubt about
what he is looking at, but we cannot help being surprised by the way he
sees it. For example, what could be a simple description of flowers turns
into a fantasy of military display:

When in the *East* the Morning Ray
Hangs out the Colours of the Day,
The Bee through these known Allies hums,
Beating the *Dian* with its *Drumms*.
Then Flow'rs their drowsie Eylids raise,
Their Silken Ensigns each displayes,

And dries its Pan yet dank with Dew,
And fills its Flask with Odours new.

These, as their *Governour* goes by,
In fragrant Vollyes they let fly;
And to salute their *Governess*
Again as great a charge they press:
None for the *Virgin Nymph*; for She
Seems with the Flow'rs a Flow'r to be.
And think so still! though not compare
With Breath so sweet, or Cheek so faire.

Well shot ye Firemen! Oh how sweet,
And round your equal Fires do meet;
Whose shrill report no Ear can tell,
But Ecchoes to the Eye and smell.
See how the Flow'rs, as at *Parade*,
Under their *Colours* stand displaid:
Each *Regiment* in order grows,
That of the Tulip Pinke and Rose. (stanzas 37–39)

Since the lord of the estate was famous as a general, the behavior of the flowers is appropriate, or would be if the flowers were soldiers. That is the way the speaker sees them. Perhaps other poets have had the same vision, but it is hardly a familiar one.

This transformation of flowers into soldiers is an example of Marvell's wit (Marvell's rather than the speaker's wit, because this kind of transformation is found throughout Marvell's poems, regardless of who the speaker is). It bears the hallmark of wit: playfulness.[5] The speaker's metamorphoses of the meadow into a sea, of grasshoppers into giants, of the wood into an ark, of the woodpecker into a forest manager, all express his delight in controlling and playing with the otherness of the world by transforming it in his mind. The speakers of many of Marvell's poems closely resemble this speaker, and the charm of his verse depends largely on his ability to surprise us with an unexpected and decidedly private view of the world.

Still, Nun Appleton was a real building in the real world. Much as he
might wish to locate it within his mind, the speaker is aware of its real
existence and its history. Part of his responsibility is to show his audience
the significance of the house in the world outside his mind. That he
devotes a comparatively small portion of the poem to this task suggests
that he prefers to present his personal vision. Even when he does live up
to this responsibility, he does so in the same playful manner that characterizes his private view.

Primarily, the house embodies the best qualities of its owner. To
begin with, it epitomizes his humility:

> *Humility* alone designs
> Those short but admirable Lines,
> By which, ungirt and unconstrain'd,
> Things greater are in less contain'd.
> Let others vainly strive t'immure
> The *Circle* in the *Quadrature*!
> These *holy Mathematicks* can
> In ev'ry Figure equal Man. (stanza 6)

In addition, in a characteristically witty way, the speaker describes the
house in terms of the aristocratic virtue of hospitality:

> A Stately *Frontispice of Poor*
> Adorns without the open Door:
> Nor less the Rooms within commends
> Daily new *Furniture of Friends*. (stanza 9)

But in comparison with Jonson's much shorter "To Penshurst," these are
merely passing references.

In considerably fuller detail, the speaker associates the house with the
religious conflicts of the preceding century. He introduces this section
(stanzas 11 through 35) with studied nonchalance:

> While with slow Eyes we these survey,
> And on each pleasant footstep stay,
> We opportunly may relate
> The Progress of this Houses Fate.

This account of origins is not to be found in other country house poems. Nor is it quite what it appears to be. The convent that became the first Appleton House was in ruins when Marvell wrote this poem. The building occupied by Fairfax had only recently been constructed.[6] A reader who did not have this information would suppose that the speaker is referring to the older house. Even assuming that his biased account is historically accurate and that the convent had, in fact, been a nest of sexual vice and greed, what is his purpose in putting 100 lines of dialogue into the mouth of a nun who is trying to seduce Isabel Thwaites? Here one can only guess at an answer. Part of it, of course, is that the speaker simply enjoys this kind of indulgence. But there is another explanation that is suggested by the reference to "this Houses Fate." In several passages the speaker traces a divine plan for the house and its master.[7] The house itself and the great descendant of its first owner play significant roles in the struggle to establish the right worship of God. The first Fairfax won legal title to the convent ("'Twas no *Religious House* till now"); his great-grandson led the Parliamentary forces that defeated Charles I and put the supporters of reformed Protestantism in power.

The civil war in which Fairfax played so great a part haunts another section of the poem:

> Oh Thou, that dear and happy Isle
> The Garden of the World ere while,
> Thou *Paradise* of four Seas,
> Which *Heaven* planted us to please,
> But, to exclude the World, did guard
> With watry if not flaming Sword;
> What luckless Apple did we tast,
> To make us Mortal, and The Wast?
>
> Unhappy! shall we never more
> That sweet *Militia* restore,
> When Gardens only had their Towrs,
> And all the Garrisons were Flowrs,
> When Roses only Arms might bear,
> And Men did rosie Garlands wear?
> Tulips, in several Colours barr'd,
> Were then the *Switzers* of our *Guard.*

> The *Gardiner* had the *Souldiers* place,
> And his more gentle Forts did trace.
> The Nursery of all things green
> Was then the only *Magazeen*.
> The *Winter Quarters* were the Stoves,
> Where he the tender Plants removes.
> But War all this doth overgrow:
> We Ord'nance Plant and Powder sow. (stanzas 41–43)

The comparison of England to a garden is hardly new. It had its greatest expression in Shakespeare's *Richard II*. Marvell uses it to contrast the present state of England with an imagined age of innocence and quiet and to introduce a compliment to Fairfax:

> And yet their walks one on the Sod
> Who, had it pleased him and *God*,
> Might once have made our Gardens spring
> Fresh as his own and flourishing.
> But he preferr'd to the *Cinque Ports*
> These five imaginary Forts:
> And, in those half-dry Trenches, spann'd
> Pow'r which the Ocean might command. (stanza 44)

In his desire to praise the estate and its master, the speaker resembles his counterparts in other country house poems: he praises the estate without reserve. There is not one aspect of it that displeases him. He is never apologetic, and his enthusiasm is infectious. Would we like to hear how the house came into the possession of Fairfax's forebears? Of course we would! There is no need to ask. So for 208 lines (by far the largest segment of the poem) he tells us about William Fairfax and Isabel Thwaites. As for Maria, she is the source of all the beauty, straightness, sweetness, and purity that the speaker finds in the gardens, woods, meadows, and rivers. Fairfax has other houses that are larger and better able to hold his greatness,

> But Nature here hath been so free
> As if she said leave this to me.

> Art would more neatly have defac'd
> What she had laid so sweetly wast;
> In fragrant Gardens, shaddy Woods,
> Deep Meadows, and transparent Floods. (stanza 10)

To anyone who has read much of his poetry, the appearance of *nature* and *art* in the same stanza will signal the presence of one of Marvell's favorite themes. We will see it treated again and again. The speaker of "Upon Appleton House" refers to nature in nine stanzas. In nearly every instance nature is personified, as in the stanza quoted above. It (or she) is associated with the four areas of the estate that are central to the poem's structure: the gardens, the meadows, the floods, and the wood. Near the beginning and the end, nature and the estate are almost synonymous:

> But all things are composed here
> Like Nature, orderly and near. (stanza 4)

> 'Tis not, what once it was, the *World*;
> But a rude heap together hurl'd;
> All negligently overthrown,
> Gulfes, Deserts, Precipices, Stone.
> Your lesser *World* contains the same.
> But in more decent Order tame;
> *You Heaven's Center, Nature's Lap.*
> *And Paradice's only Map.* (stanza 96)

The last four lines above spell out the relation between nature and the estate: Nun Appleton is a microcosm. It is a world to itself, more decent, more orderly than the world outside. This aspect is seen most clearly when nature responds to the young Maria Fairfax:

> See how loose Nature, in respect
> To her, it self doth recollect;
> And every thing so whisht and fine,
> Starts forth with to its *Bonne Mine*.
> The *Sun* himself, of *Her* aware,
> Seems to descend with greater Care;

And lest *She* see him go to Bed;
In blushing Clouds conceales his Head. (stanza 83)

Nature, not art, accounts for the charms of the estate. But nature itself responds to the powerful virtues of Fairfax and his daughter. It becomes more decent and orderly. In an appropriate way, the speaker himself is at one with nature. He too feels the power of the great man and the sweetness of Maria. Oddly enough, however, he denies the claims of art in a poem that displays the art of Andrew Marvell in every line. The strangeness of this attitude toward nature and art will strike us many times in Marvell's poetry. Again and again we meet speakers who praise the simplicity of nature in complex and witty verse.[8] It is one of the sources of the charm we respond to in these poems and, as much as anything else, defines the individuality of Marvell's art.

One aspect of the real world that is fully excluded from "Upon Appleton House" may make modern readers uncomfortable: the speaker never calls himself Maria's tutor. As far as the fiction of the poem is concerned, therefore, he is not. But Andrew Marvell was. He was not independently wealthy; to some extent he depended on Fairfax—was, in fact, a member of his household.[9] Just as in his poems to Cromwell, he praises a patron lavishly. Nothing in our modern experience of authors corresponds to this kind of relationship. If the speaker's witty hyperboles put his seriousness in doubt, his enthusiastic championing of his patron and his pupil may seem to spring from Marvell's self-interest. There is, of course, a long history of poems written by writers of demonstrated integrity in praise of rulers, generals, nobles, and patrons. No one questions the integrity of John Milton. He also wrote in praise of Fairfax and Cromwell. Ben Jonson's sturdy independence did not prevent him from extolling the greatness of several patrons. It was a way of fulfilling one of the poet's obligations: to give a public statement of public virtues in order to inspire emulation in others. Marvell had good reason to flatter his patron, but he distances himself from the charge of flattery by putting the praises in the mouth of a speaker who has no acknowledged connection with the great man or his daughter. In fact, the speaker does not at any point enter the house; although in the last stanza he invites us to go in, his attention throughout has centered on the grounds. He seems not to belong in the house.

What has the speaker accomplished by this tour of the estate? Given his fantastic imagination and his playfulness, it appears that he has no purpose other than to indulge his fancy.[10] For a poet this is no small matter. A perfectly valid response to Marvell's lyrics is simply a sense of delight that probably matches the poet's delight in composing them. There is no obvious logical progression in "Upon Appleton House," no thesis to sustain, no working up to a conclusion.[11] Aside from paying a witty and graceful compliment to Fairfax and Maria, the poem has nothing to offer beyond the pleasure of following a nimble and creative mind at work, touching on serious themes but never solemnly.

This poem gave Marvell an unusual opportunity. Because it is considerably longer than most of his lyrics, he is able to develop his images and themes at leisure. For example, as in several of his other poems, there is a biblical subtext that makes possible a number of witty allusions. In "Upon Appleton House" the subtext is the narrative of the exodus from Egypt and the wandering in the wilderness:

> No Scene that turns with Engines strange
> Does oftner then these Meadows change.
> For when the Sun the Grass hath vext,
> The tawny Mowers enter next;
> Who seem like *Israalites* to be,
> Walking on foot through a green Sea.
> To them the Grassy Deeps divide,
> And crowd a Lane to either Side.
>
> With whistling Sithe, and Elbow strong,
> These Massacre the Grass along:
> While one, unknowing, carves the *Rail*,
> Whose yet unfeather'd Quils her fail.
> The Edge all bloody from its Breast
> He draws, and does his stroke detest;
> Fearing the Flesh untimely mow'd
> To him a Fate as black forebode.
>
> But bloody *Thestylis*, that waites
> To bring the mowing Camp their Cates [cakes],
> Greedy as Kites has trust it up,

And forthwith means on it to sup:
When on another quick She lights,
And cryes, he call'd us *Israelites*;
But now, to make his saying true,
Rails rain for Quails, for Manna Dew. (stanzas 49–51)

Into these few lines Marvell crowds several witty comparisons. The
"Engines strange" probably refers to the elaborate machinery used in the
court masques that intrigued James I and Charles I, and it is possible
that Marvell deliberately modeled his portrayal of the estate on the
scene-changing techniques of the masque.[12] The mowers resemble the
children of Israel crossing the parted waters of the Red Sea. The mow-
ing, figuratively a massacre, actually becomes one when a nesting bird
falls victim to the scythe, and the mower fears that his own fate is pre-
saged by his unwitting slaughter. All this is imaginative enough. But
the invention of "bloody *Thestylis*" is quintessentially Marvellian. A
woman might well supply refreshment to the mowers, but Thestylis is a
name from ancient Greek pastoral poetry; it has no place in rural England. Marvell brings together elements from divided and distinguished
worlds to create a scene that is both naturalistic and mythical. Then he
allows this same bloody Thestylis to overhear the speaker and to
improve on his analogy with a learned and syntactically nimble wit that
could hardly be expected from a farm laborer. It does not appear that
the biblical references have any serious implications. They are simply
playful, a part of the delight Marvell took in turning an ordinary occasion into an opportunity to find unexpected resemblances.

In both large and small ways this discovery and elaboration of resemblances is a constant feature of Marvell's verse. He takes two stanzas to
compare the green woodpecker (the hewel) to a forest warden who singles out and destroys unsound trees. He then complicates and moralizes
his comparison, offers a brief consolation, and concludes by attributing
to the fallen tree the satisfaction of seeing its betrayer justly punished.
In just three stanzas (68–70) based on a simple natural phenomenon
(the woodpecker's search for food), he outlines a short morality play on
the fall of mankind and finds a catharsis for the fallen tree.[13] A criticism
that required every detail to be a part of a single grand vision might
judge these three stanzas to be superfluous. A seventeenth-century
reader, familiar with the traditional view of poetry as a source of delight,
could simply take pleasure in this display of wit.

Marvell must have enjoyed the long speech he invented for the nun (stanzas 13–28). His aim is to personify the moral bankruptcy of the Roman Catholic ideal of withdrawal from the world.[14] The nun explains the purpose of cloistered life:

> 'Within this holy leisure we
> 'Live innocently as you see.
> 'These Walls restrain the World without,
> 'But hedge our Liberty about.
> 'These Bars inclose that wider Den
> 'Of those wild Creatures, called Men.
> 'The Cloyster outward shuts its Gates,
> 'And, from us, locks on them the Grates.
>
> 'Here we, in shining Armour white,
> 'Like *Virgin Amazons* do fight.
> 'And our chast *Lamps* we hourly trim,
> 'Lest the great *Bridegroom* find them dim.
> 'Our *Orient* Breaths perfumed are
> 'With insense of incessant Pray'r.
> 'And Holy-water of our Tears
> 'Most strangly our Complexion clears. (stanzas 13 and 14)

The terms she uses are explicitly sexual, but the image of the bridegroom derives from scripture: nuns are brides of Christ. Marvell plants the first seed of doubt in the second stanza. The nun's odd reference to the cosmetic benefits of contrition suggests a concern for the flesh that jars with the innocence of convent life. In the following stanzas the nun praises Isabel Thwaites's beauty and virtually promises that she will become the next abbess and a worker of miracles:

> 'Your voice, the sweetest of the Quire,
> 'Shall draw *Heav'n* nearer, raise us higher.
> 'And your Example, if our Head,
> 'Will soon us to perfection lead.
> 'Those Virtues to us all so dear,

'Will straight grow Sanctity when here:
'And that, once sprung, increase so fast
'Till Miracles it work at last. (stanza 21)

To this point the nun has flattered Thwaites and appealed to her
ambition. A more subtle temptation emerges in the concluding stanzas
of her speech:

'Nor is our *Order* yet so nice,
'Delight to banish as a Vice.
'Here Pleasure Piety doth meet;
'One perfecting the other Sweet.
'So through the mortal fruit we boyl
'The Sugars uncorrupting Oyl:
'And that which perisht while we pull,
'Is thus preserved clear and full. (stanza 22)

This stanza introduces the theme of pleasure and rationalizes it in terms
of a most unusual analogy with the process of making fruit preserves. The
following stanza, with its ambiguous references to "handling parts" and
"sweet sins," leads to the most overtly sexual temptation in the speech:

'Each Night among us to your side
'Appoint a fresh and Virgin Bride;
'Whom if *our Lord* at midnight find,
'Yet Neither should be left behind.
'Where you may lye as chast in Bed,
'As Pearls together billeted.
'All Night embracing Arm in Arm,
'Like Chrystal pure with Cotton warm. (stanza 24)

Four stanzas later, Fairfax warns Thwaites:

'I know what Fruit their Gardens yield,
'When they it think by Night conceal'd.
'Fly from their Vices. 'Tis thy state [estate],
'Not Thee, that they would consecrate.

Marvell invented all of these speeches. As dramatic representations of the forces of greed and immorality that might have thwarted the great destiny of Thomas Fairfax, they are relevant to the poem. Still it is odd that the nun should have the longest of the speeches, especially since she did not, in fact, succeed in her scheme. Marvell concludes the episode with a mock battle between William Fairfax and the nuns. He has come to claim his bride, to carry her off from the convent. The efforts of the nuns to oppose him are presented in comic terms:

> Some to the Breach against their Foes
> Their *Wooden Saints* in vain oppose.
> Another bolder stands at push
> With their old *Holy-Water Brush*.
> While the disjointed *Abbess* threads
> The gingling Chain-shot of her *Beads*.
> But their lowd'st Cannon were their Lungs;
> And sharpest Weapons were their Tongues.
>
> But, waving these aside like Flyes,
> Young *Fairfax* through the Wall does rise.
> Then th'unfrequented Vault appear'd,
> And superstitions vainly fear'd.
> The *Relicks false* were set to view;
> Only the Jewels there were true.
> But truly bright and holy *Thwaites*
> That weeping at the *Altar* waites. (stanzas 32 and 33)

Much more troubling than the prominence given to this episode is the fact that this portrayal of convent life as morally questionable occurs in a poem that praises the master of Nun Appleton for making the same kind of withdrawal from the world that the nun advocates. The elusiveness that critics have found in the "Horatian Ode" appears to be at work in this poem too, not only in the section just analyzed but especially in the part of the poem (the episode in the wood) that closely resembles a poem that critics have taken to be Marvell's most personal utterance: "The Garden."

The speaker's rapturous experience in the wood (stanzas 61–78) differs from the rest of the poem in that he ceases to be an observer. He

becomes totally involved. Just before he enters the wood, he resigns his
role as onlooker and describer:

> Let others tell the *Paradox*,
> How Eels now bellow in the Ox;
> How Horses at their Tails do kick,
> Turn'd as they hang to Leeches quick;
> How Boats can over Bridges sail;
> And Fishes do the Stables scale.
> How *Salmons* trespassing are found;
> And Pikes are taken in the Pound. (stanza 60)

The following stanzas are not less witty than before. If anything, the wit
becomes even more striking. The wood is a sanctuary, an ark, a place
very much like the convent described by the nun. The thick growth of
trees shuts out the world; within, it *is* a world, a place for peaceful contemplation, where every natural creature ministers to the speaker's
needs. In the wood he can "confer" with birds and trees; he can almost
become a bird or tree. He can speak to birds, read prophecies from the
"light *Mosaick*" of the leaves. Grotesquely, he wears a priestly vestment
of oak leaves and ivy.

> And see how Chance's better Wit
> Could with a Mask my studies hit!
> The Oak-Leaves me embroyder all,
> Between which Caterpillars crawl:
> And Ivy, with familiar trails,
> Me licks, and clasps, and curles, and hales.
> Under this *antick Cope* I move
> Like some great *Prelate of the Grove*. (stanza 74)

He has, it appears, become something like a Druid priest, devoted to
the worship of nature. In the wood he is safe from the darts of beauty
and from the world's attacks. He has no desire to leave this security:

> Bind me ye *Woodbines* in your 'twines,
> Curle me about ye gadding *Vines*,

> And Oh so close your Circles lace,
> That I may never leave this Place:
> But, lest your Fetters prove too weak,
> Ere I your Silken Bondage break,
> Do you, *O Brambles*, chain me too,
> And courteous *Briars* nail me through. (stanza 77)

There is more than a tinge of masochism in this stanza and in the next, in which he asks to be chained and staked down. How could anyone explain his return to the meadow in stanza 79? Marvell doesn't even try. The *"easie Philosopher"* is suddenly able to see the meadows again. How or when he left the wood is a mystery.

The entire episode in the wood is dominated by first-person pronouns: *I, me, my*. Like the gardens and the flooded meadow, it is part of the estate, but no other person shares it with the speaker. It is his special place of retreat and contemplation. Its sensuous detail and its emphasis on withdrawal recall the picture of convent life painted by the nun, and her long speech of temptation suggests that Marvell's imagination responded positively to the contemplative ideal. The preference for inwardness and inaction characterizes Marvell's lyrics. Because the speaker in this episode resembles the speakers of so many of Marvell's poems, perhaps it is time to ask whether, in this episode at least, he is Andrew Marvell.

The simple answer is that he both is and isn't. He is, in the sense that Marvell wrote the words he speaks. He isn't, in the sense that he does not exist in the same way Marvell did. However talented he may have been as a poet, Marvell did not speak in rhyming couplets. Nor is it likely that he would have opened himself up so fully to a listener he did not even know. But Marvell is not imitating another writer; no one else wrote anything like "Upon Appleton House." The nearest comparison to this poem is not another country house poem but Milton's *L'Allegro* and *Il Penseroso*. Like "Upon Appleton House," Milton's twin poems are longer than the country house norm, both are spoken by solitary observers, both portray a complicated temperament, both utilize tetrameter couplets. Since the speakers of these twin poems contrast in several ways, neither can be identified with Milton. Yet each resembles some aspects of Milton: his love of music, literature, drama, nature. The problem with Marvell's poems is that so little is known about him that we are more apt to use his verse to answer questions about his life than to look to his life to illuminate his verse.

This being the case, it might be useful to look for any signs of consistency in his speakers, on the assumption that a writer's personality will show itself in his predilections, in the topics that interest him, and the themes he treats repeatedly. An interest in religion, for example, shows itself in several of Marvell's poems, but a personal commitment to Christianity of the sort that characterizes Donne's and Herbert's devotional verse is nowhere to be found. The most intense religious experience in "Upon Appleton House" is pagan—the rapture in the wood, so much like the experience of the speaker in "The Garden." Often in Marvell's poems the contrasts between art and nature are central, nature always being regarded as superior. Other poems exhibit a preference for contemplation over action, for innocence over experience, for spirit over body.

But there is another kind of speaker and another set of attitudes in, for example, "To his Coy Mistress" and "An Horatian Ode upon Cromwel's Return from Ireland," two of Marvell's best-known works. This speaker admires action, prizes body over spirit, shows no interest in religion. Still another kind of speaker appears in "Tom May's Death" and in Marvell's many political satires. He is a partisan, using his wit to discredit his opponents, excited by the opportunity to mock their hypocrisy and to strip their disguises. Both of these speakers can be heard briefly in "Upon Appleton House," in the praise of Fairfax's military prowess and in the discrediting of the hypocritical nun.

The one characteristic that all these speakers share is wit. It is the only constant in Marvell's art. His elusive and ambivalent poems are no less witty than his partisan satires. In this sense Marvell *is* the speaker in all his poems. When we look for consistency in his work, in prose as well as in verse, we find it in this one characteristic. Marvell cannot treat any subject, not even the death of Cromwell, without the play of imagination. Usually he matches his wit to the occasion. Some of his poems are almost pure play (e.g., "Fleckno, an English Priest at Rome" or "The Character of Holland"). His dedicatory poem to Milton, in contrast, shows a sober and serious kind of wit. Between these extremes lies the bulk of his verse. And the poems for which he is best known are much nearer to "Fleckno" than to the poem on *Paradise Lost*.

The other characteristic of Marvell's verse that is virtually a constant is his use of couplets. "Upon Appleton House" provides an excellent example of Marvell's skill in manipulating his verse form. The poem is composed of tetrameter couplets in eight-line stanzas, a form Marvell used in seven other poems, most notably in "The Garden." If the short-line couplet is a restrictive form, the couplet stanza is doubly so. The difficulty the poet faces in avoiding monotonous patterns in two-line units is compounded. Not only must the couplets be varied; the stanzas too must be constructed differently. Marvell's couplets and stanzas exhibit almost every conceivable combination of variables offered by English syntax and sentence structure. Marvell's commitment to the couplet is best seen in the fact that only two lines of the poem are designed to stand alone:

> The *Nuns* smooth Tongue has suckt her in. (stanza 25)

> We Ord'nance Plant and Powder sow. (stanza 43)

Each line occurs at the end of a stanza as a kind of summation. Although other lines in the poem are grammatically independent, their companion line continues the statement they introduce, as in the following couplet:

> For now the Waves are fal'n and dry'd,
> And now the Meadows fresher dy'd. (stanza 79)

In many couplets, the first line ends in such a way that the reader must not pause before beginning the next line:

> Within this sober Frame expect
> Work of no Forrain *Architect*. (stanza 1)

This is an enjambed couplet. Nearly every stanza includes at least one. This couplet illustrates another kind of variety. It is an imperative sentence, a command addressed to the reader. There are only about a dozen imperatives in the poem, not all of them directed to the reader. There are also 11 sentences in the form of questions. But, as one would expect in any extended discourse, most of the sentences are declarative. They best illustrate the variety of couplet structure in the poem.

Most of the couplets consist of two unenjambed lines that make a complete statement, illustrated by two couplets in stanza 35:

> For if the *Virgin* prov'd not theirs,
> The *Cloyster* yet remained hers.
> Though many a *Nun* there made her Vow,
> 'Twas no *Religious House* till now.

The antithesis between the first and second lines of each couplet is characteristic of Marvell's wit. Both of these couplets exhibit the most common line form: a clause containing a subject and a finite verb. They avoid monotony (but only narrowly) by the placement of the negative ("not" in the first line of one couplet and "no" in the second line of the other) and by the slight distinction between a compound and a complex sentence.

Many of Marvell's couplets do not involve antithesis. These couplets from stanza 39 exemplify a different structure: the second line finishes the statement in the first line or adds details to it:

> See how the Flow'rs, as at *Parade*,
> Under their *Colours* stand displaid:
> Each *Regiment* in order grows,
> That of the Tulip Pinke and Rose.

The witty identification of flowers with soldiers is developed in a leisurely fashion not only in these lines but in the two preceding stanzas as well. The same kind of structure appears in two enjambed couplets from stanza 47:

> They, [grasshoppers] in there squeking Laugh, contemn
> Us as we walk more low then them:
> And, from the Precipices tall
> Of the green spir's, to us do call.

These couplets use a sentence structure that ties the four lines into a syntactical unit, since the subject of the last word ("call") is expressed in the first word of the first line ("they"). The same kind of structure is found in stanza 49:

> And yet their walks one on the Sod
> Who, had it pleased him and *God*,
> Might once have made our Gardens spring
> Fresh as his own and flourishing.

The enjambment of these couplets ties all four lines into a tight unit. In a few instances, an entire stanza is made up of two four-line structures such as this one:

> When first the Eye this Forrest sees
> It seems indeed as *Wood* not *Trees*:
> As if their Neighbourhood so old
> To one great Trunk them all did mold.
> There the huge Bulk takes place, as ment
> To thrust up a *Fifth Element*;
> And stretches still so closely wedg'd
> As if the Night within were hedg'd. (stanza 63)

An even rarer kind of stanza pits the couplet structure against the grammatical structure. The couplets appear to be closed, but the sentence marches on through the entire eight lines:

> But I, retiring from the Flood,
> Take Sanctuary in the Wood;
> And, while it lasts, my self imbark
> In this yet green, yet growing Ark;
> Where the first Carpenter might best
> Fit Timber for his Keel have Prest.
> And where all Creatures might have shares,
> Although in Armies, not in Paires. (stanza 61)

Many stanzas are composed of four independent couplets (independent in the sense that each couplet stands alone as a complete statement). The second stanza of the poem illustrates this structure:

> Why should of all things Man unrul'd
> Such unproportion'd dwellings build?
> The Beasts are by their Denns exprest:
> And Birds contrive an equal Nest;
> The low roof'd Tortoises do dwell
> In cases fit of Tortoise-shell:
> No Creature loves an empty space;
> Their Bodies measure out their Place.

The metrical regularity of these lines comes close to being tedious; only the first and seventh lines allow a departure from the iambic pattern. The stanza illustrates the need for variation in a form that could become unbearably predictable.

In a very few instances Marvell breaks his line in such a way that an independent clause occupies one line and a portion of another. The 23rd stanza shows several examples of this construction (the slanted lines indicate divisions within a line):

> 'For such indeed are all our Arts;
> 'Still handling Natures finest Parts.
> 'Flow'rs dress the Altars; / for the Clothes,
> 'The Sea-born Amber we compose;
> 'Balms for the griv'd we draw; / and Pasts
> 'We mold, as Baits for curious tasts.
> 'What need is here of Man? / unless
> 'These as sweet Sins we should confess.

This survey only begins to illustrate the variety of couplet and stanza structure in "Upon Appleton House." But it shows something of the ingenuity with which Marvell handled a highly restrictive medium. Such variety does not come about by accident; it is the product of a deliberate attempt by a skillful poet to avoid the tedium that is the chief liability of the couplet form.

But why did Marvell choose to write this poem in stanzas? Since couplets can stand quite well on their own, why combine them in eight-line groupings? It cannot be simply to make a long poem easier to read by providing a rest every eighth line. Closed couplets are not long-winded. Marvell's longest poem ("The last Instructions to a Painter") consists of 495 couplets; it is not divided into stanzas. An examination of his use of stanzas suggests an explanation.

The most striking fact about Marvell's stanzas is that, with one exception, all of them conclude with some form of end-stop punctuation: a period, a question mark, or an exclamation point. Even the exception (stanza 75),

> Under this *antick Cope* I move
> Like some great *Prelate of the Grove*,

although it ends with a comma, makes a complete statement in its final couplet. The stanza, therefore, is a unit for Marvell. It may contain one, two, three, four, or even more independent clauses, but it never ends in such a way that one must go to the next stanza to find the conclusion of a sentence.

But the stanza is not necessarily independent of what precedes or follows it. Just as a prose paragraph may carry on a discussion that begins in a preceding paragraph, any stanza may be a part of a larger unit. The stanzas comparing the flowers to soldiers, for example, are part of a section describing the gardens that begins with stanza 26 and concludes with stanza 46. The meadow section occupies stanzas 47 through 60. Indeed, it would be difficult to find any stanza that stands completely alone, with the possible exception of the last stanza of the entire poem.

Therefore, since "Upon Appleton House," like any well-constructed composition, exhibits an unbroken continuity, what is the point of chopping it up into 97 eight-line units? Any answer will be a guess about the mind of Andrew Marvell, but there are clues that suggest an answer. Judging by his poems, Marvell's imagination was extraordinarily active. Without hinting at deep psychological insights, one can see that Marvell might be attracted to a form that kept his exuberant fancy in check at the same time that it gave him an excellent opportunity to express his wit.

Another answer involves a kind of paradox: the stanza form allows a variety not achievable in a nonstanzaic form. Stanzas appear to be restrictive, but they set up a pattern within which variations are more noticeable than in an unrestricted flow of couplets. In isolated couplets, there are very few possible variations. A stanza, whether of four, six, eight, or ten lines (Marvell used all these), gives the poet a chance to manipulate the relationship between units defined by rhyme and units defined by grammatical structure. Four consecutive independent units of two lines each (2, 2, 2, 2) constitute the simplest stanza. By drawing out sentences over two couplets, Marvell can create a 4, 4 structure. Other variations are 4, 2, 2 and 2, 2, 4. But some lines can stand alone, as in the second stanza, which might be figured as 2, 2, 2, 1, 1. If the poem were composed simply of couplets, the same variety would still be obtained but the reader would be less conscious of it. Judging by his fondness for them, Andrew Marvell was certainly aware of the advantages offered by stanzas.

In a short chapter, the complexity of this poem can only be suggested.[15] It has been studied as a political allegory,[16] as a pastoral, as an epic journey to the underworld, as an exercise in verbal trickery, and in numerous other guises. The aim of this chapter is simply to recognize important aspects of Marvell's verse, above all his wit and his skill in handling the short-line couplet. As in many of his poems, his goal in "Upon Appleton House" appears to be the enjoyment of making poetry, the free play of fancy disciplined by the demands of form. Marvell's famous elusiveness blurs all messages, and his wit undermines any fixed position. The best way to read his verse is to recognize that it is usually the journey, not the destination, that counts.

In other poems, however, there is a clear sense of destination, of the speaker's commitment to a fixed goal. All of the satirical pieces exhibit this commitment; almost all of them deal with public issues. The preceding chapter proposed a division of Marvell's poems into the categories of public, private, and personal. A study of "Upon Appleton House" points up some difficulties in the application of this method. In that it addresses English history and praises a man who helped to make it, the poem may be called public. But it is much more fully concerned with the responses of its speaker to the estate and to Mary Fairfax. In this respect it belongs in the category of private poems. When the speaker tells of his ecstatic mood in the wood, he is presenting a highly personal experience. If all of Marvell's poems were as long and varied as this, they could not be contained in three simple categories. Fortunately, most of the lyrics are short and fit easily into one of the proposed divisions. The next chapter examines the first of these, the private poems.

Chapter Four
Private Poems

The thirteen poems treated in this chapter are concerned with private issues. Although some of them impinge on the larger world, their emphasis is on private experience. They are presented by a speaker who is not personally involved. Nothing identifies him. In some poems he is simply in a position to overhear what others are saying. In some he provides a framework for other speakers. In several poems we do not hear his voice at all: the entire poem is a dialogue.

While these poems are all technically lyrics, Marvell uses several different methods to present his material. The most familiar is the single-speaker lyric: we hear only one voice. Such poems tend to be reflective or meditative; they look back on past experiences and reach conclusions based on them. "The Mower against Gardens" is a good example of this kind of lyric. Most of Marvell's poems, whether public or private, are of this type, though many fail to arrive at a well-defined conclusion. A variation on this manner of presentation is the framed lyric: most of the poem resembles the single-speaker lyric, but another voice introduces the speaker and is heard again either at or near the conclusion. "Damon the Mower" and "Bermudas" illustrate this technique.

Marvell tried other methods, two of which are illustrated in this chapter. The first involves a narrative: the poem tells a story. But it is not the speaker's story. His attitude may be sympathetic, as in "The unfortunate Lover," or detached and mildly cynical, as in "Daphnis and Chloe." In the latter poem the speaker reports the words of a character in his story; in the former he does not. What is striking about these poems is their originality. Many of Marvell's poems fit or nearly fit into established, traditional types. The story poems do not, and for that reason they are strange and puzzling.

The other method is dramatic. Marvell obviously enjoyed the possibilities of a form in which two or more speakers are heard without the mediation of a narrator. It is not surprising that a poet who became a member of Parliament should have an interest in debate, which we find in the "Dialogue" poems. Significantly, these debates are not always resolved, suggesting that Marvell enjoyed the dramatic possibilities rather than the resolution of debate. Although all the poems in this chapter may be called private, they show the surprising variety of Marvell's poetry, each giving evidence of his originality and elusiveness.

"On a Drop of Dew" is presented by a single speaker. In its theme and method it resembles many other seventeeth-century poems. The theme is the familiar Platonic and Christian view of the soul as an exile from an eternal home toward which it yearns. The method is comparison: in 18 lines the speaker describes the drop of dew; in 22 lines he shows that the soul behaves in the same way. Finally the speaker compares both the dew and the soul to the manna that God sent to relieve the children of Israel in the wilderness (Exodus 16).

> Such did the Manna's sacred Dew destil;
> White, and intire, though congeal'd and chill.
> Congeal'd on Earth: but does, dissolving, run
> Into the Glories of th'Almighty Sun.

The poem resembles a popular Renaissance form—the emblem, a kind of developed comparison between a visible object and a spiritual reality. In this case the comparison is fairly obvious. Only one instance of Marvell's wit is worth mentioning. Referring to the drop of dew, the speaker notes that it

> Shines with a mournful Light;
> Like its own Tear,
> Because so long divided from the Sphear.

It is tempting to regard this as one of Marvell's earliest compositions. The mature poet would not have felt the need to explain why the drop of dew was mournful. The metrical variety of this poem reinforces this impression. The three lines quoted above only begin to represent the irregularity of line length (from four syllables to ten) and the unpredictability of rhyme scheme. If Marvell had continued to compose poems like this, he would rightfully be considered an imitator of George Herbert and Henry Vaughan.[1]

"Musicks Empire" is closer to the mature Marvell. The speaker sketches the history of music, in part with the aid of Genesis and in part as an exercise of his own wit. Puns abound:

> *Jubal* first made the wilder Notes agree;
> And *Jubal* tuned Musicks *Jubilee*.

Subsequent lines pun on the words *consort* (with a play on *concert*) and *Mosaique* (with a pun on "Musick"), while "the Mosaique of the Air" is paralleled with "the Empire of the Ear." At the conclusion of this brief history (six stanzas, each composed of two iambic pentameter couplets), the speaker addresses music itself:

> Victorious sounds! yet here your Homage do
> Unto a gentler Conqueror then you;
> Who though He flies the Musick of his praise,
> Would with you Heavens Hallelujahs raise.

Who is this "gentler Conqueror"? If we knew when and where this poem was written, it might be possible to guess. But even if we knew precisely who Marvell was referring to, a more important question would remain: what logical connection ties the first five stanzas to the sixth? As it stands, the poem appears to be a witty tribute to someone whose identity, if it were known, might lend coherence to the whole.[2] It is not surprising that "Musicks Empire" is seldom included in selections of Marvell's verse.

"The Mower against Gardens" is the first of a series of four poems in which Marvell seems to be determined to avoid making any one like any other. Although the word *mower* appears in the title of all four, in only one is he given a name. In three poems the deleterious effect of Juliana, his beloved, is the chief subject. Even though Juliana is central to these poems, not one of them is addressed to her. No two poems exhibit the same metrical pattern. Because they are printed sequentially in the 1681 edition, it is easy to assume that Damon is the speaker of all four, but the attitudes exhibited in the first poem of the sequence do not resemble those in the other three. Consequently there is no advantage in discussing them as a group; two will be treated where they logically belong— in the next chapter.

The speaker of "The Mower against Gardens" sounds like an early Romantic. He accuses "Luxurious Man" of corrupting "plain and pure" nature by a process of seduction. The plants and flowers have taken on human personalities:

> The Pink grew then as double as his Mind;
> The nutriment did change the kind.
> With strange perfumes he did the Roses taint.
> And Flow'rs themselves were taught to paint.

The more they become like human beings, the worse they are. Human ingenuity has destroyed not only the innocence of nature; it has robbed the plants and flowers of their inheritance:

> No Plant now knew the Stock from which it came;
> He grafts upon the Wild the Tame:
> That the uncertain and adult'rate fruit
> Might put the Palate in dispute.

Meanwhile "the sweet Fields do lye forgot." But, the speaker concludes, outside the garden nature still dispenses "A wild and fragrant Innocence." The imagery of this attack is predominantly sexual. The very first word, *Luxurious*, in seventeeth-century usage meant "licentious." Such words as *seduce*, *allure*, *procreate*, and *Seraglio* maintain the undertone of sexual aggression against pure nature.

The title plainly identifies the speaker as a mower. As such, he has a vested interest in "the sweet Fields." But he advances a general principle that Marvell might have encountered in Montaigne's essay "Of Cannibals" and in Shakespeare's *The Winter's Tale* (4.4), in which Perdita refuses to allow striped flowers in her garden. Marvell makes him speak in a meter that resembles Latin elegiac verse and with a wit that one would not expect of a field worker. All the Mower poems make use of the pastoral convention that allowed shepherds to speak of country matters with urbane sophistication. Perhaps Marvell wrote lines 13–16 —"The Tulip, white, did for complexion seek; / And learn'd to interline its cheek: / Its Onion root they then so high did hold, / That one was for a Meadow sold"—to remind the reader of the mower's limited perspective: in his view, land is the highest conceivable value.

The tone of this poem is unusually sober, even plaintive:

> 'Tis all enforc'd; the Fountain and the Grot;
> While the sweet Fields do lye forgot:
> Where willing Nature does to all dispence
> A wild and fragrant Innocence:

And *Fauns* and *Faryes* do the Meadows till,
　More by their presence then their skill.
Their Statues polish'd by some ancient hand,
　May to adorn the Gardens stand:
But howso'ere the Figures do excel,
　The *Gods* themselves with us do dwell.

There is a genuine poignancy in this vision of human perversity, this turning away from the "wild and fragrant Innocence" of nature. As is so often the case in Marvell's lyrics, this poem draws an extended contrast between art and nature. Whatever ambiguity there is in it springs from the fact that the speaker makes a highly artful use of language in praise of nature. The poem might have been a diatribe, an angry accusation, but Marvell makes it a celebration of innocence and sweetness.[3] Still there is an irony in the reference to the "polish'd" statues of the gods that adorn the gardens. It would be hard to imagine how those statues could show a higher polish than these verses.

"Damon the Mower" is one of two poems, both identified as songs, in which the first voice is that of a presenter who introduces the occasion and the singer of the song. But the mower he introduces in this poem bears little resemblance to the mower who inveighed against gardens. This mower is too caught up in his own problems to worry about general principles. Though he speaks in the same stanza as the guide in "Upon Appleton House," he has none of the guide's wit and fantastic imagination. The burden of his song is a complaint against the scornful shepherdess Juliana. In a tradition going back to ancient Greek and Latin pastoral verse, shepherds lamented their unrequited love for fair shepherdesses. But Damon is a mower, not a shepherd. In his own opinion, he is famous and favored by nature.

I am the Mower *Damon*, known
Through all the Meadows I have mown.
On me the Morn her dew distills
Before her darling Daffadils.
And, if at Noon my toil me heat,
The Sun himself licks off my Sweat.
While, going home, the Ev'ning sweet
In cowslip-water bathes my feet.

Amusingly, he sees the whole pastoral enterprise in terms of his own occupation and judges himself to be a better catch than any keeper of sheep.

> What, though the piping Shepherd stock
> The plains with an unnum'red Flock,
> This Sithe of mine discovers wide
> More ground then all his Sheep do hide.
> With this the golden fleece I shear
> Of all these Closes ev'ry Year.
> And though in Wooll more poor then they,
> Yet am I richer far in Hay.

As any lovesick shepherd would, he brings presents to Juliana:

> To Thee the harmless Snake I bring,
> Disarmed of its teeth and sting.
> To Thee *Chameleons* changing-hue,
> And Oak leaves tipt with hony due.

In a tradition going back to ancient Greece, poetic shepherds had brought gifts to their beloved ranging from bear cubs to delicate flowers, but no swain had ever showed up with a snake, a chameleon, or oak leaves—with or without honey. No wonder the shepherdess scorns his offerings. It seems that Marvell's playfulness is expressing itself at the expense of Damon and that there is a kind of parody in this poem.[4] Although he boasts of his prowess as a mower, Damon actually cuts himself with his own scythe and then perceives a comically disproportionate resemblance between himself and Death, who is also a mower. Yet this rather clownish laborer enjoys a close and happy relation to both nature and the supernatural world.

> The deathless Fairyes take me oft
> To lead them in their Danses soft;
> And, when I tune my self to sing,
> About me they contract their Ring.

The presenter (the speaker of the first and the tenth stanzas) stands in a peculiar relation to the rest of the poem. While Damon blames the withering heat on *"Juliana's* scorching beams," the presenter has already informed us that the day was fair, "But scorching like his am'rous Care." His use of "scorching" precedes Damon's and undercuts Damon's explanation. Marvell is playing with the traditional themes of pastoral poetry, amusing himself and his reader with an original view of the pastoral world. His speaker is both comic and pitiable,[5] but the poem never loses its perfect balance.

There is a similar construction in "Bermudas." The bulk of the poem is a song, but it is framed by a presenter.

> Where the remote *Bermudas* ride
> In th'Oceans bosome unespy'd,
> From a small Boat, that row'd along,
> The listning Winds receiv'd this Song.

The presenter, who has the privilege of hearing the song, describes the setting. The song alludes to a public issue[6] (the Bermudas were a place of refuge for Puritans menaced by "Prelat's rage"), but the chief theme of the poem is that of an earthly paradise, and the aim of the singers is to "sing his Praise / That led us through the watry Maze." Their description of the island does not differ in any significant way from accounts found in numerous printed sources or from Edmund Waller's *Battle of the Summer Islands* (1645).

> He gave us this eternal Spring,
> Which here enamells every thing;
> And sends the Fowl's to us in care,
> On daily Visits through the Air.

There is a biblical subtext in the visits of the fowls (who recall the ravens sent to succor Elijah), but why such help would be needed in a paradise is not clear. "The Gospels Pearl" probably alludes to the pearl of great price in one of Jesus' parables. In a general way, the song resembles a psalm, though it is not addressed to God. The boatmen are strangely reticent about identifying the person who has done these wonderful things: they praise God without ever naming him.

But the framework of this poem raises the most interesting questions. Why should this song of praise issue from a small boat (it is small enough to be "row'd along")? Apparently the singers know the islands well and have been living there long enough to realize that there is no change of seasons. Why should they be out in a small boat? Nothing suggests that they have been fishing. Their song is apparently more important than their rowing because, in an inversion of the traditional practice, they use the strokes of their oars to keep time, "to guide their Chime" (their song). As Marvell presents it, the song does require some introduction, but he could have presented it otherwise and without a framework.

In "Damon the Mower," the presenter comes between us and the rest of the poem, creating a kind of distance. The result is mildly comic. In "Bermudas" the presenter is sympathetic to the singers. He calls their song "An holy and a chearful Note." Perhaps more than anything else it is a simple song, its charm springing from naïveté and directness. In its setting it achieves a purity of purpose. "What should we do but sing his praise?" the singers ask, with a kind of wondering, childlike simplicity, as if the expression of their gratitude had become the sole end of their lives.[7] In modern anthologies "Bermudas" is second only to "To his Coy Mistress" in number of appearances. It is hard to imagine a greater contrast between two poems by a single author or a clearer indication of the difficulty faced by those who wish to identify Marvell with the speakers of his verse.

The role of presenter becomes that of narrator in the next three poems. Each of them tells or hints at a story. Each begins with the narrator's voice; in one of them a character in the story speaks at length. Because each story is presented so briefly, these are among the most elusive of Marvell's poems.

Of the three, "The unfortunate Lover" is the most difficult. Some of its details resemble those associated with myths (e.g, the cormorants that both nourish and consume the lover). Several critics have argued that it is based on a series of emblems.[8] The narrator does not explain why the lover undergoes such torments. Some of them are exaggerations of the traditional lovers' complaints found in countless sonnets, but this lover does not have anyone to *be* in love with. At the end he becomes a heraldic device: "In a Field *Sable* a Lover *Gules*," a blood-red figure against a black background. Nothing in the poem suggests parody or satire. If, as in so many of his poems, Marvell is playing, he has neglected to give us the rules of the game. Like any insoluble puzzle, the poem frustrates all attempts to enjoy it.

"Mourning" begins with a challenge:

> You, that decipher out the Fate
> Of humane Off-springs from the Skies,
> What mean these Infants which of late
> Spring from the Starrs of *Chlora's* Eyes?

Here the game is clearly defined: we are to guess the meaning of Chlora's tears. Perhaps she is mourning for Strephon, "her dead Love." But "some affirm" that she is merely indulging herself, while "others, bolder" interpret her tears as completely hypocritical invitations to a new love. The next to last stanza refutes these suppositions:

> How wide they dream! The *Indian* Slaves
> That sink for Pearl through Seas profound,
> Would find her Tears yet deeper Waves
> And not of one the bottom sound.

And so the question would seem to be settled: the tears are expressions of Chlora's deepest feelings (though the fact that "sound" may be an adjective, not a verb, produces an ambiguity). Apparently her detractors are wrong.

But there is one more stanza, quintessentially Marvellian:

> I yet my silent Judgment keep,
> Disputing not what they believe:
> But sure as oft as Women weep,
> It is to be suppos'd they grieve.

Withholding judgment is Marvell's specialty. So is the tactful irony of the closing couplet. "It is to be suppos'd" is as fine a piece of undermining as could be imagined. The effect of the final stanza is to imply that Chlora's detractors are right. How can this stanza be reconciled with the one that precedes it? Only by supposing that Chlora's deepest feelings are neither sorrow for a lost lover nor expressions of self-indulgence. But what, then, do they express?

Whatever Chlora's tears mean, this poem embodies Marvell's spirit of playfulness. It offers a problem, several solutions, and a conclusion that,

in its irony, refuses to give an authoritative answer. The pleasure we get
from it derives from the wit that allows the narrator to win the game he
is playing with us, for surely nothing is at stake.

"Daphnis and Chloe" is the longest of the poems in this chapter. The
narrator quickly sketches the situation. It is both delicate and complicated.[9] Inexperienced in love, Chloe has fended off the advances of
Daphnis. For some unstated reason, he must part from her. To prevent
his leaving, she makes it clear that she will yield to his desire. In a
speech of 52 lines, Daphnis refuses to mingle joy with his now-perfect
sorrow:

> Farewel therefore all the fruit
> Which I could from Love receive:
> Joy will not with Sorrow weave,
> Nor will I this Grief pollute.

He leaves Chloe, but, as the narrator informs us, he has since slept with
Phlogis and is ready to take on Dorinda. As for Chloe, we are not told
how she is affected.

> But hence Virgins all beware.
> Last night he with *Phlogis* slept;
> This night for *Dorinda* kept;
> And but rid to take the Air.

So much for the story. But the narrator has one final question:

> Yet he does himself excuse;
> Nor indeed without a Cause.
> For, according to the Lawes,
> Why did *Chloe* once refuse?

Clearly the narrator's sympathies lie with Daphnis. Whatever the
"Lawes" are, Chloe has broken them by refusing. The narrator seems to
accept an assumption that is common to many witty libertine poems of
the seventeenth century—namely, that women by nature are as libidi-
nous as men and that to deny that fact is to break the laws of nature. As
the speaker of Suckling's "The Siege" says, "I hate a fool that starves her
love / Only to feed her pride." But Daphnis is not without fault:

> He, well read in all the wayes
> By which men their Siege maintain,
> Knew not that the Fort to gain
> Better 'twas the Siege to raise.

To his credit, Daphnis has not manipulated Chloe into surrender. But he has refused to seize an opportunity. His long speech attempts to explain why. His reasoning makes sense only if his separation from Chloe is permanent and unavoidable. Since the narrator has failed to explain why Daphnis has to part from Chloe, we cannot judge his decision to refuse her favors. He talks like a condemned man who, having resolved to leave the world, rejects a last-minute reprieve. Is his decision noble, sensitive, high-minded, or stupid? Similarly, the narrator's cryptic reference to the "Lawes" leaves us unable to assess Daphnis's solace in the arms of Phlogis and Dorinda. Where does Andrew Marvell stand on this issue?

As usual, Marvell eludes the question. He has shaped the poem to leave us without an authoritative interpretation. Neither the narrator nor Daphnis supplies an answer. We can be sure of only one thing: this is an entirely original poem. It offers Marvell an opportunity to develop a brief narrative containing a dramatic speech in which a lover, having expressed through a series of witty analogies his reasons for refusing what he has been ardently seeking, immediately turns to other women who provide what he has just rejected.[10]

The five remaining poems differ from those already discussed in that there is no mediating voice to provide a framework. The speakers in each poem are identified in the title and by speech prefixes. Three of the poems belong to the pastoral tradition, but like all of Marvell's experiments in pastoral poetry they are quite unusual. The other two reflect another well-established tradition: the body-soul debate. All these poems are essentially dramatic.

The pastoral poems can be dealt with briefly. Neither the names nor the settings suggest the English countryside. We have already encountered the names *Damon* and *Thestylis* in other poems, but there is no reason to suppose that they are the speakers who bear the same names in the poems we are now concerned with. The situations do not belong to the pastoral tradition. "Clorinda and Damon" presents the attempt of a shepherdess to seduce a shepherd. Apparently she fails because Damon has encountered Pan and is now devoted to singing his praise. When John Milton, following an established tradition, referred to Pan in "On the Morning of Christ's Nativity," a reader could know that he was simply viewing the nativity through the eyes of shepherds. But Marvell provides no such framework. His Pan may be the ancient pagan god. In any case, the poem is only a vignette of 30 lines, graceful and delicate, but quite isolated from an interpretive tradition.[11]

"A Dialogue between Thyrsis and Dorinda" poses special problems for an editor[12] as well as for a commentator. Thyrsis has painted so idyllic a picture of "Elizium" that Dorinda apparently wants him to join her in a suicide that will carry them directly to this perfect place. It is a shepherd's vision of paradise—plenty of grass and flowing springs, no wolves or foxes, perpetual morning, cool winds, and an ideal social structure:

> Shepheards there, bear equal sway,
> And every Nimph's a Queen of *May*.

Only the phrase "Everlasting day," which Marvell may have borrowed from Lovelace's "The Grasshopper," implies that this poem might have a Christian subtext. It appears to be exactly like "Clorinda and Damon," an experiment in pastoral drama.

In its 16 lines of seven-syllable verse, "Ametas and Thestylis making Hay-Ropes" plays out a short debate between a rustic and his love. She will not yield to his advances and counters his arguments with an ingenious analogy based on the process of making hay-ropes. If Ametas wants to make comparisons between love and hay-ropes, as he does in his first two speeches, she is ready to make some of her own. But the poem ends with Ametas's invitation:

> Then let's both lay by our Rope,
> And go kiss within the Hay.

Since Thestylis does not reply, we are free to imagine our own conclusion to this short drama.[13] Like the other pastorals, it is no more than a sketch and quite unlike any other poem in the pastoral tradition. Since it involves a kind of debate, the fact that no resolution is provided indicates that Marvell enjoyed the process of argument even when it did not lead to a victory for either side.

The remaining two poems belong to a Christian tradition of debate between the soul and an antagonist. Following that tradition in one poem, Marvell allows the soul to triumph and to receive its commendation. The other poem suspends the contest, giving the last word to the body.

"A Dialogue Between The Resolved Soul, and Created Pleasure" offers three speakers, the two named in the title and a Chorus that cheers on the Soul. The Soul speaks only in eight-syllable couplets. Pleasure, offering various forms of gratification, is allowed a variety of line lengths and rhyme schemes, as well as eight lines more than the Soul. The result is that the Soul sounds dogged, inflexible, and curt in its dismissals. Only the praise of music evokes an answer as long as the tempter's speech.

The dialogue begins with 10 lines in which the Soul persistently uses the imagery of battle:

> Courage my Soul, now learn to wield
> The weight of thine immortal Shield.
> Close on thy Head thy Helmet bright.
> Ballance thy Sword against the Fight.

It is somewhat confusing to find the first speaker addressing "my Soul," since we assume that it is the Soul speaking. An alternative would be to suppose that the first 10 lines are given to an unidentified speaker, presumably a human being who sees that his soul must sustain the burden of combat. He is oddly uncertain about the status of the soul:

> Now, if thou bee'st that thing Divine,
> In this day's Combat let it shine:
> And shew that Nature wants an Art
> To conquer one resolved Heart.

Whatever the status of the soul, if it wins, the result will be a victory over Nature.

The other speaker, Pleasure (in some respects synonymous with Nature), never uses the imagery of battle. It simply offers an assortment of gratifications—pleasures of taste, touch, smell, sight, sound, a woman, wealth, glory, and wisdom—all summarily rejected by the Soul. None of Pleasure's speeches even vaguely recalls the Nun's subtle appeals in "Upon Appleton House." That is, they are not presented as invitations to sin. But the Soul sees them as occasions for sinfulness. The following exchange is typical:

Pleasure

If thou bee'st with Perfumes pleas'd,
Such as oft the Gods appeas'd,
Thou in fragrant Clouds shalt show
Like another God below.

Soul

A Soul that knowes not to presume
Is Heaven's and its own perfume.

It is logical that Pleasure should argue literally and the Soul metaphorically. In every exchange the Soul finds some reason for rejecting what Pleasure has to offer.

Pleasure

On these downy Pillows lye,
Whose soft Plumes will thither fly:
On these Roses strow'd so plain
Lest one Leaf thy Side should strain.

Soul

My gentler Rest is on a Thought,
Conscious of doing what I ought.

The real issue is not even stated in the dialogue: the Soul sets no value on anything Pleasure has to offer. Its aim is to mount to Heaven, to surpass Nature. The Soul is truly resolved. In the concluding lines a Chorus sings its triumph:

Triumph, triumph, victorious Soul;
The World has not one Pleasure more;
The rest does lie beyond the Pole,
And is thine everlasting Store.

We can hardly disagree with the Chorus: the World has offered all its pleasures in vain. The "rest" may mean what remains of the Soul's existence. It may mean the end of the Soul's contest. There is no reason why it should not mean both.

But Marvell has left us with a question that this dialogue cannot answer: is it a Christian poem? Pleasure refers to the gods; the Soul does not object to the plural, nor does it ever call upon God. The speaker at the beginning of the poem is not certain that the Soul is divine. The Chorus is unidentified, and the term *Heaven* is not uniquely Christian. The assumptions that the Christian tradition would allow us to make may not apply to this poem. Not only are the central Christian doctrines of grace and atonement not mentioned, but the Soul appears to have an innate urge to rise above its earthly home and to find its rest elsewhere. Surely this is nearer to Platonism than to Christianity.[14]

The elusiveness of this dialogue suggests that it is a more mature poem than "On a Drop of Dew," which also deals with the soul's yearning for its heavenly origin. There is a contest in "A Dialogue" and a clear indication of a decisive outcome. But the significance of Marvell's lyric eludes us because we do not know what kind of universe the poem is portraying. His refusal to make the kind of commitment that Milton makes in *Paradise Regained* (also a poem about a victory over temptation) gives this poem the opportunity to play out a witty game in which the reader's pleasure depends entirely on the restrained, polite parry and thrust of combatants who seem to have nothing to gain or to lose.

A similar lack of commitment pervades "A Dialogue between the Soul and Body." There are two speakers but no contest and no decision. Each accuses the other of deliberate torment. Yet they speak in the same voice: a witty deployment of puns and paradoxes neatly packed into eight-syllable closed couplets. The point of this game is to portray a fundamental estrangement between the two parts of human existence. The method is to show that the powers of each component are precisely designed to frustrate the desires of the other. It is a simple game, but Marvell plays it for all it is worth. He does not make the mistake of trying to resolve the conflict or of slanting it in favor of either speaker,[15] although the Body does get four more lines than the Soul. In modern terms, the Body and the Soul are the odd couple. Their plight is essentially comic.[16]

When editors of poetry anthologies choose selections from Marvell's verse, they frequently include "A Dialogue between the Soul and Body." There are good reasons for this. It is brief and wonderfully witty. It provides an excellent example of Marvell's skill in manipulating tetrameter couplets. Its subject matter seems to justify the term *meta-physical*. And, while the speakers are totally committed to their own arguments, Marvell is characteristically elusive.

Despite the title, the poem is not a dialogue. Only in its final speech does the Body address the Soul; the Soul never speaks directly to the Body. Apparently, each speaker listens to the other as every speech is a direct response to the one preceding it. The poem belongs to a long tradition,[17] but Marvell breaks with tradition by leaving the issue suspended. As we have seen, the Resolved Soul wins its contest with Created Pleasure, but the struggle between Soul and Body appears to be unending.

The essential position of each speaker is presented in images: for the Soul the Body is a dungeon, for the Body the Soul is a disease. Each wields tyrannical power over the other. The dilemma is not presented in Christian terms. In fact, the Body's accusation that the Soul has fitted it for sin reverses the traditional Christian (and Platonic) contrast between flesh and spirit. Marvell's abandonment of traditional imagery frees his imagination to make this contest original and open. Neither speaker can rely on an established response to its complaints.

This original handling of traditional material accounts in part for the pleasure this poem provides. But its wit is even more striking. It consists of a nearly unbroken string of puns and paradoxes—statements that appear to contradict themselves or contain contradictory elements. For a very simple example, the Body complains that the Soul "Has made me live to let me dye." Similarly, the Soul must share the Body's griefs:

> Where whatsoever it complain,
> I feel, that cannot feel, the pain.

These, however, are mild compared to the outrageous charges leveled elsewhere in the poem. In its first speech the Soul presents a detailed picture of itself as a prisoner of the Body:

> O who shall, from this Dungeon, raise
> A Soul inslav'd so many wayes?
> With bolts of Bones, that fetter'd stands
> In Feet; and manacled in Hands.
> Here blinded with an Eye; and there
> Deaf with the drumming of an Ear.

The last line offers a simple play on "drum." There is more wit in the play on "Feet" and "fetter'd." But to be "manacled in Hands" is to participate fully in the same sort of paradox that "blinded with an Eye" expresses: all the powers of the Body are shackles for the Soul. The Body is no less witty in voicing its complaint:

> O who shall me deliver whole,
> From bonds of this Tyrannic Soul?
> Which, stretcht upright, impales me so,
> That mine own Precipice I go.

The Body is actually impaled on the Soul, forced to adopt an upright position that leaves it in constant danger of falling. Worse still, the Body has *become* the precipice from which it may fall.

Perhaps the wittiest line in the poem occurs in the Soul's second speech:

> And all my Care its self employes,
> That to preserve, which me destroys.
> Constrain'd not only to indure
> Diseases, but, whats worse, the Cure:
> And ready oft the Port to gain,
> Am Shipwrackt into Health again.

The Soul's port is its release from the Body and return to its creator. This seafaring metaphor explains the paradox of being shipwrecked into health. The wittiness of the line may lead us to overlook the weakness of rhyming "gain" with "again." But it is the only weakness in a poem which demonstrates Marvell's skill in handling short-line couplets, taking advantage of their brevity, and snapping them like a whip.

> Constrain'd not only to indure
> Diseases, but, whats worse, the Cure.

The second line not only balances perfectly on the two objects of "indure"; it also explodes into paradox in its final syllable.

Scholars have found a troubling problem in this poem: the final speech of the Body is four lines longer than the preceding speeches, yet it hardly sounds conclusive. Here are the last four lines:

What but a Soul could have the wit
To build me up for Sin so fit?
So Architects do square and hew,
Green Trees that in the Forest grew.

Is this poem finished? Certainly not if we expect Marvell to signal a victory for one of the speakers. But to end with a simile implying that the Soul has acted against the Body's nature is merely to repeat what the Body has already said with far greater force. The effect is anticlimactic. The Soul's most effective lines come at the end of its second speech. Why does the Body's second speech end so feebly? The simplest explanation is that Marvell did not finish the poem. It is unfinished not because Marvell failed to tell who won the argument but because he failed to give a clear signal—not that the argument was over but that the poem was over. Since he does not fail to do this in any other poem, there is good reason to consider this one incomplete.[18]

Among the poems in this chapter, there is only one ("Bermudas") that is almost always anthologized and none for which Marvell is famous. Although they vary in prosody, topic, and rhetorical approach, these poems share one characteristic: none of them is spoken in the unmediated voice of the singer, the "I" whose experience is conveyed directly to us. Poems of this sort are the subject of the next chapter.

Chapter Five

Personal Poems

The eleven poems in this chapter are personal in the sense that in each the reader hears the voice of one speaker who calls himself or herself "I" and who is concerned with his or her own experiences. There is no narrator or presenter who stands between the reader and the speaker. These poems fit the pattern usually found in English lyric poetry. In them the reader is most tempted to suppose that the speaker is Andrew Marvell. Consequently, it will be useful to begin with a poem whose speaker is certainly not the poet.

"The Nymph complaining for the death of her Faun" is one of the most enigmatic and most frequently anthologized of Marvell's poems. Like "The unfortunate Lover" it presents a situation for which there is no useful parallel in literature. It seems designed to keep a reader consistently off balance, yet its poise and polish suggest that it is the work of a mature, confident poet.

The speaker is a young woman. The situation is made clear in the first two lines:

> The wanton Troopers riding by
> Have shot my Faun and it will dye.

For the rest of the poem the speaker laments the loss of her faun, remembers how she received it, lovingly recalls its unusual habits, resolves to join it in death, and plans a monument as their memorial. Summarized in these flat, general terms, the poem loses all the qualities that make it fascinating and disturbing. But the details tell another story.

From the very beginning the reader is thrust into a world that frustrates all attempts to give it a time or place. The word *Troopers* in line one first appeared in the English language in 1640. It referred to the cavalry of the Covenanting Army. It locates the place and time of the events in the poem. But the nymph recalls that "Unconstant *Sylvio*" gave her the faun. Sylvio is hardly a common English name. The nymph's resolution to place a vial of tears in "*Diana's* Shrine" puts the

poem in the ancient pagan world; so does her reference to "Elizium."
But her declaration that "Heavens King / Keeps register of every thing"
echoes Jesus' promise that God observes the death even of a sparrow.
The faun itself has no place in the real world. The nymph insists on its
whiteness and the softness of its feet. Its preferred diet consists of roses
and lilies. It challenges the nymph to races, plays hide-and-seek, kisses
her, and weeps as it is dying. There is no other animal in literature that
even vaguely resembles this faun.

But the most disconcerting aspect of the poem depends on the mixture of narrative and dramatic elements that makes it impossible for the
reader to understand the nymph's state of mind. The faun is dying at
the beginning of the nymph's lament. Its death occurs in line 94. The
dramatic situation calls for a total concentration on the suffering animal.
Instead, most of the first 93 lines display the sort of thinking that would
be natural in someone who had put the initial shock behind her. Over
the body of the dying faun, the nymph feels resentment toward Sylvio
and is able to wonder whether the faun in time might also have betrayed
her as Sylvio did:

>   Had it liv'd long, I do not know
>   Whether it too might have done so
>   As *Sylvio* did: his Gifts might be
>   Perhaps as false or more than he.

Since the faun has never done anything to justify this speculation, it is
hard to imagine why such a thought would come into the nymph's
mind.

While the faun is still dying, she remembers the day Sylvio brought
it as a present:

>   Unconstant *Sylvio*, when yet
>   I had not found him counterfeit,
>   One morning (I remember well)
>   Ty'd in this silver Chain and Bell,
>   Gave it to me: nay and I know
>   What he said then; I'me sure I do.
>   Said He, look how your Huntsman here
>   Hath taught a Faun to hunt his *Dear*.

> But *Sylvio* soon had me beguil'd.
> This waxed tame, while he grew wild,
> And quite regardless of my Smart,
> Left me his Faun, but took his Heart.

She has not gotten over Sylvio's falsehood. She can even recall the ambiguous words he spoke, or thinks she can ("I'me sure I do" does not bolster confidence in her memory). Then she devotes 48 of the following 56 lines to remembering the faun's behavior, as if it were already dead. She seems to be reconciled to the faun's death before it occurs, while Sylvio's falsehood still rankles.

Near the end the nymph resolves to join the faun in death. The last section of the poem describes her funeral monument:

> First my unhappy Statue shall
> Be cut in Marble; and withal,
> Let it be weeping too: but there
> Th' Engraver sure his Art may spare;
> For I so truly thee bemoane,
> That I shall weep though I be Stone:
> Until my Tears, still dropping, wear
> My breast, themselves engraving there.
> There at my feet shalt thou be laid,
> Of purest Alabaster made:
> For I would have thine Image be
> White as I can, though not as Thee.

The nymph's concentration on herself and the preservation of her grief hints at a kind of narcissism, a sentimental pleasure in dwelling on her loss that expresses itself most clearly in her witty conceit regarding her tears. On the other hand, the simplicity and straightforwardness of her language through most of the poem give an impression of tender innocence that is found in several other poems discussed in this chapter.

Another kind of dislocation arises from the fact that the nymph begins by referring to the faun as *it*, as if she were speaking to some unspecified hearer. In lines 3 through 12 she speaks directly to the faun. Thereafter she regularly uses *it* (with the exception of line 53) until line 110. From there to the end she addresses the now-dead faun. If she

spoke directly to the faun while it was still alive and switched to *it* after
its death, there would be no problem. But most of her lines to the faun
occur after its death.

As if this were not confusing enough, Marvell's lines appear to offer
clues to an allegorical interpretation. Near the beginning the nymph
declares that the troopers who shot the faun cannot possibly be cleansed
of guilt:

> Though they should wash their guilty hands
> In this warm life-blood, which doth part
> From thine, and wound me to the Heart,
> Yet could they not be clean: their Stain
> Is dy'd in such a Purple Grain.
> There is not such another in
> The World, to offer for their Sin.

The concept of the last couplet is presented in specifically Christian
terms. If the faun had been a lamb, an allegorical interpretation would
be inescapable. Other lines point to a parallel with the Song of Songs
(sometimes called The Song of Solomon), which itself had been treated
as an allegory by Christian interpreters for over a thousand years. Marvell's poem has been read as a lament for the destruction of the Anglican
Church or as a symbolic expression of Christ's love for the Church or as a
parallel to the sacrificial death of the Lamb of God.[1]

But the allegorical interpretations face at least one great difficulty:
Sylvio and the romantic attraction the nymph feels for him. Though he
is not the principal figure in the poem, it is still hard to fit him into any
allegory. In addition, allegory tends to point us away from the human
situation that *is* the principal focus of the poem. Simply put, the nymph,
betrayed by Sylvio, has lavished her affection on the faun. Their kisses
and game-playing imply a sexual content in this relationship of which
the nymph is totally unaware. On the other hand, the power of this sexual attraction is called into question by the nymph's unresolved feelings
for Sylvio, which distract her even as she is witnessing the death of the
faun. Her resolution to join the faun in death is both a natural consequence of her present sorrow and, if she carries it out, a grotesque exaggeration of normal human behavior.

We have already seen Marvell's propensity for creating unusual situations and for presenting lyric verse in a narrative or dramatic frame-

work. This poem is dramatic in that it presents a sequence of events as occurring while we read of them. But the nymph's recollection of past events gives the poem a narrative character. The tension between dramatic and narrative impulses added to the tension between the nymph's awakening sexuality and her tender innocence makes this one of Marvell's most appealing lyrics. An allegorical interpretation, even a convincing one, should not discourage readers from responding to this charming portrait of a naive young girl's first experience of love and loss.[2]

In each of the next two poems, the speaker is a mower. Some scholars assume that he is the Damon of "Damon the Mower" and that he is also the speaker of "The Mower against Gardens." In the 1681 volume the mower poems appear as a group, and in three of the four the speaker is hopelessly in love with Juliana.[3] But there is an important distinction between the first two mower poems discussed in the preceding chapter and the two in this chapter: these poems are spoken, or sung, by an unmediated voice. The speaker states his complaint directly, without presentation or framework.

In "The Mower to the Glo-Worms," only the title identifies the speaker. Nothing that he says indicates that he is a mower, and his one reference to mowers does not obviously include himself. A tradition stretching back to ancient Rome associates glowworms (beetles that emit light from the abdomen) with haying. The speaker attributes to them three useful though quite fanciful functions. They provide light for the nightingale to study her songs; they signal the time for cutting grass; and they show the way to mowers who are lost in the dark. But, he concludes, the glowworms cannot help him:

> Your courteous Lights in vain you wast,
> Since *Juliana* here is come,
> For She my Mind hath so displac'd
> That I shall never find my home.

More than any of the other mower poems, this one impresses us by its poise and finish.[4] Perhaps for that reason it is the most frequently anthologized of the group. Each of the first three stanzas begins with an address: "Ye living Lamps," "Ye Country Comets," "Ye Glo-worms." Each stanza defines one of the glowworms' functions. In no stanza is it possible to take the speaker seriously. He speaks the language of courtly compliment, of hyperbole and delicate fancy. If he is Damon, he has learned to express his complaint lightheartedly and with a humility that makes the glowworms, not the vainglorious mower, the center of interest.

The speaker, or singer, of "The Mower's Song" clearly *is* a mower. He speaks of the "fellowship" between himself and the meadows. They have been "Companions of my thoughts more green." His song complains of the faithless behavior of the meadows, which continue to grow and flourish while he has been mowed down by Juliana. His revenge will be to cut down both flowers and grass and use them to adorn his tomb. He does not sound like the speaker of the preceding poem. His tone is not so light, and the refrain that concludes each of the five stanzas,

> When *Juliana* came, and She
> What I do to the Grass, does to my Thoughts and Me,

although it is not inappropriate in a song, makes him appear to be obsessive. He shows something of Damon's exalted opinion of himself, but his childish impulse toward revenge on the meadows makes Damon look mature by comparison.

It is probably most appropriate to regard the mower poems as Marvell's experiments with a new kind of pastoral. The three in which Juliana is named differ from each other in prosody, and because the speakers have little in common it is not possible to trace a development in them. Nor is there any need to: each poem stands as an independent achievement.

In the eight poems that remain to be discussed, it could be supposed that the speaker is Andrew Marvell. Each presents a situation or an attitude that might reflect his experience. In fact, some of them almost demand to be read as autobiographical. If more were known about Marvell's life, perhaps a connection could be established. But, following the method we have been using, each poem will be read as a personal utterance without any assumption that the person speaking is the poet himself.

"The Coronet" appears to be an act of contrition by a Christian lamenting his sinfulness. Like "On a Drop of Dew" it centers on an image, an emblem whose significance will be interpreted during the course of the poem. The speaker wants to crown his Savior's head with a garland of flowers to make amends for the crown of thorns with which he has wounded Him. But he finds "the Serpent old" disguised among the flowers, and, realizing that his contrition itself is mingled with

"Fame and Interest," he calls on his Savior to free him from his dilemma. The poem may be read as a statement of orthodox Christian doctrines: the innate depravity of humankind and the freely offered grace of God. Two aspects of "The Coronet" are puzzling. First, though its topics are sin and grace, those words do not appear in the poem. For that matter, neither do the words *God* or *Christ*. Second, the speaker's reference to "my Shepherdesses head" (*Shepherdesses* is possessive, not plural) suggests that he is a shepherd, a piece of information apparently irrelevant to his situation, which is universal, according to Christian doctrine. Desirable as it might be to base an interpretation of the poem on these two features, they do not lead anywhere.[5]

But there is another aspect of "The Coronet" that does appear to be significant. Its meter and rhyme scheme work together to produce an effect of weaving and winding. The lines vary from three to five feet in length. The rhyme scheme is unusually complicated and marks the turns in thought. The first 12 lines rhyme *abba*. The turn in lines 13–16 is marked by a new rhyme scheme: *abab*. The last 10 lines begin with a couplet showing the speaker's recognition that his dilemma is one he shares with all mankind:

Ah, foolish Man, that would'st debase with them,
And mortal Glory, Heavens Diadem!

The following six lines rhyme *abcabc*, and the whole poem concludes with a couplet that, in its last line, states the speaker's humble realization of how little he can do to honor his Savior:

That they [flowers], while Thou on both their Spoils dost tread,
May crown thy Feet, that could not crown thy Head.

The variety of line length and rhyme scheme in this poem link it to "On a Drop of Dew" and suggests that it is an early work. Whenever it was composed, it is the only poem by Marvell that is an unambiguous statement of Christian doctrine. The weaving effect of its prosody might justify the conclusion that the speaker's coronet is, in fact, his lines of verse. If so, the effect is much more subtle than in Herbert's "Sin's Round" or "The Wreath" or Donne's sonnet sequence *La Corona*.[6] No other poem by Marvell makes a comparable attempt to unite form and content. And very few of his lyrics exhibit so unambiguous an attitude toward their subject.

"Eyes and Tears" is one of several seventeeth-century poems about tears (Donne's "A Valediction: Of Weeping" and Crashaw's "The Weeper" are the best-known examples). The eyes and tears are the speaker's own, and the cause of the tears is only hinted at. There is no narrative behind this poem, no particular event that led the speaker to weep. Stanza five exemplifies the vagueness of his sorrow:

> I have through every Garden been,
> Amongst the Red, the White, the Green;
> And yet, from all the flow'rs I saw,
> No Hony, but these Tears could draw.

For some unstated reason, the speaker admires eyes swollen with weeping and compares them to other rounded objects,

> Not full sailes hasting loaden home,
> Nor the chast Ladies pregnant Womb,
> Nor *Cynthia* Teeming [the full moon] show's so fair,
> As two Eyes swoln with weeping are.

The final stanza calls for eyes and tears to become identical:

> Thus let your Streams o'reflow your Springs,
> Till Eyes and Tears be the same things:
> And each the other's difference bears;
> These weeping Eyes, those seeing Tears.

Apparently Marvell was trying his hand at a popular subject. The appearance of Mary Magdalen in stanza eight is to be expected. But her weeping was for a cause. Since we know of no good reason for the speaker's sorrow, the poem resembles a finger exercise for pianists, a witty playing in an ocean of grief that is merely puddle-deep.[7] It is among the least frequently anthologized of Marvell's lyrics in our century. Oddly enough, a portion was reprinted in a seventeeth-century anthology, and the poem was praised in a medical textbook published in 1747 (Margoliouth, 1:245).

The six remaining poems are concerned with love. In all but one the speaker is clearly a man, but only four are spoken to the person he loves.

Two of these persons can hardly be referred to as women, since the poems dwell on the fact that they are close to the beginning of their lives. None of these poems implies that there has been a sexual consummation or even looks forward to one. Nor is there evidence that the speaker has any interest in the feelings of the person he professes to love.

"The Fair Singer" is Marvell's only poem in the Venus and Adonis stanza (so named because Shakespeare used it for his narrative poem, *Venus and Adonis*). The speaker is love's unwilling victim, conquered by his lady's beauty and her voice. Beauty alone he could resist, but her voice captivates his mind, and the combination is overwhelming. The imagery throughout the poem derives from warfare. Marvell's witty use of martial terminology is well illustrated by the final stanza:

> It had been easie fighting in some plain,
> Where Victory might hang in equal choice,
> But all resistance against her is vain,
> Who has th'advantage both of Eyes and Voice,
> And all my Forces needs must be undone,
> She having gained both the Wind and Sun.

This is certainly a reluctant lover. Were the odds fairer, he would have fled, but he is now the singer's slave. Clearly "The Fair Singer" has taken an unfair advantage of him. In choosing the Venus and Adonis stanza, Marvell might well have thought it appropriate for his speaker, since Adonis fled from all of Venus's attempts to seduce him. But Shakespeare's poem is lush and erotic. Marvell's speaker has no intentions of any kind except to complain of the "fatal Harmony" that has made him a prisoner. Although this is a poem about love, it is hardly a conventional love poem.

"The Match," Marvell's only poem in common meter (alternating tetrameter and trimeter lines rhyming *abab*) is so carefully planned that its form undermines its substance. Four stanzas praise the perfect beauty of Celia: she is a compound of all of Nature's choicest treasures. The next five stanzas describe the fiery passion the speaker feels for Celia. The final stanza presents an unexpectedly sedate account of the lovers' happiness:

> So we alone the happy rest,
> Whilst all the World is poor,

And have within our Selves possest
All Love's and Nature's store.

In the first line, "rest" is a verb that calls attention to itself by its syntactical ambiguity. We expect "happy" to be an adjective, not a noun. After
the speaker's description of his burning passion, "rest," while it clearly
means "remain," implies a passive condition quite at odds with his declaration, "None ever burn'd so hot, so bright."

There is a puzzling shift of focus in the poem. The stanzas praising
Celia's beauty are not addressed to her. Neither are the stanzas devoted
to the lover's passion until the last line of stanza nine, which is spoken to
Celia. The final stanza, quoted above, shifts to first-person plural pronouns ("we," "our Selves"). This blurring of focus deprives the poem of
dramatic force. So does the mythological narrative, which makes Nature
and Love the chief characters and places the speaker and Celia in the
same realm of idealized embodiment. The result is that Marvell is dealing with passion in terms that deny its human reality.

Something of this same retreat from physical embodiment informs
"The Gallery." In seven eight-line stanzas of tetrameter couplets the
speaker asks Clora to view the pictures of her that make his soul a portrait gallery.[8] There are more than a thousand of them, "In all the Forms
thou can'st invent / Either to please me, or torment." He describes two
of each—an "Inhumane Murtheress" and an enchantress, a sleeping
goddess and Venus "in her pearly Boat"—and then concludes with a
description of his favorite portrait:

> But, of these Pictures and the rest,
> That at the Entrance likes [pleases] me best:
> Where the same Posture, and the Look
> Remains, with which I first was took.
> A tender Shepherdess, whose Hair
> Hangs loosely playing in the Air,
> Transplanting Flow'rs from the green Hill,
> To crown her Head, and Bosome fill.

Although this poem is a remarkable witness to Clora's power over the
speaker, both to please and torment, in fact each of these portraits is a
retreat from the "real" Clora, a fantasy that the speaker indulges in to
avoid confronting the flesh-and-blood woman.[9] Certainly it is a graceful

form of compliment and an early indication of Marvell's fascination with portrait poetry (each portrait is a vivid evocation of sensory effects, especially that of Venus, which is comparable to Enobarbus's wonderful description of Cleopatra in Shakespeare's *Antony and Cleopatra*, 2.2). Significantly, the last portrait, the speaker's favorite, emphasizes innocence and naturalness. Like "The Match," "The Gallery" presents love in terms of disembodied images. Its artifice functions to replace rather than to reveal passion.

Even if the speakers of these poems are not to be identified with Andrew Marvell, their ways of speaking about a beloved woman suggest that Marvell, who invented them, may himself have been reluctant to take on the guise of a passionate lover. The speakers of the next two poems have found a way to experience love without passion: each addresses a child.

"Young Love" begins with an invitation:

> Come little Infant, Love me now,
>   While thine unsuspected years
> Clear thine aged Fathers brow
>   From cold Jealousie and Fears.

This teeters on the brink of perversion, and the fact that similar poems might have served as models for Marvell (see Leishman, 165–171) does little to relieve our anxiety, for this poem's language is full of implications. What are we to make, for example, of stanza four?

> Love as much the snowy Lamb
>   Or the wanton Kid does prize,
> As the lusty Bull or Ram,
>   For his morning Sacrifice.

This language of sacrifice emphasizes the physical demands of love. The second stanza is similarly suggestive.

> Pretty surely 'twere to see
>   By young Love old Time beguil'd:
> While our Sportings are as free
>   As the Nurses with the Child.

Apparently it is the father who will be beguiled. And if this love is innocent, why should their "sportings" not be free? The stanza seems to say
that the youth of the "little Infant" will let the lover get away with anything. The final stanzas, recalling Donne's passionate statements of a
mature love that makes the lovers rulers of their own private world,
drive home the inappropriateness of such a relationship between a man
and a child:

> Thus as Kingdomes, frustrating
>   Other Titles to their Crown,
> In the craddle crown their King,
>   So all Forraign Claims to drown,
>
> So, to make all Rivals vain,
>   Now I crown thee with my Love:
> Crown me with thy Love again,
>   And we both shall Monarchs prove.

The two stanzas that lack this kind of language are disturbingly reminiscent of Marvell's most famous poem, "To his Coy Mistress":

> Now then love me: time may take
>   Thee before thy time away:
> Of this Need wee'l Virtue make,
>   And learn Love before we may.
>
> So we win of doubtful Fate;
>   And, if good she to us meant,
> We that Good shall antedate,
>   Or, if ill, that Ill prevent.

As in "To his Coy Mistress," this speaker argues that, in any case, the
lovers cannot lose by seizing their opportunity. But when the speaker in
"Mistress" refers four times to love, there is no reason to question what
he means. What does the speaker in "Young Love" mean when he says,
"Now then love me"?

No one should presume to psychoanalyze Andrew Marvell by reading
a handful of his lyrics, especially since most of them were published after

his death. He may not have wanted any of them to appear in print. Furthermore, we have noted that he frequently treated traditional themes in unusual ways, experimenting with different kinds of speakers and points of view. Surely the poet who could invent the tempting speeches of a subtle nun could imagine a speaker whose intentions toward the "little Infant" are, at best, ambiguous. Still it is not surprising that "Young Love" is seldom included in anthologies of seventeeth-century poetry.

"The Picture of little T. C. in a Prospect of Flowers," another poem about a girl's youth and innocence, is usually found in anthologies, however. It presents none of the problems of "Young Love." The speaker makes no invitations to this young girl. Foreseeing the power that her beauty will have, he only wants to "see thy Glories from some shade." Rather than invitations, he offers advice. We can be comfortable with this speaker. He knows that this girl will break some hearts; he just wants to admire her from afar.

Was little T. C. a person whose identity can be established? She might have been Theophila Cornewall,[10] whose older sister (also named Theophila) died two days after being born. If Marvell was writing for this T. C. (born 1644), the ominous final stanza would have to be taken seriously. But to a considerable extent Marvell has mythologized his subject, as he does in several poems about historical persons.

The poetry of courtly compliment and public praise has virtually ceased to be written, and modern readers are unfamiliar with its rules. We have already seen, in "Upon Appleton House," how far it was permissible for a poet to go in praising a patron. What counted more than anything else was the graceful and witty invention that defined the poet as worthy. Any sycophant could heap compliments on a patron; only a fool would desire such praise. Marvell's accomplishment in this poem is to make, with grace and charm, a number of preposterous statements.

In the first stanza the reader is invited to see "This Nimph" taming the "wilder" flowers and giving them names. "Nimph" is conventional enough to have lost its evocative power, but the giving of names to the flowers was the work of Eve, and the idea of taming "wilder" flowers, fantastic as it is, hints at a more than human capacity to affect the natural world. Another kind of power is described in the second stanza:

> Yet this is She whose chaster Laws
> The wanton Love shall one day fear,

> And, under her command severe,
> See his Bow broke and Ensigns torn.

Even Love itself will yield to "This Darling of the Gods." No wonder the speaker concludes this stanza with the exclamation,

> Happy, who can
> Appease this virtuous Enemy of Man!

In the fourth stanza the speaker asks T. C. to perform tasks that call for a godlike power—to give fragrance to tulips, to take the thorns from roses, and to endow violets with a longer life.

The final stanza presents a startling turn: the Nimph is cautioned to gather flowers but to spare the buds, lest Flora (the goddess of flowers) be angered by the killing of her infants and make an example of little T. C. The girl, after all, is just a human being, vulnerable to the anger of the gentlest of gods. And so the preposterous statements of the earlier stanzas are seen to be the heartfelt exaggerations of a true admirer.

But how are we to understand the title? Is the poem itself the picture or is it a response to a picture (a painting)? Although the speaker foresees the increasing power of her beauty, the picture presents no indication of change in her. The speaker begins with a command to the reader:

> See with what simplicity
> This Nimph begins her golden daies!

For two stanzas he speaks *of* T. C. In the last line of stanza three he first speaks *to* her. The last two stanzas continue the direct address to T. C., the fourth stanza made up of supplications to this darling of the gods, the last stanza a warning to a mortal child. In the last two lines the speaker includes us in his fear for her: "And, ere we see, / Nip in the blossome all our hopes and Thee."

In what sense, then, is this poem a picture? Only the first stanza offers pictorial details (T. C. lying in the grass, talking to and playing with flowers). The rest of the poem is not at all like "The Gallery," which really does imagine several pictures. When the speaker addresses T. C. he does not speak as if to a picture. Only by taking the word in a figurative sense (as a vivid verbal description) can we call this poem a picture. But "in a Prospect of Flowers" plainly indicates a setting for a literal picture.

All this worrying over a title might be a waste of time if this poem fitted into some traditional category.[11] But it is not known whether T. C. was even a real person. The kind of compliment Marvell pays her has parallels in the work of poets as different as Jonson, Donne, and Milton. The gentle concern for flowers in stanza four is the same as Robert Herrick's. The mildly mythological atmosphere characterizes courtly compliment throughout the seventeeth century. But nobody else wrote a poem like this one. Its wide appeal is demonstrated by its inclusion in 13 of the 20 most important modern anthologies of seventeenth-century poetry. As much as any of his poems, this one illustrates the delicacy, the charm, and the elusiveness of Marvell's verse.

The final personal poem discussed here is an enigma. "The Definition of Love" is as purely abstract a treatment of love as could be imagined. It begins with a mystery:

> My Love is of a birth as rare
> As 'tis for object strange and high:
> It was begotten by despair
> Upon Impossibility.

"My Love" could very well mean "the woman I love," and her high birth might explain the speaker's reference to despair. But the "It" of line three rules out such an interpretation. As the third and fourth stanzas make clear, this love is opposed by Fate:

> And yet I quickly might arrive
> Where my extended Soul is fixt,
> But Fate does Iron wedges drive,
> And alwaies crouds it self betwixt.

> For Fate with jealous Eye does see
> Two perfect Loves; nor lets them close:
> Their union would her ruine be,
> And her Tyrannick pow'r depose.

Therefore Fate has made the lovers like the opposite poles, "Not by themselves to be embrac'd."

The poem is a definition in the literal sense of the word: it marks off the limits of this love.[12] But, in ways that Marvell may not have intended, it suggests other limits. For example, the other person in this relationship is neither named nor addressed, though she is at least included in the pronouns of the last four stanzas ("us," "ours"). The speaker has found wonderfully apt explanations for this separation (with analogies from mapmaking, geometry, and astronomy), but nothing implies that he has any serious objection to it. In fact, it confers on him and his beloved a special status:

> Therefore the Love which us doth bind.
> But Fate so enviously debarrs,
> Is the Conjunction of the Mind,
> And Opposition of the Stars.

In the face of this hopeless situation (for who would be fool enough to challenge Fate?), the speaker may be allowed the luxury of witty analogies. Our problem as readers is that his love seems to be as devoid of human feeling as his geometry.

Why then is this poem so frequently reprinted (in 16 out of 20 modern anthologies of seventeeth-century poetry)? Only "Bermudas," "To his Coy Mistress," and "The Garden" appear more often. I suspect that the compilers of these anthologies found that "The Definition of Love" fitted one of their definitions of metaphysical poetry. Its abstract treatment of love might be called metaphysical, and its use of imagery from cartography and astronomy is reminiscent of learned images in Donne's love poetry.[13]

The speaker of this poem illustrates the same reluctant attitude toward sexual passion that we have seen in all the first-person love lyrics in this chapter. He has found the perfect solution to the problem: fall in love with someone from whom you are separated by an insuperable barrier. Of course the barrier may increase the passion, and the intensity of the poetry in which it is expressed. But Marvell's lovers convey no more than a mild regret. Not for them the desperate yearning of Romeo for Juliet or, to come nearer to Marvell's time and temperament, the impassioned pleading of the repentant Eve to Adam in *Paradise Lost*. Marvell is no less a poet for this lack of powerful feeling. He is simply not a major poet, and could not have been had he written 10 times as many poems.

I do not think Marvell would object to this observation. He appears to have had no desire to be measured against the great poets of Western civilization (as Milton clearly did). He wrote a small body of lyrics and during his lifetime published only a few, none of them among his finest. Typically his poems shy away from a deep passionate engagement with their subject. His best-known lyric is unlike all the rest of his verse precisely because it does speak passionately and single-mindedly of love and death. Still, it is no small achievement to have written one of the most famous poems in the English language. And a poet who speaks in a unique voice, as Marvell does, will always provide a special kind of pleasure that no other poet can offer. So to call him a minor poet is not to devalue his poetry or his worth.

Marvell is still a major presence in the modern response to seventeeth-century English poetry. Over 700 books and articles devoted entirely or in part to Marvell's poems have been published in the past 90 years. The revival of interest in metaphysical poetry received a tremendous impetus from T. S. Eliot's analysis of Marvell's verse. In 1978 there was a huge outpouring of books and scholarly articles commemorating the 300th anniversary of his death. Since then, a dozen books concerned solely with Marvell's poems have appeared. Although there is a remarkable amount of interest in nearly all of Marvell's poetry, three poems—the ones that will be examined in the next chapter—are largely responsible for this flood of scholarship and criticism.

Chapter Six

Three Masterpieces

While it is difficult to anticipate the tastes of future generations of readers, the three poems in this chapter will probably form the basis for Marvell's continuing reputation. It is hard to imagine that "To his Coy Mistress" will ever fall out of favor. During the past 90 years "The Garden" has elicited nearly as much attention from scholars and has been anthologized almost as often as "Mistress." "An Horatian Ode" is not far behind. Consequently it is all the more striking that these poems have so little in common. To be sure, all three are spoken by a single voice and are relatively short, but they differ in subject matter, in verse form, in the speaker's attitude toward his subject, and in their relation to the rest of Marvell's poetry.

"To his Coy Mistress" is certainly Marvell's best-known poem. Nearly 200 scholarly studies are devoted to its explication.[1] It appears in every modern anthology of seventeenth-century poetry. No analysis of metaphysical poetry can afford to ignore it. Its power and passion are undeniable. Yet it is the least Marvellian of all his poems. To begin with, "To his Coy Mistress" fits perfectly into an identifiable poetic tradition. The carpe diem theme received memorable treatment from Marlowe, Donne, Jonson, Herrick, and Carew. Marvell's poem stands out only because of its grim vision of the grave and its passionate urging of the lover's case. In other words, it does what a typical carpe diem poem does, but it does so with unparalleled power.[2]

In the last chapter we saw that Marvell's first-person speakers hold ambiguous attitudes toward amorous passion. They suffer from the lady's coldness or they idealize her or they declare their love for a person who is unattainable. Even if the lady is compliant, the speaker is reluctant to press for a consummation. The speaker of "To his Coy Mistress" exhibits no reluctance or ambiguity. Whether his appeal is logical or not,[3] it is absolutely free of doubt about the desirability of a passionate relationship. And though it offers some of the light playfulness of other carpe diem poems—the same playfulness that is characteristic of most of Marvell's verse—it does so only to intensify the contrast with the grim seriousness that takes over after the first 20 lines.

90

Finally, "To his Coy Mistress" develops a rhythmic intensity and drive that are foreign to Marvell's verse. His usual treatment of the tetrameter couplet is relaxed, fanciful, playful. It is, in fact, just what we observe in the first 20 lines of this poem. There is no way to anticipate the sudden turn that sweeps up the poem and carries it into a realm that Marvell had never explored before and would never enter again.[4]

An acquaintance with Marvell's love poetry reveals several aspects of this poem that set it apart almost from the beginning. The speaker is not talking to a shepherdess or to a woman whose name implies a pastoral or a mythical setting. She is simply "Lady." While that form of address seems a bit stilted for a lover, it does not allow the woman to escape into some fictitious literary never-never land. Furthermore, the speaker locates himself in England by his reference to "the Tide of *Humber*," a real river, not a name from poetic tradition. The opening couplet, "Had we but World enough, and Time, / This coyness Lady were no crime," plainly implies that, in the world of the poem, the lady's coyness *is* a serious offense. This speaker is not at all reluctant to urge his case.

But the first 20 lines manage to lull any suspicions about the speaker. He indulges in the familiar hyperbole of courtly compliment. The exaggerations are witty and gracefully phrased:

> An hundred years should go to praise
> Thine Eyes, and on thy Forehead Gaze.
> Two hundred to adore each Breast:
> But thirty thousand to the rest.
> An Age at least to every part,
> And the last Age should show your Heart.

Surely so patient a lover will be considerate of the lady's natural reluctance. One more couplet completes this soothing prologue: "For Lady you deserve this State; / Nor would I love at lower rate."

What follows is doubly unexpected: unexpected because the calm and courtly opening offers no preparation, and unexpected because this is one of Marvell's poems. It should be elusive, ambiguous, cool. But, in one of the most powerfully moving reversals of rhythm and tone in English poetry, the speaker presents a vision of human mortality that evokes a chill along the spine:

> But at my back I alwaies hear
> Times winged Charriot hurrying near:

> And yonder all before us lye
> Desarts of vast Eternity.
> Thy Beauty shall no more be found;
> Nor, in thy marble Vault, shall sound
> My ecchoing Song: then Worms shall try
> That long preserv'd Virginity:
> And your quaint Honour turn to dust;
> And into ashes all my Lust.

The turn is almost literally breathtaking. The leisurely movement of "For, Lady, you deserve this state," with its two pauses and the necessary hesitation between the *s* sounds of "this" and "state," suddenly gives way to the haste of two enjambed couplets. There is no place to pause and catch a breath. The hurrying of "Times winged Charriot" is mirrored by the hurrying lines in which it appears. "Desarts of vast Eternity" is the sort of line that defies all attempts to account for its evocative power.[5] Nowhere else in his lyrics does Marvell create a picture of human mortality. Few poets have presented it in terms so vivid and so grim.

The wit that previously was playful is here sardonic: "then Worms shall try / That long preserv'd Virginity." Marvell's use of *try* is both simple and inspired. Of course it means "test" or "make a trial of." In this sense *try* is purely ironic. No part of the body can pass this test. But *try* can also mean "taste." In either sense, the word both masks and reveals the gruesome truth: the lady's body will be food for worms. Long before her honor turns to dust, she will be a hideous banquet.

Then comes the unforgettable couplet: "The Grave's a fine and private place, / But none I think do there embrace." We have already commented on the wit of these lines. Seeing them now in context, the full force of "I think" becomes evident. Nothing in the preceding 10 lines appears to be open to debate. Everything that we know about death supports the speaker's grim portrayal. Nevertheless, no one has ever returned to tell us what it is like *to be* in the grave. So he draws his modest conclusion, as if there were some room for doubt, as if it would not be polite to hammer home so distasteful and so obvious a point to a "Lady."

The last 14 lines carry the argument to a logical conclusion, the conclusion of all carpe diem poems: the lovers must take their pleasure now before they become time's victims. But no other poem of this type presents the lovers' actions in such violent terms. The speaker's first invitation, "Now let us sport us while we may," sounds light and pleasant enough; the images that follow do not. The lovers are to become "like am'rous birds of prey." They will "tear [their] Pleasures with rough strife / Thorough the Iron gates of Life." The desperation of their struggle reflects the desperation of the speaker's view of the grave that awaits them. In that respect, "To his Coy Mistress" develops logically. Desperate situations call for desperate measures. In the face of death and dissolution, human love can only summon up a desperate resolve to fend off the inevitable end.[6]

But the final couplet brings about a curious change of tone: "Thus, though we cannot make our Sun / Stand still, yet we will make him run." The sun image appears often in carpe diem poems, going back at least to Catullus. Ben Jonson's version of it is practically a translation of the Latin:

> Suns that set may rise again;
> But if once we lose this light,
> 'Tis with us perpetual night.

It is a serviceable image, contrasting the eternal order of the heavens with the short duration of human existence. It manages to avoid the repellent aspects of mortality that Marvell's speaker faces in his vision of the grave. But there is a different source and a different use for this sun image. The source is the biblical narrative of the battle at Gibeon, in which God "hearkened unto the voice" of Joshua and caused the sun to stand still while the Israelites slaughtered the Amorites (Joshua 10:9–14). The biblical writer offers a comment in verse 14: "And there was no day like that before it or after it." Clearly the lovers cannot make the sun stand still. But they can make it run. On the face of it, making the sun move faster would shorten their "long Loves Day." Apparently the speaker's meaning is that the lovers can make time hurry to keep up with them. The idea may not be new, but the expression is witty and compressed. The tone, however, is puzzling. The neatness of the closing couplet, with its easy assertion of a human means to frustrate the inevitable force of decay, clashes with the vivid picture of mortality that the speaker has just presented.

Like most carpe diem poems, "To his Coy Mistress" says nothing of marriage. It is, to borrow the title of another seventeenth-century poem of this type, a persuasion to love. Is it persuasive? In one sense it is the most persuasive of all of Marvell's poems: that is, it is single-mindedly devoted to moving the listener to a belief and to a course of action based on that belief. In another sense, the one we commonly have in mind when we use the word *persuasive* (does it succeed in persuading?), it can hardly hope to be persuasive. While we are reading it, we are caught up in its hyperbole and its passionate vision of life's brevity. It presents an intensely dramatic view of the lovers' need to seize the moment, to fill their brief time with pleasure. Its own brevity and the strength of its passion enact the speaker's message. It does what all great poetry does: it takes us into a world that is more vividly alive than the world we live in. But much of the pleasure we get from it depends on our awareness of how little it has to do with the real world, the world in which we have many days and love sometimes dies before the lovers. The speaker's "Lady" may find his arguments persuasive. As readers we can admire them for their brilliant sophistry only if they fail to persuade us.[7]

"The Garden" is so unlike "To his Coy Mistress" that it is hard to believe that the same person wrote both poems.[8] For the speaker of "The Garden," solitude fulfills the deepest needs of human beings. The soul, not the body, dominates this poem. The amorous passion that moves the speaker of "To his Coy Mistress" will cool because its object offers no lasting satisfaction. The struggle to achieve fame of any kind will be rewarded by a wreath made of just a small gathering of the leaves the garden offers freely and in endless profusion. There the soul can divest itself of the body that encumbers it and prepare "for longer flight."

The contrasts between the two poems should not be surprising. Once it is clear that Marvell enjoys experimenting with various forms and attitudes, his inconsistency can be seen as an aspect of his delight in creating different kinds of speakers, adopting different attitudes, and conveying a variety of messages. The romantic view of the poet as a man speaking to men was unknown in Marvell's time. The poet's skill was in making poems, not in baring his soul.[9]

In "The Mower against Gardens" we saw how skillfully Marvell could convey a message precisely the opposite of that presented in "The Garden." The mower argues that gardens are a perversion of innocent nature, a sort of horticultural prostitution. The vegetable kingdom has been corrupted by human intervention. In "The Garden" the speaker praises just such intervention: "How well the skilful Gardner drew / Of flow'rs and herbes this Dial new." The flowers and herbs form the face of a sundial, a highly artificial arrangement. The nectarines and peaches referred to in stanza five could not survive in an English climate unless the trees were planted against the south face of a brick or stone wall. The fountain in stanza seven suggests another human intervention.

Clearly Marvell's speaker is describing a cultivated garden of the same kind that the speaker in "Upon Appleton House" admires.

In several ways the speaker of "The Garden" resembles the "Appleton" speaker. Both adopt the eight-line stanza composed of four tetrameter couplets. Both respond enthusiastically to the order imposed upon nature by the garden. Both assign human characteristics to the vegetable inhabitants. But the "Appleton" speaker has his mystical experience in the woods, not in the garden, and his interest in the natural world extends to the meadows as well. As befits a much shorter poem, "The Garden" is more narrowly focused.

The speaker of "The Garden" is not addressing another person. We seem to be overhearing his thoughts. His only direct address is to "Fair Quiet," "Innocence," and "Fair Trees." There is no logical progression of thought, no argument that moves from point to point. Nor is there a movement in space such as we find in "Upon Appleton House." Praise of the garden begins in the first stanza and is sustained throughout the poem. Development, such as it is, involves a gradual revelation of the benefits of solitude, for it is solitude that makes the garden worthy of praise.

But why is solitude so precious? And what is the logical connection between solitude and the garden? We can best begin with the latter question. In his long and highly detailed essay "Of Gardens," Francis Bacon shows an enthusiasm that is unmatched in his other essays, an enthusiasm for formal gardens widely shared by many seventeenth-century Englishmen.[10] But he makes no mention of solitude or contemplation. The delight he takes in the garden is a delight in order and in a well-regulated variety. It is largely visual, a heightening of the sense of sight rather than a withdrawal from the body. Bacon's essay shows one kind of response to the garden—a planned, enclosed, artificial place—as it was experienced by a cultured gentleman of the seventeenth century. Marvell's speaker exhibits a different response, one not necessarily to be expected in his time and place.

The connection between solitude and the garden depends on the belief (nowhere stated directly in the poem) that anything the world outside the garden has to offer is more simply and satisfyingly available in the garden. That is to say, human needs do not require human society for their fulfillment. The garden satisfies every need. Put in so prosaic a fashion, this proposition drains all the wit and charm out of the poem. Nevertheless, it is the thread that runs through the whole composition and gives it continuity. The first stanza illustrates both the central idea of the poem and Marvell's witty presentation of it:

How vainly men themselves amaze
To win the Palm, the Oke, or Bayes;
And their uncessant Labours see
Crown'd from some single Herb or Tree.
Whose short and narrow verged Shade
Does prudently their Toyles upbraid;
While all Flow'rs and all Trees do close
To weave the Garlands of repose.

Although solitude and repose are not synonymous, the speaker treats
them as if they were. The garden offers both. The victor's garland that
Milton describes in *Areopagitica* as to be won "not without dust and
heat" consists of leaves woven into a crown, but the flowers and trees of
the garden offer "Garlands of repose." The human desire to wear a
crown that is a symbol of fame and achievement can be satisfied without
"uncessant Labours," whereas the crown society awards "upbraid[s]"
(that is, *reproaches*, with a play on *braid*) the wearer "prudently," presumably for his unnecessary strivings. The garden provides a better crown
and requires no effort from the recipient.

An attentive reader might well wonder why anyone would want a
crown so completely lacking in significance. But such a question never
occurs to the speaker. It must be understood that no part of "The Garden" presents an argument for the value of solitude and repose. Their
value is simply taken for granted. If one assumes, as the speaker does,
that solitude and repose are the crown of life, it is quite appropriate to
praise the garden for making them available to all.

But there is still no logical connection between solitude and the garden. The flowers and trees provide material for many crowns. There is
room in the garden for more than one person. With the second stanza
we begin to see a connection:

Fair quiet, have I found thee here,
And Innocence thy Sister dear!
Mistaken long, I sought you then
In busie Companies of Men.
Your sacred Plants, if here below,
Only among the Plants will grow.
Society is all but rude,
To this delicious Solitude.

There are two plants that will grow only in the garden—those that symbolize quiet and innocence. For some reason, the speaker has looked for them "In busie Companies of Men," presumably the same men whose "uncessant Labours" win the stunted crowns described in the first stanza. The final couplet proclaims a paradox: society, which is usually associated with manners and refinement, is almost crude in comparison to the solitude of the garden. The couplet, in its neatness and its wit, is itself an excellent example of the very refinement that the speaker finds wanting in society. Among the multiple ironies that play about this poem, not the least is the fact that gardens are products of society and require a certain amount of labor both to create and to maintain. There is no garden without a gardener.

The speaker resembles the "Appleton" speaker in his enthusiasm. Long before he describes the mystical ecstasy of the soul's escape from the body, it is clear that he is more concerned with a state of mind than with a physical location. Bacon described the garden as a place; Marvell's speaker conveys an ideal, a concept that may be associated with a garden. But he does so only by ignoring nearly every aspect of the garden as a real place.

This state of mind cannot be shared with anyone. The business of the next two stanzas is to proclaim a special relation between the speaker and the vegetable inhabitants of the garden: it is a form of love that is fully compatible with quiet and innocence.

> No white nor red was ever seen
> So am'rous as this lovely green.
> Fond Lovers, cruel as their Flame,
> Cut in these Trees their Mistress name.
> Little, Alas, they know, or heed,
> How far these Beauties Hers exceed!
> Fair Trees! where s'eer your barkes I wound,
> No Name shall but your own be found.
>
> When we have run our Passions heat,
> Love hither makes his best retreat.
> The *Gods*, that mortal Beauty chase,
> Still in a Tree did end their race.
> *Apollo* hunted *Daphne* so,
> Only that She might Laurel grow.

> And *Pan* did after *Syrinx* speed,
> Not as a Nymph, but for a Reed.

The garden provides a retreat for love, a refuge from "Passions heat."
We hear the authentic voice of Marvell's lover, turning away from the
pursuit of amorous passion and the consummation of sexual desire. In a
witty reinterpretation of classical mythology, the speaker attributes to
the gods the same love of plants and trees that he claims to feel. There is
no better example of Marvell's comic inversion than the speaker's apos-
trophe to the trees:

> Fair Trees! where s'eer your barkes I wound,
> No Name shall but your own be found.

The preposterousness of signaling one's love for a tree by carving its
name in the bark should let sober-minded readers know that they are
having their leg pulled by a reductio ad absurdum.[11]
   The next stanza claims that the plants in the garden actively minister
to the speaker's pleasure:

> What wond'rous Life in this I lead!
> Ripe Apples drop about my head;
> The Luscious Clusters of the Vine
> Upon my Mouth do crush their Wine;
> The Nectaren, and curious Peach,
> Into my hands themselves do reach;
> Stumbling on Melons, as I pass,
> Insnar'd with Flow'rs, I fall on Grass.

This picks up the implication found in the final couplet of the first
stanza: that the inhabitants of the garden offer themselves freely and in
profusion, so much so that they actually ensnare the speaker. He
becomes a willing prisoner. At least his body does.
   But the greatest benefit of the garden is to free the mind and soul
from imprisonment in the body:

> Mean while the Mind, from pleasure less,
> Withdraws into its happiness:

The Mind, that Ocean where each kind
Does streight its own resemblance find;
Yet it creates, transcending these,
Far other Worlds, and other Seas;
Annihilating all that's made
To a green Thought in a green Shade.

Here at the Fountains sliding foot,
Or at some Fruit-trees mossy root,
Casting the Bodies Vest aside,
My Soul into the boughs does glide:
There like a Bird it sits, and sings,
Then whets, and combs its silver Wings;
And, till prepar'd for longer flight,
Waves in its Plumes the various Light.

Oddly enough the greatest benefit the garden can bestow is to allow the speaker to transcend the natural forms with which it surrounds him. In the preceding three stanzas he has described its beauty and its special appeal to the senses. Now he tells us that it is a kind of launching pad for the spirit. The mind, "from pleasure less" (that is, because it finds less pleasure in the physical beauty of the garden), withdraws into itself, as it might in a quiet room or a deserted place. In fact, the mind would be *more* likely to retreat into itself in any place that offered solitude and repose without the distractions of physical beauty. Just as there is no logical connection between the garden and solitude, there is no logical connection between the garden and the soul's escape from the body.

The reason for insisting on this gap in logic is to point out a kind of arbitrariness in this poem. It is neither more nor less successful as a poem because it is arbitrary. One could argue that its charm is enhanced by the speaker's illogical claims. Like the "Appleton" speaker, he is an enthusiast who carries us along on the strength of his feelings. As in "To his Coy Mistress," we take pleasure in observing his wit even while we are aware of his quite limited, exaggerated views. Especially for American readers, he may suggest that mysterious, slightly comic English passion for gardening. The one thing we must not do is to regard this poem as a serious effort to convey a mystical experience or an argument for the superiority of the mind over the body.

The mind *is* different. It possesses a creative power that surpasses nature. It can even annihilate "all that's made," turning it into "a green Thought in a green Shade." Nothing in the poem implies that such a prodigious power is harmful or dangerous. But it is odd that the mind should turn away from the natural world. It wouldn't be odd if the natural world had been represented as deceptive or corrupted, a fairly conventional Christian interpretation. Marvell's speaker, it appears, is a Platonist of sorts. His soul is able to take flight, "Casting the Bodies Vest aside," and, like a bird, prepare its wings "for longer flight." But, of course, a Platonist has no business taking all that pleasure in natural forms that are merely shadows of reality unless he uses them as steps in a ladder of ascent to true beauty. Perhaps that is what the speaker intends to imply, but he never says so directly.

If we have accepted his view of the mind/soul as genuinely Platonic, we are in for a surprise in the next stanza:

> Such was that happy Garden-state,
> While Man there walk'd without a Mate:
> After a Place so pure, and sweet,
> What other Help could yet be meet!
> But 'twas beyond a Mortal's share
> To wander solitary there:
> Two Paradises 'twere in one
> To live in Paradise alone.

Here is a reference to a garden that has nothing to do with Platonism. Since the speaker has already described the garden as a place ideally suited to human needs, he can easily associate it with the place God designed for the first man. But his concluding couplet suggests that God made a mistake in providing a companion for Adam. The speaker plays on the biblical phrase "a help meet" (*meet* meaning "appropriate," literally "measured") in exclaiming that the garden was all the help Adam needed. It would be as absurd to take this for blasphemy as it would be to take seriously anything else the speaker says.[12] Marvell is trying on an attitude and finding witty ways to express it. But this particular attitude is one we have encountered before in his verse: it signals a retreat from passion and a love of innocence.

To the extent that this poem allows for a logical conclusion, that conclusion is stated at the end of stanza eight: "Two Paradises 'twere in one

/ To live in Paradise alone." The last stanza provides a return to the literal garden that emphasizes its artificiality:

> How well the skilful Gardner drew
> Of flow'rs and herbes this Dial new;
> Where from above the milder Sun
> Does through a fragrant Zodiack run;
> And, as it works, th'industrious Bee
> Computes its time as well as we.
> How could such sweet and wholsome Hours
> Be reckon'd but with herbs and flow'rs!

It has been argued that "this Dial" describes the whole garden. But the reference to the gardener's skill asks us to imagine an arrangement of herbs and flowers which mimics the face of a sundial. The acknowledgment of the gardener's contribution comes as a surprise, since the speaker has not previously acknowledged the need for labor or design in the garden. In the witty conceit that makes the bee into a chronologist as it gathers nectar from the dial, there is a reminiscence of the bee in "Upon Appleton House" who serves as a sentry guarding his flower. The whole poem ends with a rhetorical question (although the seventeenth-century punctuation disguises it as an exclamation).

This conclusion does not seem completely appropriate. Perhaps the emphasis on flowers and herbs is unexpected, since they were so seldom mentioned earlier. This garden possesses an unusually large number of trees. Perhaps it is because the speaker has abandoned the comic inversion of myth and the search for high significance in favor of looking (for the first time?) at a real garden. It is not that the conclusion is wrong. It is just not the one we might expect the speaker to make. The emphasis on solitude appears to be forgotten. So also is the role of the garden as a place of spiritual growth and as a reminder of Eden. After his ecstasy, the speaker has returned to the world of time; he cannot live in the garden.

Before leaving "The Garden," it will be useful to spend a few paragraphs on an aspect of Marvell's poetry that he shared with Carew, Lovelace, Suckling, Cowley, Thomas Randolph, Aurelian Townshend, Cleveland, Waller, and many lesser writers of his time. Perhaps it is best indicated by Pope's condescending reference to seventeenth-century poets as "The mob of gentlemen who wrote with ease" (*Imitations of Horace*, II:1:108). The key words are "gentlemen" and "ease" (although

Pope's attitude is most clearly conveyed by his calling them a "mob"). They were all gentlemen in the sense that they held a certain position in society and had received a university education. But the implications of "gentlemen" as Pope uses the word point toward something different. A gentleman is an amateur. Poetry for him is an avocation. He will show no itch for publication or for praise. The reason he writes with ease (or appears to) is that he must at all costs not betray the real labor that goes into composing a graceful trifle. As much as these poets admired Donne and Jonson, neither could serve as a model. And Milton would have been impossibly demanding. All three were far too seriously engaged in their verse, even when they meant it to be light.[13]

Wit, as Marvell and his contemporaries practiced it, was the perfect means of creating an impression of grace and freedom from effort, provided that it was *their* kind of wit. George Herbert's verse is as witty as Marvell's, and the twentieth century has come to recognize Herbert as a great poet. But his wit functions to perceive God's message written in the heart and in a kind of hieroglyphic to be discovered whenever the Holy Spirit grants a poet the grace to see it. In most of Herbert's lyrics the speaker is addressing God. Marvell and the poets who resemble him made very few attempts at devotional poetry. Love, friendship, honor, the country life are their subjects, and on these subjects they wrote wonderfully entertaining poems. No doubt they took their writing seriously. Poetry came no more naturally to them than it ever has to anyone. But they labored to give an impression of ease. Modern readers are apt to make two mistakes about their verse: first, to suppose that it really was easy, and second, by taking it too seriously, to miss all the fun it offers.

Some lines in "The Garden" give the appearance of ease:

> Two Paradises 'twere in one
> To live in Paradise alone.

The neatness and straightforward syntax of the couplet make it seem natural and obvious. But anyone who has ever tried to write an epigram will recognize the labor that went into that couplet and into this one:

> Society is all but rude,
> To this delicious Solitude.

For one thing, Marvell has managed to put the antithetical terms at opposite ends of the couplets: "two"/"alone," "society"/"solitude." And in the first line of each couplet he creates another antithesis: "two/one," "society"/"rude." As a stressed syllable at the point where we expect an unstressed syllable, "Two" is emphatic and balances with the stress on "one" in the last syllable. The three light syllables at the beginning of the line "To this delicious Solitude" cause a heavy emphasis to fall on an adjective that is interesting enough to bear the weight. For reasons that I am unable to explain, the following couplet is both easy and inspired:

> No white nor red was ever seen
> So am'rous as this lovely green.

And the celebrated line "To a green Thought in a green Shade" manipulates the accented and unaccented syllables perfectly to emphasize the significant words. But the art is so carefully concealed that it is nearly impossible to conceive of any other way of constructing the line.

It is easy to point out flaws in Marvell's verse. He relies far too frequently on *do*, *did*, and *does* to produce a rhyme or make up the requisite number of syllables:

> While all Flow'rs and all Trees do close
> To weave the Garlands of repose.

> The *Gods*, that mortal Beauty chase,
> Still in a Tree did end their race.

> The Luscious Clusters of the Vine
> Upon my Mouth do crush their Wine;
> The Nectaren, and curious Peach,
> Into my hands themselves do reach.

There is an awkward repetition in

> Your sacred Plants, if here below,
> Only among the Plants will grow.

The word order of "No Name shall but your own be found" is badly distorted to fit the meter (the straightforward English syntax of "no name but your own shall be found" produces exactly the kind of bouncy line

in triple meter that appears in some of the satirical poems attributed to
Marvell). In the first couplet of the last stanza, "How well the skilful
Gardner drew / Of flow'rs and herbes this Dial new," the need for a
rhyme wrenches the syntax, and the significance of "new" is not clear.
Such flaws are exactly what one might expect from a gifted amateur.
Considering the pleasure this poem gives us, to dwell on its shortcom-
ings would be ungrateful, but they are an aspect of Marvell's poetry that
he was willing to accept.

The other mistake modern readers often make is to take poems like
"The Garden" too seriously. Like many of Marvell's poems (but more
than any other), it has been burdened with a heavy weight of scholarship and criticism. A chapter devoted to "The Garden" in a recent book
on Marvell (Rees, *Judgement*, 179–197) refers to 63 books and articles. I
know of some 70 articles and 13 books that contain extended discussions of this poem. Some, concerned with the symbolic significance of
the garden, interpret the poem according to Platonic, Neoplatonic,
Stoic, Epicurean, Hermetic, scholastic, or Cartesian philosophy. It has
been read as a religious poem, a Christian meditation on the soul and
the promise of immortality with sources in the Song of Songs. The gardener mentioned in the final stanza has been identified as God or as
Christ.[14] One critic sees the poem as "a personal vision of the good life,"
a view with which this chapter is in agreement if it is understood that
the "personal" vision was not necessarily Andrew Marvell's.[15] This outpouring of criticism and interpretation testifies to the poem's power to
fascinate and mystify readers.

But it is probably a mistake to encumber a poem like "The Garden"
with a heavy message. Marvell deliberately chose to make his speaker
both earnest and mildly funny. How could anyone take seriously a man
who thinks of carving the names of the trees in their bark as a token of
his love? The picture of him stumbling on melons and ensnared with
flowers is inescapably comic. His plain implication that God made a
mistake in creating a companion for Adam does not brand the speaker
as a misogynist, but it does make him out to be a rather odd duck. Yet
his message is conveyed in a perfectly sociable tone. He is not one of
those men who frighten away little children and are never seen in company. Perhaps he does not speak directly to us, but he plainly reaches out
to us more than once (for instance, when he asks us to admire the gardener's skill and closes his panegyric with a rhetorical question). Neither
a crank nor a fanatic, Marvell's speaker certainly is an enthusiast.[16] He
gets carried away by his topic. Although he sees the vanity of human

striving, he does not suffer for the human condition. Except in a very limited way he doesn't even seem to be aware of it. What he does see is that he enjoys being alone and the garden is a perfect place for solitude and contemplation. And he wants us to agree.

Up to this point all the poems we have examined are essentially private. They do not impinge on matters of public interest. Whether we agree with the speaker of "The Garden" or not is of little consequence. He speaks for himself only. It does not appear that agreeing with him will make any difference to us or to the world. The elusiveness of Marvell's speakers sometimes makes it hard to know what they believe. With one exception, these are the poems that Marvell's fame rests upon. The exception is the work that bridges the gap between Marvell's private poems and his public ones: "An Horatian Ode upon Cromwel's Return from Ireland."[17]

The events referred to in this poem are a part of English history. At the time Marvell wrote it (presumably around May 1650 when Cromwell had just come back from subduing the rebels in Ireland and was about to begin a campaign in Scotland), the English were in the midst of a revolution that had cost Charles I his life and established Parliament as the governing body. For a country with a centuries-old tradition of monarchical rule, it was difficult to imagine a government not headed by a king. At least it would have been difficult had it not been for the example of republican government that was familiar to every educated person: ancient Rome. Marvell's "Horatian Ode" is doubly a public poem. It deals with events in the public life of England in terms of the public life of ancient Rome.[18]

But the example of Rome was not simple. There was a Roman empire as well as a Roman republic. And before the republic, there had been a Roman kingdom. Thus Marvell's decision to view events in England in terms of Roman history does not imply a particular attitude or political philosophy. In fact, the reason the "Horatian Ode" may be said to bridge the gap between public and private poems is that Marvell's speaker proves to be as elusive as any we have yet encountered.

There are three individuals in the "Ode": Cromwell, Charles I, and "The forward Youth that would appear." Considering that the events in the poem have already involved two countries and are about to involve a third, this is a strikingly limited cast. Two of these individuals are important figures in the history of England. But who is the "forward Youth"? Perhaps he exists merely as part of a simile, not so much "the" as *any* young man who has been forced by the events of his time to abandon poetry and learning and take up arms. "So restless *Cromwel* could not cease / In the inglorious Arts of Peace." But the word *So* is mystifying. Why should Cromwell's actions be compared to those of a fictitious young poet? The simile can only diminish the great general. Nor can Cromwell *be* this young man. In 1650 he was 51 years old and had never showed any devotion to the Muses.

The "forward Youth" could be the speaker of the poem who, because of the dignity and weight of the occasion, chooses to relinquish the first person "I" and to adopt an impersonal point of view. To the extent that this poem is Horatian (that is, based on the example of the ancient Roman poet Horace), the speaker may dare to give advice to a great leader. Since the speaker is a fictitious person, there is no reason why he should not be preparing to go into battle, but if this poem is his act of combat, how can he be said to "forsake his *Muses* dear"?

Could the "forward Youth" be Andrew Marvell? He was only 29 in 1650; he was devoted to books and the writing of poetry; and his life had been lived almost entirely "in the Shadows." But what would be indicated by the imagery of rusted armor and a corselet that had been hanging on a wall? Did Marvell see the composition of this poem as an entry into combat? If so, which side was he on?[19]

Unless we want to accuse Marvell of beginning his poem with a piece of irrelevance, we have to worry about this simile. Taken in the most general sense, it merely says that there are times when even a peaceful and retired person has to fight. Later in the poem, the speaker reminds us that Cromwell came

> . . . from his private Gardens, where
> He liv'd reserved and austere,
>   As if his highest plot
>   To plant the Bergamot.

But planting pears, even though it qualifies as one of "the inglorious Arts of Peace," is not work for Muses. Neither Cromwell nor Cincinnatus, the ancient Roman general whose memory the speaker seems to be evoking, was reputed to be a poet or a scholar.

Whether or not he is the forward youth, the speaker clearly is a student of Roman history who tends, as many Renaissance writers did (Machiavelli is the best example[20]), to validate his interpretation of events in his own time by finding parallels with ancient Rome. He is impressed by Cromwell's apparently irresistible power, but he feels some sympathy for the royal victim of Cromwell's policy. His confidence in Cromwell's humble obedience to the Parliamentary government sounds a bit like whistling past the graveyard. Still, the prospects for future conquests excite him, and he counsels the general to keep his sword erect. Like Julius Caesar, Cromwell is a great soldier. Although such men can be dangerous to any state, there is not much point in opposing them, for they seem to have the force of fate behind them.

It is important to note some of the issues the speaker does not raise in the "Ode." The poem's generally pagan atmosphere obscures the fact that the civil war was fought largely over religious differences. Nor does the speaker concern himself with contemporary political theory (e.g., the sanctity of monarchy) or the legality of a king's subjects bringing him to trial and executing him (these may be among "the antient Rights" that "Justice" pleads in vain). Apparently the idea of extending English rule over France or Italy appeals to him. When Marvell looked for a position in Cromwell's government, this poem would not have been held against him.

The speaker of the "Ode" appears to laud precisely the kind of activity that the speaker of "The Garden" finds so empty. This is worth remembering only because scholars have hoped to find Andrew Marvell in both poems. The world of "The Garden" may be fictitious, the speaker no more than part of the fiction. But the "Ode" portrays events in the world of history, English and Roman, and the speaker, we feel, ought to be a part of that world. Crucial happenings in English history are not properly the basis for the witty comments of an imagined speaker.

Certainly the speaker *is* witty, and we have argued that wit is the one constant in all of Marvell's verse. In chapter two we examined the wit involved in the most vividly imagined lines in the poem: the scene of Charles's beheading. The kind of ambiguity haunting that episode can be seen in many other passages. For example, the speaker struggles with the question of whether it was a just act to destroy the monarchy, to "cast the Kingdome old / Into another Mold." His conclusion draws upon an analogy with physics:

> Nature that hateth emptiness,
> Allows of penetration less:
>> And therefore must make room
>> Where greater Spirits come.

ANDREW MARVELL REVISITED

The comparison suggests that, like the natural world, the world of politics resists any kind of moral judgment. It is simply a fact that two bodies cannot occupy the same space simultaneously. The analogy overlooks the fact that Charles, by the laws and customs of England, was entitled to occupy that space. Another analogy draws a related conclusion: "'Tis Madness to resist or blame / The force of angry Heavens flame." This couplet concludes a section that compares Cromwell to a bolt of lightning. Truly it would be ludicrous to suppose that lightning bears some kind of moral responsibility for the damage it does. The wit in both of these passages produces an odd effect: if Cromwell cannot be blamed for his actions because he is a force of nature, neither can he be praised. Yet the "Ode" praises him for "industrious Valour" and for "wiser Art"; it calls him good and just. Cromwell is also compared to a falcon, a bird that kills by nature but can be trained to deny its instincts and obey its master. He is also "The *English Hunter*" stalking "The *Caledonian* Deer." These witty analogies tend to blur the image of Cromwell and to make it difficult to determine the speaker's attitude toward him.[21]

The Roman analogies produce a similar effect. The pagan atmosphere of the "Ode" is conveyed in a number of passages. Sometimes a single word ("Pict" instead of "Scot," "Gaul" instead of "France," "Caledonian" instead of "Scottish") establishes the ancient Roman point of view. On the scaffold, Charles kept his dignity, "Nor call'd the *Gods* with vulgar spite." An ancient Roman might well have called the gods to avenge him, but to deny that a Christian king did such a thing is, at the very least, superfluous. The "Fate" against which "Justice" complains has no place in Christian belief, having been replaced by God's providence (the word *providence* is not found in the poem). Caesar appears twice in the poem, first as Charles, then as Cromwell. If there had been a consensus concerning Julius Caesar among Renaissance students of Roman history, it might establish the speaker's view of Cromwell, but no consensus was available. And even if it were, the "Ode," by identifying both Charles and Cromwell with Caesar, would nullify its application to this poem.

In the last eight lines, the speaker finally addresses Cromwell:

> But thou the Wars and Fortunes Son
> March indefatigably on;
> And for the last effect

> Still keep thy Sword erect.
> Besides the force it has to fright
> The Spirits of the shady Night,
> The same *Arts* that did *gain*
> A *Pow'r* must it *maintain*.

Following the example of Horace, the speaker advises the great general. The advice is characteristically witty. A sword held erect resembles a cross, whence the reference to the "Spirits of the shady Night." But that is only "Besides." The main point of the image is that to be held erect the sword must be unsheathed and ready for battle. Cromwell has gained power by the sword; he must be prepared to fight to keep it. These lines express both warning and encouragement. What they do not express is judgment.

In the end we must accept the fact that the "forward Youth" cannot be identified. Perhaps Marvell intended to surround the "Ode" with ambiguity. The topic was dangerous (so dangerous that the "Ode" was canceled from all but two copies of the 1681 volume and not printed again until the 1776 edition of Marvell's works), and if the poem was composed in the summer of 1650, neither Marvell nor anyone else could have known what lay ahead for Cromwell and his supporters. His later Cromwell poems, composed when the general had become the de facto head of the English government, show no signs of ambiguity. For students of English history, the "Ode" can be read as a memorable statement of the mixed feelings with which Cromwell was regarded. But its value for most readers lies in the speaker's struggle to come to terms with the threat and the promise embodied in the conquering general.[22] The greatness of this poem is based on the speaker's refusal to gloss over either aspect of Cromwell's power—its capacity to destroy an old order and its potential to create a new one. The poem's wit serves to emphasize the impossibility of adopting a single-minded attitude toward the man who, in 1650, appeared to be the instrument of a destiny that could hardly be imagined.

It may be odd to praise a poem that leaves us wondering which side the speaker is on. The latter half of the seventeenth century produced an enormous outflowing of political poetry, some of it contributed by Marvell. In the poems that we will examine in the next chapter, there is no question which side Marvell was on. Yet none of those poems and none of the political poems of his contemporaries even begins to compare with the "Ode." The reason is not hard to find. Marvell's "Ode" cannot be read as political propaganda.[23] It confronts Cromwell's power with the same kind of dignity that it attributes to Charles on the scaffold. In the face of a revolution, it conveys the speaker's desire to praise the destroyer without forgetting the value of what was lost.

Chapter Seven
Satirical and Political Poems

Most of the poems in this chapter respond to matters of public interest. In almost all of them the speaker has chosen a side and either supports it or derides the opposite side. Neither cool nor elusive, he is a partisan. His wit is a weapon of attack, and there is nothing subtle about the way he uses it. Although he speaks in couplets, he has abandoned the tetrameter line in favor of the longer pentameter, a line less suited to the lyric. Or he uses a bouncy triple rhythm that conveys a sense of ridicule. These are the poems for which Andrew Marvell was famous in the century following his death. Not one of them is usually found in modern anthologies of seventeenth-century poetry.

In fact, many of them were not printed in the 1681 folio edition of Marvell's poetry.[1] The three Cromwell poems, printed in 1681, were stricken from all but two copies. Poems that attack the government of Charles II did not appear in the folio. Many poems attributed to Marvell in *Poems on Affairs of State* (in the editions of 1689 and 1697) may not have been his work; those that almost certainly were will be discussed. The speakers in this chapter will be much less interesting than most of the speakers we have previously encountered. Their concerns are much more narrowly focused on the events and politics of their time. Although these poems could be discussed in chronological order, it is convenient to begin with the two that deal with Oliver Cromwell since they continue the topic of the last chapter.

"The First Anniversary of the Government under O. C." was published anonymously in 1655. In 402 lines of iambic pentameter couplets, the speaker praises Cromwell and derides his enemies. The first 12 lines illustrate the general thesis of the poem: Cromwell is like no other man.

> Like the vain Curlings of the Watry maze,
> Which in smooth streams a sinking Weight does raise;
> So Man, declining alwayes, disappears
> In the weak Circles of increasing Years;

> And his short Tumults of themselves Compose,
> While flowing Time above his Head does close.
>   *Cromwell* alone with greater Vigour runs,
> (Sun-like) the Stages of succeeding Suns:
> And still the Day which he doth next restore,
> Is the just Wonder of the Day before.
> *Cromwell* alone doth with new Lustre spring,
> And shines the Jewel of the yearly Ring.

The speaker devotes 30 lines to a description of other rulers, inactive
drones who oppress their people and accomplish nothing. Cromwell,
like Amphion, builds the Commonwealth through the power of harmony. Disdaining the offer of a crown, "For to be *Cromwell* was a greater
thing, / Then ought below, or yet above a King," he becomes the instrument of divine power:

>   What since he did, an higher Force him push'd
> Still from behind, and it before him rush'd,
> Though undiscern'd among the tumult blind,
> Who think those high Decrees by Man design'd.

Numerous allusions to the Old Testament associate Cromwell with
judges and prophets who carried out God's purposes. The poem concludes by identifying Cromwell with the angel referred to in John 5:4.

>   Pardon, great Prince, if thus their [other princes'] Fear or Spight
> More then our Love and Duty do thee Right.
> I yield, nor further will the Prize contend;
> So that we both alike may miss our End:
> While thou thy venerable Head dost raise
> As far above their Malice as my Praise.
> And as the *Angel* of our Commonweal,
> Troubling the Waters, yearly mak'st them Heal.

There is no reason to doubt that Marvell wrote this poem or to question
his sincerity. If the praise of Cromwell seems exaggerated, we need only
compare it with the praises of kings and princes in dozens of seven-

teenth-century poems. The many allusions to biblical figures serve to define Cromwell as God's agent, a man whose exceptional powers are not his own.

But it is easy to see why this poem and "A Poem upon the Death of O. C." hardly ever appear in modern anthologies of seventeenth-century poetry: they fail to engage us as poetry. "An Horatian Ode" remains interesting because it dramatizes in vivid terms a basic human response to power: we are both frightened by it and attracted to it. When it is embodied in human beings, it is mysterious. Marvell found the poetic means to convey this response. Although he wrote the "Ode" for his contemporaries, he managed to make it permanently interesting. The other two Cromwell poems fail to rise above a simply partisan view of their subject. However sincerely Marvell admired the Protector, he conveyed only that admiration, not the basis on which readers might feel the same.[2]

This comment applies with equal force to most of the poems in which Marvell commends his subject. A striking exception, "On Mr. Milton's Paradise lost" (one of the small number of Marvell's poems published in his lifetime), appeared in the second edition of *Paradise Lost* (1674), signed A. M. It is an encomium, not a work of criticism.[3] Its most unexpected aspect for us, since we now look back on Milton's epic as an acknowledged masterpiece, is Marvell's awareness of the dangers of failure in such an ambitious undertaking.

> When I beheld the Poet blind, yet bold,
> In slender Book his vast Design unfold,
> *Messiah* Crown'd, *Gods* Reconcil'd Decree,
> Rebelling *Angels*, the Forbidden Tree,
> Heav'n, Hell, Earth, Chaos, All; the Argument
> Held me a while misdoubting his Intent,
> That he would ruine (for I saw him strong)
> The sacred Truths to Fable and old Song,
> (So *Sampson* groap'd the Temples Posts in spight)
> The World o'rewhelming to revenge his Sight.

As this fear subsided, two others took its place: that Milton would perplex his readers with mysteries beyond human comprehension, and that someone less skilled might make a play based on Milton's poem. The

disparity between these two fears—the first a response to the inherent
difficulty of the material, the second to Dryden's attempt to turn the
epic into a play (published in 1677 but apparently never presented in
the theater)—is unintentionally comic. Marvell's tribute conveys both a
decorous reverence for Milton and an indecorous animosity toward Dryden, who is an intrusive presence only because Marvell has brought him
into the poem.

   After complimenting the strength and majesty of Milton's style,
Marvell concludes by commenting on a facet of *Paradise Lost* so puzzling
to seventeenth-century readers that Milton had to supply an explanation: the poem did not rhyme.

> Well mightst thou scorn thy Readers to allure
> With tinkling Rhime, of thy own Sense secure;
> While the *Town-Bays* writes all the while and spells,
> And like a Pack-Horse tires without his Bells.
> Their Fancies like our bushy points appear,
> The Poets tag them; we for fashion wear.
> I too transported by the *Mode* offend,
> And while I meant to *Praise* thee, must Commend.
> Thy verse created like thy *Theme* sublime,
> In Number, Weight, and Measure, needs not *Rhime*.

The "Town-Bays" is a coded reference to Dryden, who again is dragged
into the poem. But Marvell confesses that he too follows the fashion.
His need for a rhyme forces him to commend where he meant to praise.
This rather self-conscious joke at his own expense, coupled with the fact
that he finds in the word "Rhime" both an appropriate companion for
"sublime" and a harmonious and witty close for his tribute, suggests
that Marvell's praise of Milton's style and his scathing picture of the
"Town-Bays" are not to be read as a repudiation of rhyming verse. This
commendatory poem may have little of interest to say about *Paradise
Lost*, but it does show us an Andrew Marvell who has deliberately chosen a medium that enables him to do what he prefers to do.

   What he prefers to do in the following poems is to use his wit as a
weapon. His aim is to bring scorn and ridicule on his subject. In seventeenth-century English poetry the closed couplet is preeminently the
medium of satire. With few exceptions, Marvell's satires are in closed

couplets. Modern anthologies of seventeenth-century poetry seldom reprint them, perhaps because they are so at odds with the Marvell that modern criticism has created. At their best they display both wit and a liberating delight in mockery. They are just as genuine a reflection of Marvell as the cultivated, cool, elusive poems for which he is known today. But he never achieved the rhetorical brilliance of Dryden's and Pope's couplets. His medium for his lyric verse is the tetrameter line. The extra foot in each line of a heroic couplet allowed Dryden and Pope to develop a style that rested heavily on parallelism and antithesis. Oddly enough, their treatment of the longer line produces an effect of epigrammatic compression. Occasionally Marvell tries for this effect, as in these lines from "The last Instructions to a Painter":

> Gain and Revenge, Revenge and Gain are sweet
> United most, else when by turns they meet.

But the sense of the couplet is hard to understand. To get the effect that Dryden and Pope aimed for, the first couplet would have to begin with a more compact statement: "Gain and Revenge united most are sweet." In a line like "Scarce them their Leaders, they their leaders knew" (meaning their leaders scarcely knew them and they scarcely knew their leaders) the compression is bought at too high a price. Marvell's most successful attempt to master this couplet rhetoric occurs in a poem celebrating an English sea victory over Spanish ships at the Canary Islands: "On the Victory obtained by Blake over the Spaniards."

> O noble Trust which Heaven on this Isle poures,
> Fertile to be, yet never need her showres.
> A happy People, which at once do gain
> The benefits without the ills of rain.
> Both health and profit, Fate cannot deny;
> Where still the Earth is moist, the Air still dry;
> The jarring Elements no discord know,
> Fewel and Rain together kindly grow;
> And coolness there, with heat doth never fight,
> This only rules by day, and that by Night.
> Your [Cromwell's] worth to all these Isles, a just right brings,
> The best of Lands should have the best of Kings.

But by the time Marvell wrote this (1657), Waller and John Denham were already more skilled at this kind of effect. Dryden and Pope perfected it. If we read Marvell's satires with Dryden and Pope in mind, they seem to sprawl.

Probably "Fleckno, an English Priest at Rome" was the first of these satires to be composed. Marvell was in Rome in 1645–1646, as was the poet Richard Flecknoe. The poem describes a visit to Flecknoe's lodgings and a dinner. It is not likely that the events narrated in the poem actually took place. The whole poem depends so much on comic exaggeration that it is best read as fiction. Even in the throes of hunger pangs, Flecknoe would hardly try "With gristly Tongue to dart the passing Flyes" or wrap himself in seven layers of paper containing his verses. The first 18 lines convey the flavor of the whole poem:

> Oblig'd by frequent visits of this man,
> Whom as Priest, Poet, and Musician,
> I for some branch of *Melchizedeck* took,
> (Though he derives himself from *my Lord Brooke*)
> I sought his Lodging; which is at the Sign
> Of the sad *Pelican*; Subject divine
> For Poetry: There three Stair-Cases high,
> Which signifies his triple property,
> I found at last a Chamber, as 'twas said,
> But seem'd a Coffin set on the Stairs head.
> Not higher then Seav'n, nor larger then three feet;
> Only there was nor Seeling, nor a Sheet,
> Save that th'ingenious Door did as you come
> Turn in, and shew to Wainscot half the Room.
> Yet of his State no man could have complain'd;
> There being no Bed where he entertain'd:
> And though within one Cell so narrow pent,
> He'd *Stanza*'s for a whole Appartement.

These lines are meant to be difficult. Marvell is writing in the style of Donne's and Joseph Hall's satires. The lines are rough, the couplets often open, and the wit both erudite and compressed. Lines 9 through 14, for example, are full of puns based on "Chamber" and "Coffin." The last couplet depends on the reader's knowing that *stanza* means both "lines of verse" and "room" in Italian. Flecknoe's "triple property" as priest, poet, and musician finds its reflection in his lodging, "three Stair-Cases high." The wit frequently involves points of theology, as when the speaker, trying to descend the narrow staircase, encounters another man coming up to visit Flecknoe and remarks,

> . . . there can no Body pass
> Except by penetration hither, where
> Two make a crowd, nor can three Persons here
> Consist but in one substance.

Marvell portrays Flecknoe as the author of excruciatingly bad poetry. In 1678 Dryden represented him as the monarch of nonsense. But the reader, caught up in the speaker's high spirits and trying to follow his abstruse turns of wit, may overlook the fact that Flecknoe is consistently mocked for being poor and hungry, misfortunes that might well elicit sympathy rather than scorn. Still, the business of satire is to make fun of its victims, and Marvell's poem is typical of seventeenth-century satire in its willingness to take every opportunity to belittle its target.

"Tom May's Death" probably dates from 1650, the year of May's death. Though it is less abstruse than the poem on Flecknoe, its references to May's drunkenness show that Marvell had not changed his tactics. Like Flecknoe, May was a poet, especially known for his translation of Lucan's *Pharsalia* (some lines in "An Horatian Ode" reflect Marvell's knowledge of May's translation), and many of Marvell's jibes depend on the reader's knowledge of that poem. The satire's chief charge against May is that he was a mercenary and a turncoat. In the fiction of the poem, May finds himself in Elysium, where he encounters Ben Jonson, the speaker of most of the poem. Jonson banishes him to a region Marvell's readers would recognize as Tartarus, an ancient concept of Hell described in Virgil's *Aeneid*. The opening lines provide a fair sample of Marvell's approach.

> As one put drunk into the Packet-boat,
> *Tom May* was hurry'd hence and did not know't.
> But was amaz'd on the Elysian side,
> And with an Eye uncertain, gazing wide,
> Could not determine in what place he was,

> For whence in Stevens ally Trees or Grass?
> Nor where the Popes head, nor the Mitre lay,
> Signs by which still he found and lost his way.

The Popes Head and the Mitre were common names for taverns in London. Many other details in the poem assume in the reader a knowledge of May's writing and of current events.

Jonson's charge against May bears some relevance to Marvell's later poems. Specifically, Jonson accuses May of betraying the poet's special mission to be a speaker of dangerous truths.

> When the Sword glitters ore the Judges head,
> And fear has Coward Churchmen silenced,
> Then is the Poets time, 'tis then he drawes,
> And single fights forsaken Vertues cause.
> He, when the wheel of Empire, whirleth back,
> And though the World's disjointed Axel crack,
> Sings still of ancient Rights and better Times,
> Seeks wretched good, arraigns successful Crimes.

This noble concept of a poet's vocation will be worth remembering in the discussion of Marvell's political satires.

The versification of this poem is relatively smooth. Most of the couplets are closed. The satire of Flecknoe appears to have been Marvell's experiment with a deliberately rough and obscure style. The satire of May moves toward an easier kind of verse. By the time he wrote "The Character of Holland," Marvell was regularly using closed couplets in his satires.

Judging by its reference to Deane, Monck, and Blake, the commanders of the British navy, "The Character of Holland" was composed after a victory over the Dutch fleet in 1653. But it scarcely matters what the occasion was. The poem is so totally and preposterously hostile to the Dutch that no knowledge of the historical background is required. The aim of the satirist is ridicule, not objective judgment. A satire is the obverse of courtly praise, but both kinds of poetry share the same need for wit and imagination. Satire is not vituperation; the satirist wields a scalpel, not an ax. Long after the circumstances that led to his attack have ceased to exist, his skill may still give us pleasure.

The entire 152-line poem rests on a single fact: a large part of Holland had been reclaimed from the sea. A friendly observer might see in this fact an example of Dutch ingenuity and determination. Here is the way Marvell presents it at the very beginning of his poem:

> *Holland*, that scarce deserves the name of *Land*,
> As but th'Off-scouring of the *Brittish Sand*;
> And so much Earth as was contributed
> By *English Pilots* when they heav'd the Lead;
> Or what by th'Oceans slow alluvion fell,
> Of shipwrackt Cockle and the Muscle-shell;
> This indigested vomit of the Sea
> Fell to the *Dutch* by just Propriety.
>   Glad then, as Miners that have found the Oar [ore],
> They with mad labour fish'd the *Land* to *Shoar*;
> And div'd as desperately for each piece
> Of Earth, as if't had been of *Ambergreece*;
> Collecting anxiously small Loads of Clay,
> Less than what building Swallows bear away;
> Or then those Pills which sordid Beetles roul,
> Tranfusing into them their Dunghil Soul.

As far as the speaker is concerned, Holland barely deserves to be called a land of any kind, and Dutch ingenuity is spent on an enterprise that is trivial in its means but desperate in its consequences: nothing less than a struggle against nature. Sometimes nature wins.

> Yet still his claim the Injur'd Ocean laid,
> And oft at Leap-frog ore their Steeples plaid:
> As if on purpose it on Land had come
> To shew them what's their *Mare Liberum*.
> A daily deluge over them does boyl;
> The Earth and Water play at *Level-coyl*;
> The Fish oft-times the Burger dispossest,
> And sat not as a Meat but as a Guest.

Ridiculing a country that struggles to overcome its vulnerability to natural forces may be as unfair as making fun of a man for being poor and hungry. But Marvell's point is that the Dutch have created their own problems: they have tried to make a country by robbing the sea. And since they, not nature, made the land, they have had to create their own special (and unnatural) forms of government and religion. Their government is a logical development of their special needs:

> Therefore *Necessity*, that first made *Kings*,
> Something like *Government* among them brings.
> For as with *Pygmees* who best kills the *Crane*,
> Among the *hungry* he that treasures *Grain*,
> Among the *blind* the one-ey'd *blinkard* reigns,
> So rules among the *drowned* he that *draines*.
> Not who first see the *rising Sun* commands,
> But who could first discern the *rising Lands*.
> Who best could know to pump an Earth so leak
> Him they their *Lord* and *Country's Father* speak.
> To make a *Bank* was a great *Plot of State*;
> Invent a *Shov'l* and be a *Magistrate*.

Even their religion, which had made them England's allies for so many years against the Roman Catholic power of Spain, comes in for ridicule:

> 'Tis probable *Religion* after this
> Came next in order; which they could not miss.
> How could the *Dutch* but be converted, when
> Th'*Apostles* were so many Fishermen?
> Besides the Waters of themselves did rise,
> And, as their Land, so them did re-baptize.

In the course of his poem, Marvell plays on several stereotyped views of the Dutch: their drunkenness, their addiction to butter and cheese, their boorishness (the word *boor* is Dutch in origin), their dedication to commerce above all other activities, their willingness to accommodate any religion for the sake of trade, and their pride.

In an evaluation of this poem, questions of fairness or factual accuracy are simply irrelevant. The poem succeeds if it derides and ridicules the Dutch in a witty fashion. It certainly succeeded with English readers in the seventeenth century. The first 100 lines were apparently printed in 1665 and printed again in 1672 during another war with the Dutch. For us the wit alone must justify the effort of following the many clever turns of thought. By this standard, the reward is slight. Although the lines are smoother than those in "Fleckno" and the conceits less abstruse, "The Character of Holland" lacks the verbal felicity of Dryden's *MacFlecknoe* (1678) and the energy and comic outrage of Cleveland's "The Rebel Scot" (c. 1644). Well-turned phrases like "Invent a *Shov'l* and be a *Magistrate*" occur too seldom, and there is a limit to the number of variations that can be played on the poem's single joke.[4]

The remaining satires are the poems for which Marvell was famous during the century following his death. They all have two things in common: none appeared in the 1681 folio, and not one is certainly by Marvell. In fact, very few were printed before 1689, chiefly because they were too dangerous. Charles II may have been a tolerant, easygoing monarch, but his government was assiduous in the discovery and prosecution of libel, broadly defined as any piece of writing that undermined the public's confidence in the King.[5] From 1667 to 1688, several thousand pieces of political satire, whether in manuscript or printed form, circulated surreptitiously despite vigorous efforts by the government to suppress such material (most notably in the case of Algernon Sidney, who was executed simply because he was in possession of a lampoon). When the English people deposed and exiled James II, booksellers quickly took advantage of the opportunity to publish collections of satirical poems, many of which they attributed to Andrew Marvell. At this time there is no general agreement among scholars as to which of them, if any, can be credited to Marvell. Two of these poems, accepted by the most recent editors of Marvell's poetry (Kermode and Walker) as genuine, are worth discussing on their own merits.

The longest and most highly regarded of the satires attributed to Marvell, "The last Instructions to a Painter" (first published in *Poems on Affairs of State* [1689] and ascribed to A. M.), was apparently composed in the autumn of 1667.[6] By this time Marvell had been a member of the House of Commons for eight years. While scholars do not agree about his political affiliations, no one can doubt that "The last Instructions" is a scathing indictment of greed, cowardice, and immorality in Parliament and in the court of Charles II. Its 990 lines deal with a series of events in 1666 and 1667 that culminated in the humiliating expedition of the Dutch fleet up the Thames and the Medway and the loss, virtu-

ally without resistance, of several English warships in full view of a
crowd of courtiers. In large part it is mock-heroic: the debates in Parliament are represented as a battle, and a long section (lines 151–302)
names and describes the combatants on each side in a parody of epic cat-
alogs. But since the speaker obviously favors one side and represents
himself as a true English patriot, the satire is mixed with some genuine
admiration and even an exalted tribute to the only person who actually
attempted to save one of the ships (lines 649–696). The speaker uses
extended similes of the sort commonly found in epics, and there is one
lyric section (lines 523–550) that blends mythology, pastoral, and remi-
niscences of the description of Cleopatra's barge in Shakespeare's *Antony
and Cleopatra*. Near the conclusion Charles II is visited by the ghosts of
his father (Charles I) and his maternal grandfather (Henry IV of France).
Along with these rather elegant passages we find some of the nastiest
lines in seventeenth-century verse. It is truly a bewildering mixture of
styles and tones.

The title indicates the fictional setting of the poem: the speaker is
addressing an artist who is going to paint a picture of England. The
device had already been used by Waller in his "Instructions to a Painter"
(1666) and was so enthusiastically received that four poems bearing the
title "Advice to a Painter" (at least two of which may have been by Marvell) appeared in 1666–1667. Sensibly Marvell does not adhere
doggedly to so limiting a format. A large part of the poem is essentially
a narrative of the Dutch incursion. But the most bitterly hostile passages of the poem are portraits of individuals. Here is a part of the portrait of Anne Hyde, the Duchess of York, daughter of the Lord
Chancellor and wife to the King's younger brother:

> Paint then again *Her Highness* to the life,
> Philosopher beyond *Newcastle*'s Wife.
> She, nak'd, can *Archimedes* self put down,
> For an Experiment upon the *Crown*.
> She perfected that Engine, oft assay'd,
> How after Childbirth to renew a Maid.
> And found how *Royal Heirs* might be matur'd,
> In fewer months than Mothers once indur'd.
> Hence Crowder made the rare Inventress free,
> Of's *Highnesses Royal Society*.
> Paint her with Oyster Lip, and breath of Fame,

> Wide Mouth that Sparagus may well proclaim:
> With *Chanc'lor's* Belly, and so large a Rump.
> There, not behind the Coach, her Pages jump.

The speaker's contempt comes across clearly, even though the references to Newcastle's wife and Crowder mean nothing to us now. While the sexual innuendo may be hard to understand, it obviously *is* sexual innuendo. But the wit involved in "made the rare Inventress free, / Of's *Highnesses Royal Society*" depends on our understanding the double meanings of "Inventress," "made . . . free," and *"Royal Society."* It is the kind of wit that makes good dirty jokes.

The problem is that the jokes depend so much on the reader's knowing what the writer is referring to. Because a modern reader is not familiar with the people and the events that are being satirized, the parts of the poem that he will likely find most impressive are the least satirical. For example, the wonderful description of the Dutch fleet sailing calmly up the river might be at home in a fully detailed mock-heroic poem:

> *Ruyter* the while, that had our Ocean curb'd,
> Sail'd now among our Rivers undisturb'd:
> Survey'd their Crystal Streams, and Banks so green,
> And Beauties e're this never naked seen.
> Through the vain sedge the bashful *Nymphs* he ey'd;
> Bosomes, and all which from themselves they hide.
> The Sun much brighter, and the Skies more clear,
> He finds the Air, and all things, sweeter here.
> The sudden change, and such a tempting sight,
> Swells his old Veins with fresh Blood, fresh Delight.
> Like am'rous Victors he begins to shave,
> And his new Face looks in the *English* Wave.
> His sporting Navy all about him swim,
> And witness their complaisence in their trim.
> Their streaming Silks play through the weather fair,
> And with inveigling Colours *Court* the Air.
> While the red Flags breath on their Top-masts high
> Terrour and War, but want an Enemy.
> Among the Shrowds the Seamen sit and sing,

And wanton Boys on every Rope do cling.
Old *Neptune* springs the Tydes, and Water lent:
(The Gods themselves do help the provident.)
And, where the deep Keel on the shallow cleaves,
With *Trident*'s Leaver, and great Shoulder heaves.
Æolus their Sails inspires with *Eastern* Wind,
Puffs them along, and breathes upon them kind.
With Pearly Shell the *Tritons* all the while
Sound the Sea-march, and guide to *Sheppy Isle*.

This description is easily understood by any reader with a moderate
knowledge of classical mythology. But it is only mildly satirical, and its
refined pastoral and mythological atmosphere is at odds with the generally cynical and combative tone that animates this portrait "of Drunk-
ards, Pimps, and Fools."

Similarly the 56 lines that celebrate the heroic death of Archibald
Douglas, a young soldier who refused to leave the ship he was guarding
even after the Dutch had set fire to it, contrast with the ridicule of Sir
Thomas Daniel, who fled in haste ("Daniel then thought he was in *Lyons*
Den"). Here is an excerpt from the praise of Douglas:

Like a glad Lover, the fierce Flames he meets,
And tries his first embraces in their Sheets.
His shape exact, which the bright flames infold,
Like the Sun's Statue stands of burnish'd Gold.
Round the transparent Fire about him glows,
As the clear Amber on the Bee does close:
And, as on Angels Heads their Glories shine,
His burning Locks adorn his Face Divine.
But, when in his immortal Mind he felt
His alt'ring Form, and soder'd Limbs to melt;
Down on the Deck he laid himself, and dy'd,
With his dear Sword reposing by his Side.
And, on the flaming Plank, so rests his Head,
As one that's warm'd himself and gone to Bed.

Satire yields to drama in the eerie visions that appear to the King near the end of the poem. The tone is solemn:

> Paint last the *King*, and a dead shade of Night,
> Only dispers'd by a weak Tapers light;
> And those bright gleams that dart along and glare
> From his clear Eyes, yet these too dark with Care.
> There, as in the calm horrour all alone,
> He wakes and Muses of th' uneasie Throne:
> Raise up a sudden Shape with Virgins Face,
> Though ill agree her Posture, Hour, or Place:
> Naked as born, and her round Arms behind,
> With her own Tresses interwove and twin'd:
> Her mouth lockt up, a blind before her Eyes,
> Yet from beneath the Veil her blushes rise;
> And silent tears her secret anguish speak,
> Her heart throbs, and with very shame would break.
> The Object strange in him no Terrour mov'd:
> He wonder'd first, then pity'd, then he lov'd:
> And with kind hand does the coy Vision press,
> Whose Beauty greater seem'd by her distress;
> But soon shrunk back, chill'd with her touch so cold,
> And th' airy Picture vanisht from his hold.
> In his deep thoughts the wonder did increase,
> And he Divin'd 'twas *England* or the *Peace*.

The vivid picture of a distressed naked maiden, bound, silent, and blind-folded, is the very epitome of vulnerability. But the King, though he feels pity, moves to take advantage of the helpless woman. When she vanishes, he guesses at her true identity. For a modern reader, his action is merely contemptible; Marvell's readers, knowing the King's lustful propensities, would have made the connection hinted at in the last line. This unattainable vision is a coded reference to Frances Stuart (referred to by name in line 762), a court beauty who had been the model for Britannia on English coins and had successfully resisted the King's advances.[7] Whether one makes the connection or not, the passage conveys with

eerie power the desperate condition of the kingdom and a sense of how
far the King is from understanding his duties as a monarch.

Eight lines later the second vision appears:

> Shake then the room, and all his Curtains tear,
> And with blue streaks infect the Taper clear:
> While, the pale Ghosts, his Eye does fixt admire
> Of Grandsire *Harry*, and of *Charles* his Sire.
> Harry sits down, and in his open side
> The grizly Wound reveals, of which he dy'd.
> And ghastly *Charles*, turning his Collar low,
> The purple thread about his Neck does show:
> Then, whisp'ring to his Son in Words unheard,
> Through the lock'd door both of them disappear'd.

The effect of these two visions is to raise the tone of the poem out of the
realm of satire. Only the connection with Frances Stuart might make
possible the response a satirist hopes to create. But the power with
which Marvell portrays the hopeless woman and the gruesome ghosts of
dead kings belongs to a tragic vision that is fatal to satire. After this,
with only another dozen couplets to come, the poem cannot regain its
satiric energy.

"The last Instructions," it should be remembered, was written for
seventeenth-century readers who would need no footnotes or explanations. Its popularity among them is indicated by its continuing appearances in poetic anthologies. It would be unfair to require of it a unity of
tone and a logical structure that reflect twentieth-century standards of
poetic excellence.[8] But it would be equally unfair to require a modern
reader to find in "The last Instructions" the kind of pleasure offered by
"An Horatian Ode" or "To his Coy Mistress."

Among the many satirical poems attributed to Marvell, there are several that make use of multisyllabic feet. Since it is nearly impossible to
avoid a comic effect in such a meter, it is perfectly suited to a satirist's
desire to make fun of his subject. Here is a stanza from "Clarindon's
House-Warming," printed in 1667 but first attributed to Marvell in
1726.

> Already he [Clarendon] had got all our Money and Cattel,
> To buy us for Slaves, and purchase our Lands;

What *Joseph* by Famine, he wrought by Sea-Battel;
Nay scarce the Priests portion could scape from his hands.

Each one of these lines has a different number of syllables, ranging from 10 to 13. But they all have exactly four feet (four accented syllables). To read them properly one must be prepared for a different pattern of accented and unaccented syllables in every line. Each line begins with an unaccented syllable followed by an accented syllable. After that the reader is on his own. The only rule is that each line will have four accented syllables and that no two accented syllables will be contiguous. The second line has the same 10 syllables that comprise a line of iambic pentameter, but only four are accented: "To *buy* us for / *Slaves* and / *pur*chase our / *lands*." The fourth line is similar: "Nay *scarce* the Priests / *por*tion could / *scape* from his / *hands*." Lines one and three exhibit another aspect of English verse that creates a comic effect: two-syllable rhyme. Though in print it is deceptively short, the first line has the most syllables: "Al*ready* he had / *got* all our / *Mon*ey and / *Cat*tel." To make it fit the pattern, it is necessary to compress five syllables into the first foot.

There is nothing essentially comic about multisyllabic feet or two-syllable rhymes, but in English poetry few poets have used them seriously. The irregular feet in "Clarindon's House-Warming" suggest the irregularity of Clarendon's tactics. When Marvell praises Cromwell for building the structure of a new government in England, he alludes to the mythical Amphion who raised the walls of ancient Thebes by the power of music:

So when *Amphion* did the Lute command,
Which the God gave him, with his gentle hand,
The rougher Stones, unto his Measures hew'd,
Dans'd up in order from the Quarreys rude;
This took a Lower, that an Higher place,
As he the Treble alter'd, or the Base:
No Note he struck, but a new Story lay'd,
And the great Work ascended while he play'd.

The stately movement of the iambic feet is well suited to a poem meant to praise its subject. The allusion to Amphion in "Clarindon's House-Warming" conveys a quite different impression:

But then recollecting how the Harper *Amphyon*
Made *Thebes* dance aloft while he fidled and sung,
He thought (as an Instrument he was most free on)
To build with the Jews-trump of his own tongue.

The rhyming of "Amphion" and "free on," the verb *fidled*, and the choice of a Jew's harp as Clarendon's instrument combine to diminish and mock the man as the unworthy imitator of a fabled builder.

In a number of ways the poem attacks the Lord Chancellor for the greed and ostentation expressed in his grand house that was nearing completion when these stanzas were published. The speaker enjoys playing on the Chancellor's family name (Hyde) in the following stanza:

Yet a President [precedent] fitter in *Virgil* he found,
Of *African Poultney*, and *Tyrian Did'*
That he begg'd for a Pallace so much of his ground,
As might carry the measure and name of an *Hyde*.

This is just the kind of witty analogy Marvell delighted in. In Virgil's *Aeneid*, Dido tricked the African ruler Iarbas into giving her, as a site for the city she intended to build, the land that could be encompassed by the hide of an ox. She cut the hide into thin strips and acquired much more land than Iarbas intended to give. Sir William Poulteney was an owner of the land granted to Clarendon, whose surname was Hyde. To complicate the pun still further, the term *hide* refers to a measure of land. The stanza succeeds in implying that the land on which Clarendon built his house was gotten by trickery.

A nastier suggestion, also involving a figure from the ancient world, appears in this stanza:

He had read of *Rhodope*, a Lady of *Thrace*,
Who was dig'd up so often ere she did marry;
And wish'd that his Daughter had had as much grace
To erect him a Pyramid out of her Quarry.

According to Herodotus, Rhodope was a courtesan who made so much money from the sale of her body that she built a pyramid. Clarendon's daughter Anne had clandestinely married the King's brother, the Duke of York, under questionable circumstances in 1660 and given birth to a son not quite two months after the wedding. The tone of this stanza depends not only on the suggestion that Clarendon profited by his daughter's unchastity but also on the coarseness of the term *dig'd up* and the reference to Anne's genitalia as "her Quarry." The reader may remember the equally coarse description of Anne in "The last Instructions."

The concluding stanza helps to fix the date of composition.

> Or rather how wisely his Stall was built near,
> Lest with driving too far his Tallow impair;
> When like the good Oxe, for publick good chear,
> He comes to be roasted next St. *James*'s Fair.

On 25 June 1667, a proclamation summoned Parliament to assemble on St. James's Day, 25 July. Between those two dates the poem was written. During that session Clarendon was impeached. He fled the country on 29 November and never returned to England. Both "The last Instructions" and "Clarindon's House-Warming" testify to the enmity the Lord Chancellor had created.

The public poems reveal a side of Marvell that his other poems never hint at: a partisan, committed attitude that leaves no room for ambiguity or elusiveness. They do not suggest that the lyrics should be read differently. Rather, they belong to another side of an author whose only unvarying trait is his irrepressible wit.

Chapter Eight
The Prose Works

For more than a century after his death, Andrew Marvell was famous as a writer of controversial prose treatises. The basis of his fame has so radically changed that there has not been a complete edition of these works since 1875.[1] Yet they are as fully a product of his mind as his poems, and they give access to some parts of his character that are not otherwise available. In keeping with the earlier chapters, this study will focus on the speaker in each treatise.

But the prose treatises differ in several ways from Marvell's poetry. To begin with, they respond in very direct ways to events in English history. Of course, Marvell's Cromwell poems also do this, but the prose treatises deal with specific issues and specific treatises by other writers. In several of them the speaker is involved in a dialogue with his opponent, quoting his words and answering them. He may be as witty as the speaker of "Upon Appleton House," but his wit is reactive, to a large extent limited by the words he is responding to. Though Marvell deliberately chose this method, it imposes a strict discipline on his speaker.

The fact that the treatises are controversial limits them in another way. The speaker's aim is to discredit his opponent, to make fun of him, to undermine his authority and his credibility: in short, to win. He can be witty, but he cannot by any means be ambiguous or elusive. Only by his apparent honesty, good sense, and candor will he convince the reader. Furthermore, he must impress on the reader the weightiness of the issues being disputed. In most of Marvell's lyrics nothing is at stake, but the prose treatises claim to be concerned with the freedom of Englishmen and the survival of England. The wonderfully amusing oddity of the guide in "Upon Appleton House" or the enthusiast who speaks in "The Garden" would be liabilities in an attack upon persecuting bishops and Catholic conspirators. So would the flights of fancy that created Damon the Mower, the Nymph, and the contentious Body and Soul.

Finally, the prose treatises are written in seventeenth-century prose. Modern English prose style emphasizes brevity and simplicity. A seventeenth-century prose writer will usually produce sentences far longer and more complicated than those of a modern writer. In addition, Mar-

vell's prose preserves peculiarities of syntax and morphology that make
it sound antiquated to a modern reader. For example, the opening sentence of *An Account of the Growth of Popery, and Arbitrary Government in
England*:

> There has now for divers years a design been carried on to change the
> lawful Government of England into an absolute Tyranny, and to convert
> the established Protestant Religion into downright Popery: than both
> which, nothing can be more destructive or contrary to the interest and
> happiness, to the constitution and being of the king and kingdom.

The sentence is clear enough, but a modern writer would probably say,
"For several years there has been a plot to change the lawful government
of England into an absolute tyranny, etc."

In Marvell's lyrics the reader is struck by the teasing, playful implications of his language. In the prose treatises the language is relatively
straightforward in meaning but antiquated in syntax and diction. The
speaker in a lyric by Marvell seems to be speaking directly to us, while
the speaker in a prose treatise is immediately distanced from us by his
language.

Yet the issues raised by Marvell's prose speakers are like some that
still trouble the twentieth century: religious freedom, persecution of
minorities, the arrogance of power, and the moral responsibility of people who are just following orders. It will not do to press the resemblance. No one in Marvell's time could have conceived of religious
freedom as a right to ignore religion, and few desired an absolute separation of Church and State. Persecution and the arrogance that causes it
in the modern world seldom rest in the hands of bishops. Nevertheless,
it would be a mistake to suppose that Marvell's prose treatises are about
dead issues.

All of these treatises are concerned with religion. During the civil war
and the Protectorate of Oliver Cromwell, the organizational structure of
the Church of England was thoroughly dismantled and something like
religious freedom as we know it prevailed. With the restoration of
Charles II in 1660, it seemed possible that the reestablished Church of
England might include both Presbyterians and Independents, united
with Anglicans in a new form of Protestantism. Charles himself leaned
toward the Roman Catholic Church, though he could hardly make that
inclination public. At the beginning of his reign he attempted to
encourage toleration of Nonconformists, probably to create an atmos-

phere in which Roman Catholics might have greater freedom of worship. The various Protestant sects attempted to work out an accommodation, but the Act of Uniformity, confirmed by Parliament in 1662, laid such difficult requirements on Nonconformists that they could not in good conscience obey it. For instance, Nonconformist ministers who were not ordained by Anglican bishops had to be reordained, in effect confessing that their previous ordination was not valid. All worship services had to follow the prescribed forms in the Book of Common Prayer, which many Nonconformists regarded as aping the religion of Rome.

Thus there arose two kinds of persecution in England: that of Roman Catholics and that of Nonconformists. Both groups comprised tiny minorities. Less than one percent of Englishmen were openly Roman Catholic, about five percent were Nonconformists. Neither group could be stamped out, although Parliament did its best to legislate against them. Both groups were suspected of conspiring to overthrow the government, either separately or together. Nonconformists who continued to worship at their conventicles were, by the Act of Uniformity, subject to heavy fines, and any minister who would not swear the prescribed oath would lose his position (as 2000 of them did).

But laws are merely words until they are enforced. Throughout Charles II's reign, conventicles flourished in spite of new and more repressive laws such as the Five Mile Act (1665) and the Conventicle Act (1670), which Marvell, in a letter to his nephew, characterized as "the Quintessence of arbitrary Malice." It is clear that in many places the local officers of the law looked the other way. Those who were at risk of fines and imprisonment regarded the health of their souls as more important than any other consideration. And while some of the supporters of the Church of England labored to represent Nonconformists as disloyal and seditious, they were predominantly loyal, hardworking citizens who simply wanted to worship in their own fashion.

Marvell's prose treatises show his sympathy for Nonconformists and his fear of Roman Catholicism. Three of them are directed against spokesmen for the Church of England who argued for the suppression of Nonconformists. In the fourth he presents evidence of a conspiracy to reestablish the Roman church in England. But all these treatises are haunted by a single specter: the tyranny of absolute government. Consequently it is legitimate to call them political, for Marvell's constant concern is to undermine the claims of authority, whether political or religious, to control the conscience of individuals. He appears not as a republican or as a defender of democracy, most assuredly not as an anar-

chist or a revolutionary, but as an Englishman who wishes to preserve
the liberties of the English people as established by English law and custom and, more importantly, by the Christian gospel.

Since Marvell's first treatise, *The Rehearsal Transpros'd* (1672), is the
most famous and accomplished of his prose works, it is appropriate to
examine it at length. Marvell wrote it as a response to three attacks on
Nonconformists by Samuel Parker, an Anglican who was rising rapidly
in the church hierarchy. In 1669 Parker had published *A Discourse of
Ecclesiastical Politie*. Responses to this work led him to issue *A Defence and
Continuation of the Ecclesiastical Politie* (1671). Finally Parker wrote a preface to a new edition of the *Vindication of Himself and the Episcopal Church
From the Presbyterian Charge of Popery* by Bishop Bramhall (1672).
Parker's fundamental contention (Marvell quotes these passages, calling
the first the "grand thesis") was that "The Supream Government of
every Commonwealth, where-ever it is lodged, must of necessity be universal, absolute, and uncontroulable in all affairs whatsoever that concern the Interests of Mankind and the ends of Government" and that "it
is absolutely necessary to the peace and government of the World, that
the supream Magistrate of every Commonwealth should be vested with
a Power to govern and conduct the Consciences of Subjects in affairs of
Religion."[2]

Although it might seem a simple matter to refute such sweeping
assertions of government authority, Marvell did not attack them
directly, for to do so would appear to deny both the King's position as
supreme governor of the English Church and the authority of Parliament. Charles had been careful in all his proclamations to represent
himself as a loving father of the established church. Knowing that his
defense of the Nonconformists could not receive official approval, Marvell published it anonymously and without a license.[3] Instead of disput-
ing the ideological bases of Parker's arguments, Marvell chose to attack
Parker himself and to impugn his character and his motives. The most
brilliant aspect of this attack accounts for the strange title of the treatise.

One of the great successes of the London stage in 1671 was a comedy
by the Duke of Buckingham titled *The Rehearsal*.[4] The chief character,
generally taken to be a satirical portrait of John Dryden, was Mr. Bayes,
a foolish writer of plays who has no concept of character or plot. Early in
the play Bayes confesses that he borrows his material from other writers,
turning their prose into verse and vice versa to hide his thefts. Another
character remarks that the process might be called "transprosing." Marvell seized the opportunity to turn Buckingham's successful burlesque of

Dryden into a weapon against Parker. Taking for granted that the reader will know Buckingham's play, the speaker of *The Rehearsal Transpros'd* consistently refers to Parker as Mr. Bayes and spices his text with brief quotations from *The Rehearsal*.

By choosing to mount a satirical attack on Parker, however, Marvell created a problem of decorum. In simple terms, it came to this: if your opponent is an egregious fool, what is the point of arguing with him? The Book of Proverbs (26:4–5) offers two apparently contradictory pieces of wisdom: "Answer not a fool according to his folly, lest thou also be like unto him," and "Answer a fool according to his folly, lest he be wise in his own conceit." The speaker of *The Rehearsal Transpros'd*, without quoting either proverb, consistently presents himself as a man of good sense who, recognizing Mr. Bayes's foolishness, nevertheless undertakes the slightly ludicrous task of answering a fool according to his folly because this particular fool has meddled with matters of serious import that are none of his business.

Marvell's subtitle, *Animadversions upon a late Book, Intituled A Preface Shewing what Grounds there are of Fears and Jealousies of Popery*, referring to Parker's third treatise, is inaccurate as a description of the scope of his work (he responds to all three treatises) but quite accurate as a characterization of his method. A seventeenth-century reader knew that an animadversion is an informal collection of comments, not a rigidly logical discourse. The writer will attack his opponent selectively, picking sentences here and there to quote and replying sarcastically. He is under no obligation to give a fair account of his opponent's opinions. He may insinuate that his opponent is a knave, a fool, or a madman (Marvell does all three). But in doing so he had better be entertaining and witty. Otherwise he can be accused of railing. Indeed, this is exactly the charge Marvell's speaker brings against Mr. Bayes:

> But the Author's end was only railing. He could never have induc'd himself to praise one man but in order to rail on another. He never oyls his Hone but that he may whet his Razor; and that not to shave, but to cut mens throats. And whoever will take the pains to compare, will find, that as it is his only end; so his best, nay his only talent is railing. (20)

To rail means to utter abusive language. Here are some passages that might justly be called examples of railing:

> Tenderness and Indulgence to such men [Nonconformists], were to nourish Vipers in our own Bowels, and the most sottish neglect of our

own quiet and security, and we should deserve to perish with the dishon-
our of Sardanapalus. (67)

For if he will not accept his own Charge, his Modesty is all impudent and
counterfeit: Or, if he will acknowledge it, why then he had been before,
and did still remain upon Record, the same lewd, wanton, and inconti-
nent Scribler. (3)

Having fixed his Center in this Nobleman's House, he thought he could
now move and govern the whole Earth with the same facility. Nothing
now would serve him but he must be a madman in print, and write a
Book of *Ecclesiastical Policy*. (31)

He doth so verily believe himself to be a Wolf, that his speech is all
turn'd into howling, yelling, and barking: and if there were any Sheep
here, you should see him pull out their throats and suck the blood. (32)

These are, indeed, bitterly abusive. But only the first is quoted from
Parker. The other three are comments made by Marvell's speaker. There
is very little wit in them. They serve as fair warning to a reader of *The
Rehearsal Transpros'd*: Marvell's intent is to make Parker look like a fool;
and, as the proverb has it, any stick will do to beat a dog. Parker's small-
est mistake will be turned against him. When Parker charges that a
well-meaning zealot is the most dangerous of all villains, Marvell's
speaker notes parenthetically, "even more dangerous it seems then a
malicious and ill-meaning Zelot" (58). After quoting a sentence in
which Parker inaccurately locates Geneva on the south side of Lake
Leman, Marvell's speaker spends several pages mocking Parker's style,
imagining a dialogue in which "some critical people" blame Parker for
mislocating the city, to which the speaker invents far-fetched defenses,
and elaborating a Rabelaisian narrative involving the capons of Geneva
and the bears of Berne. Seizing upon a phrase from Parker's first treatise
("in matters of a closer and more comfortable importance"), Marvell's
speaker deduces that this "comfortable importance" must be a woman
and embarks on a series of sexual innuendoes.

The fact is that *The Rehearsal Transpros'd* includes a great deal of railing. The treatise is largely an attack upon the morals and motives of
"Mr. Bayes." Marvell's speaker explains why he chooses to call his opponent "*Bayes* the Second": first, because Parker's attacks were published
anonymously ("he hath no Name or at least will not own it"); second,
because he is "a lover of Elegancy of Stile";

But chiefly, because *Mr. Bayes* and he do very much Symbolize [agree]; in their understandings, in their expressions, in their humour, in their contempt and quarrelling of all others, though of their own Profession. (9)

Marvell's strategy of identifying Parker with Buckingham's addled playwright allows him to attribute to Parker all of Bayes's foolish pride and incompetence. It establishes the decorum of his attack.

For a modern reader, *decorum* suggests polite behavior, and making fun of people hardly seems polite. But for Marvell's readers, decorum had a broader significance that involved aesthetic and moral issues as well as social. Marvell's awareness of the need for decorum is clearly indicated more than once in his treatise:

For, as I am obliged to ask pardon if I speak of serious things ridiculously; so I must now beg excuse if I should hap to discourse of ridiculous things seriously. But I shall, so far as possible, observe *decorum*, and, whatever I talk of, not commit such an Absurdity, as to be grave with a Buffoon. [Marvell's speaker had already given Bayes the title of Buffoon-General to the Church of England.] But the principal cause of my Apology is, because I see I am drawn in to mention Kings and Princes, and even our own; whom, as I think of with all duty and reverence, so I avoid speaking of either in jest or earnest, lest by reason of my private condition & breeding, I should, though most unwillingly, trip in a word, or fail in the mannerliness of an expression. (49)

Here, if ever in Marvell's prose, is a passage that amply supports the notion that Swift was indebted to Marvell for his satiric style. The phrase, "though most unwillingly," has all the naive sincerity of Swift's Gulliver or the speaker of *A Modest Proposal*. One has only to recall Marvell's portrait of Charles II in "The last Instructions to a Painter" to put this unwillingness in perspective.

For the most part, Marvell's speaker observes decorum: he is not grave with Mr. Bayes, the buffoon. One of the funniest passages in *The Rehearsal Transpros'd* burlesques the combative nature of the Anglican clergy who attempt to do battle with Nonconformists. The speaker pictures them as warriors donning armor in preparation for battle:

Great variety there was, and an heavy doo. Some clapp'd it on all rusty as it was, others fell of oyling and furbishing their armour: Some piss'd in their Barrels, others spit in their pans, to scowr them. Here you might see one put on his Helmet the wrong way: there one buckle on a Back in place of a Breast. Some by mistake catched up a Socinian or Arminian Argument, and some a Popish to fight a Papist. Here a Dwarf lost in the accoutrements of a Giant: there a *Don-Quixot* in an equipage of differing pieces, and of several Parishes. Never was there such Incongruity and Nonconformity in their furniture. . . . And no less sport was it to see their Leaders. Few could tell how to give the word of Command, nor understood to drill a Company: They were as unexpert as their Soldiers aukward. (120)

Bayes himself is associated with the ridiculous Drawcansir, a character in *The Rehearsal* who ends a battle by killing everyone on both sides:

But it is a brave thing to be the Ecclesiastical *Draw-Can-Sir*; He kills whole Nations, he kills Friend and Foe; *Hungary, Transylvania, Bohemia, Poland, Savoy, France,* the *Netherlands, Denmark, Sweden,* and a great part of the Church of *England,* and all *Scotland* (for these, beside many more, he mocks under the title of *Germany* and *Geneva*) may perhaps rouse our Mastiff, and make up a Danger worthy of his Courage. A man would guess that this Giant had promised his *Comfortable Importance,* a Simarre [a woman's undergarment, also a bishop's gown] of the beards of all the *Orthodox Theologues* in Christendom. (21)

Lest anyone suppose that the entire treatise is an exercise in foolery, Marvell's speaker concludes by hoping his reader "shall learn by this Example, that it is not impossible to be merry and angry as long time as I have been writing, without profaning and violating those things which are and ought to be most sacred" (145). This echoes an observation made earlier in the work: "But truth, you see, cannot want words: and she will laugh too sometimes when she speaks, and rather than all fail too, be serious" (117). Marvell's speaker is a truth-teller, and, when he wishes, can abandon his drollery and his wit to speak soberly and straightforwardly. Bayes may be a buffoon, and laughter may be the most appropriate response to his treatises. But the issues he raises are far too serious to be laughed off the stage. And he is not alone in his opinions. He is one of a class of men whom Marvell's speaker portrays in a description that recalls the seventeenth-century genre known as the *character*:

They are the *Politick Would-be's* of the Clergy. Not Bishops, but Men that have a mind to be Bishops, and that will do anything in the World to compass it. . . . They are Men of a fiery nature that must always be uppermost, and so they may increase their own Splendor, care not though they set all on flame about them. You would think the same day that they took up Divinity they divested themselves of Humanity, & so they may procure & execute a Law against the Nonconformists, that they had forgot the Gospel. They cannot endure that Humility, that Meekness, that strictness of Manners and Conversation, which is the true way of gaining Reputation and Authority to the Clergy; much less can they content themselves with the ordinary and comfortable provision that is made for the Ministry: But, having wholly calculated themselves for Preferment, and Grandeur, know or practise no other means to make themselves venerable but by Ceremony and Severity. (106–107)

"Ceremony and Severity" are the two main issues that Marvell's speaker addresses in *The Rehearsal Transpros'd.* "Ceremony" refers to the various aspects of ritual (e.g., the requirement that a minister wear a surplice and that the congregation kneel to receive communion) prescribed by the Book of Common Prayer that the Nonconformists could not accept. "Severity" is a shorthand expression for Parker's attempt to bring the whole authority of the state down upon the Nonconformists. Marvell's speaker contrasts the humanity and meekness of genuine Christians with the greedy ambition of would-be bishops like Parker, who climb the steps to advancement by trampling on the private conscience of sincere believers. While he continues to address "Mr. Bayes" on these issues, the speaker, no longer a wit or a railer, becomes the spokesmen for all Christians who have an earnest desire for peace in the church and in the kingdom.

In dealing with these serious matters, Marvell's speaker is quite different from the Andrew Marvell who served in the government of Oliver Cromwell and wrote poems that praise his greatness. The speaker presents himself as a loyal subject of the King (certainly not a Nonconformist) and a believer in the prudence and moderation of princes.[5] References to the happy restoration of Charles II and statements of trust in his wisdom serve to mask Andrew Marvell's growing distrust of the King. But there is an excellent reason for this pose. Marvell knew that one hope for the Nonconformists was the King's repeated attempts to secure toleration for their forms of worship (Charles II issued a Declaration of Indulgence in 1672), even though he probably suspected the King's motives. A passage like the following might help to strengthen the King's resolve or win support in Parliament:

[Princes] do not think fit to command things unnecessary, and where the profit cannot countervail the hazard. But above all they consider, that God has instated them in the Government of Mankind, with that incumbrance (if it may so be called) of Reason, and that incumbrance upon Reason of Conscience. . . . That men therefore are to be dealt with reasonably: and conscientious men by Conscience. . . . That the Prince therefore, by how much God hath indued him with a clearer reason, and by consequence with a more enlightned judgment, ought the rather to take heed lest by punishing Conscience, he violate not only his own, but the Divine Majesty. (111–112)

Here the speaker has dropped all traces of wit or railing. The measured pace of the argument (much more sustained than this brief quotation can illustrate), the patient piling up of parallel clauses, the repeated emphasis on reason, the dignified vocabulary—all attest to the speaker's sincerity and sober-mindedness. And this is not the only example. The last pages of *The Rehearsal Transpros'd* consist largely of serious argument. Having proved that Bayes is a fool, the speaker turns to showing how dangerous such foolishness can be. Earlier he had made an ironic apology to his opponent: "I ask you heartily pardon, Mr. *Bayes*, for treating you against *Decorum* here, with so much gravity. 'Tis possible I may not trouble you above once or twice more in the like nature; but so often at least, I hope, one may in the writing of a whole Book, have leave to be serious" (83). There will be no more apologies.

The final pages are shadowed by the darkest moment in English history: the beheading of Charles I. Marvell's speaker charges Bayes with blaming the civil war and the execution of the King on the Nonconformists:

And, I observe, that all the Argument of your Books is but very frivolous and trivial: onely the memory of the late War serves for demonstration, and the detestable sentence & execution, of his late Majesty is represented again upon the Scaffold; and you having been, I suspect, better acquainted with Parliament Declarations formerly upon another account, do now apply and turn them all over to prove that the late War was wholly upon a Fanatical Cause [i.e., caused by the Nonconformists], and the dissenting party do still goe big with the same Monster [i.e., still want to foment rebellion]. (124–125)

In this battle for the possession of English history, Marvell's speaker counters by tracing the cause of the civil war to the pride and ambition of the Anglican clergy. The King's tragedy was that he trusted them while they, to serve their own ends, led him to believe that his power was absolute.

But he that will do the Clergyes drudgery, must look for his reward in another World. For they having gained this Ascendent upon him,

resolv'd whatever became on't to make their best of him; and having
made the whole business of State their *Arminian* Jangles, and the persecution for Ceremonies, did for recompence assign him that imaginary
absolute Government, upon which Rock we all ruined. (134)

In effect, Marvell's speaker argues, Bayes advocates exactly the same
policies that led to the civil war. His predecessors betrayed Charles I;
Bayes is an enemy of Charles II and a danger to the kingdom: "by what
appears, I cannot see that there is any probability of disturbance in the
State, but by men of his spirit and principles" (138). Bayes is a danger
because he imagines that a ruler's power can be unlimited:

The truth is in short and let *Bayes* make more or less of it if he can; *Bayes*
had at first built up such a stupendious Magistrate, as never was of God's
making. He had put all Princes upon the Rack to stretch them to his
dimension. (92)

Marvell's speaker does not, here or elsewhere, contend that absolute
government is wrong. Rather, he argues that princes are too wise to
want such power:

. . . the care I say of all these [common people, nobles, and clergy], rests
upon them [princes]. So that they are fain to condescend to many things
for peace-sake, and the quiet of Mankind, that your proud heart would
break before it would bend to. (108)

He then cites several examples of princes who came to grief because of
their arrogance. As for the King of England, the speaker is confident of
his wisdom:

Do not you think that the King has considered all these things? I believe
he has; and perhaps, as you have minced the matter, he may well think
the Nonconformists have very nice [finicky] Stomachs, that they cannot
digest such chopp'd hay: But on the other side, he must needs take you
to be very strange men, to cram these in spite down the throats of any
Christian. (110)

It is not possible in this chapter to do justice to the variety of *The
Rehearsal Transpros'd*.[6] To a modern reader, it is a strange combination of
foolery, personal abuse, and enlightened concern for an oppressed minority.
It has no logical structure; it refuses to challenge the fundamental points of

Parker's treatises; it alternates between burlesque, pedantry, railing, and what appear to be deeply felt statements of the speaker's true feelings. One of these is the most frequently quoted passage in Marvell's prose:

> Whether it [the civil war] were a War of Religion, or of Liberty, is not worth the labour to enquire. Which-soever was at the top, the other was at the bottom; but upon considering all, I think the Cause was too good to have been fought for. Men ought to have trusted God; they ought and might have trusted the King [Charles I] with that whole matter. The *Arms of the Church are Prayers and Tears*, the Arms of the Subjects are Patience and Petitions. The King himself being of so accurate and piercing a judgment, would soon have felt where it stuck. For men may spare their pains where Nature is at work, and the world will not go the faster for our driving. Even as his present Majesties happy Restauration did it self, so all things else happen in their best and proper time, without any need of our officiousness. (135)

Anyone who recalls the "Horatian Ode" will be struck by the next-to-last sentence, for it echoes the view of Cromwell as a force of nature, not to be withstood. But that view is at odds with the confidence in Charles's judgment expressed in the preceding sentence. The final sentence, appearing to advocate a totally passive attitude, is difficult to reconcile with Marvell's career in Parliament and even with his writing of this treatise. Although the whole passage reads like a sincere statement of belief, it may be no more than a rhetorical device to suggest that a defense of the Nonconformists is not an invitation to civil disobedience.

One fact about *The Rehearsal Transpros'd* is certainly clear: it was an enormous success. The demand for the book was so great that there was a second issue, with Marvell's name on the title page. Charles II was reported to have read it more than once with considerable enjoyment, and it could hardly have been reissued without his approval. According to a contemporary, this book by "the liveliest droll of the age" was so entertaining that "from the king to the tradesman, his books were read with great pleasure."[7] Within a year no fewer than six replies were in print, one of them, *A Reproof to the Rehearsal Transpros'd*, by Samuel Parker himself. In a letter to Sir William Harley dated 3 May 1673, Marvell calls Parker's reply "the rudest book . . . that ever was publisht (I may say), since the first invention of printing." He tells Harley that he intends to answer it, though he is reluctant "to intermeddle in a noble and high argument wch therefore by how much it is above my capacity I shall use the more industry not to disparage it" (Margoliouth, 2:328).

His answer, published in 1673, was *The Rehearsal Transpros'd: The Second Part*. The title page includes some additional information:

> *Occasioned by Two Letters: The first*
> *Printed, by a nameless Author,*
> *Intituled,* A Reproof, &c.
> *The Second Letter left for me at a Friends*
> *House, Dated* Nov. 3.
> *1673. Subscribed* J. G. *and*
> *concluding with these words*; If
> thou darest to Print or Publish
> any Lie or Libel against Doctor
> *Parker*, By the Eternal God I
> will cut thy Throat.

In this context the next line—*Answered by* ANDREW MARVEL—is a gesture of defiance.

The second part of *The Rehearsal Transpros'd*, published late in 1673, resembles the first part in several ways. After an introductory section in which he makes it clear that his adversary is Samuel Parker, Marvell's speaker still calls him Mr. Bayes, "For indeed, 'tis too ceremonious and tiresome to repeat so often upon all occasions the *Author of the Ecclesiastical Politie*" (199). The personal abuse is, if anything, even more severe, the speaker suggesting that Bayes's madness may be the result of syphilis. The whole treatise is as formless as its predecessor. But there are significant differences. In 1673 Parliament had forced the King to withdraw the Declaration of Indulgence and was debating the passage of a Bill of Ease to lighten the persecution of Nonconformists. Marvell's speaker no longer needs to present the King as the model of a prudent ruler. He can and does address more directly the basic tenets of Parker's argument. There is less burlesque and more sober argument.

While the main points are the same as in the first part, several passages suggest that Marvell is finding the contest less enjoyable. The speaker comments on the peculiar character of satirical writing:

> But, among all the differences of writing, he that does publish an Invective, does it at his utmost peril, and 'tis but just that it should be so. For a mans Credit is of so natural and high concernment to him, that the preserving of it better, was perhaps none of the least inducements at first to enter into the bonds of Society, and Civil Government. . . . Yet if for once to write in that stile may be lawful, discreet or necessary, to do it a second time is lyable to greater Censure. (160–161)

The problem is that readers will not only get tired of "personal and passionate discourses," but will conclude that "justice lies on the weaker side":

> And yet nevertheless, and all that has been said before being granted, it may so chance that to write, and that Satyrically, and that a second time and a third; and this too even against a Clergy-man, may be not only excusable but necessary. (163)

A good deal of the brio with which Marvell's speaker attacked Mr. Bayes in the first part has disappeared.

But, as the speaker makes clear, Parker must be attacked because he has made his erroneous opinions public.

> But he that hath once Printed an ill book has thereby condens'd his words on purpose lest they should be carried away by the wind; he has diffused his poyson so publickly in design that it might be beyond his own recollection; and put himself deliberately past the reach of any private admonition. In this Case it is that I think a Clergy-man is laid open to the Pen of anyone that knows how to manage it; and that every person who has either Wit, Learning or Sobriety is licensed, if debauch'd to curb him, if erroneous to catechize him, and if foul-mouth'd and biting, to muzzle him. (164)

The speaker will be as serious as Bayes allows him to be: "If at any turn he gives me the least opportunity to be serious I shall gladly take it: but where he prevaricates or is scurrilous (and where is he not?) I shall treat him betwixt Jest and Earnest" (187).

The prevailing tone of the second part is earnest. Marvell's speaker finally confronts Bayes's grand thesis: the necessity of absolute power in government. He begins by pointing out that Bayes imagines a world that does not exist: "You do hereby seem to imagine, that Providence should have contrived all things according to the utmost perfection, or that which you conceive would have been most to your purpose." But "we must nevertheless be content with such bodies, and to inhabit such an Earth as it has pleased God to allot us." In this world "Slaughter and War has made up half the business" and God has "distinguish'd the Government of the World by the intermitting seasons of Discord, War, and Publick Disturbance" (231–232). It is not God's will that mankind should find tranquillity, although "'tis indeed the very thing proposed in your *Ecclesiastical Politie*, that you might be row'd in state over the Ocean of Publick Tranquillity by the publick

Slavery" (232). In this fallen world there must be government and power to govern:

> The Power of the Magistrate does most certainly issue from the Divine Authority. The Obedience due to that Power is by Divine Command; and Subjects are bound both as Men and as Christians to obey the Magistrate Actively in all things where their Duty to God intercedes not, . . . or if they cannot do that (the Magistrate or the reason of their own occasions hindring them) then by suffering patiently at home, without giving the least publick disturbance. (232–233)

The question is not whether the magistrate has the authority to command obedience. It is, rather, whether it is wise to use it to the limit: "But the modester Question . . . would be how far it is advisable for a Prince to exert and push the rigour of that Power which no man can deny him" (233). The speaker's approach is pragmatic, not theoretical. "A Prince that goes to the Top of his Power is like him that shall go to the Bottom of his Treasure" (235). The prince's safety is best assured by the affection of his people. As for the absolute power Bayes is so fond of, "there is not any so proper and certain way of attaining it, as by this softness of handling" (234). But Marvell's speaker, imagining a kingdom in which princes rule benevolently and the people always obey, even to the point that "the very memory or thoughts of any such thing as Publick liberty would, as it were by consent, expire and be for ever extinguish'd," presents a fantasy as unrealistic as Bayes's concept of tranquillity based on absolute power.

In the last section of the Second Part the speaker drops all pretense of witty urbanity and amused detachment in favor of a series of bitter charges against his opponent. Nowhere is his anger more apparent than in the section in which he defends "J. M." (John Milton). It is too long to quote in full, but even a portion of it illustrates the speaker's feelings:

> But he never having in the least provoked you, for you to insult thus over his old age, to traduce him by your *Scaramuccios*, and in your own person, as a School-Master, who was born and hath lived much more ingenuously and Liberally then your self; to have done all this, and lay at last my simple book to his charge, without ever taking care to inform your self better, which you had so easie opportunity to do; nay, when you your self too have said, to my knowledge, that you saw no such great matter in it but that I might be the Author: it is inhumanely and inhospitably done, and will I hope be a warning to all others as it is to me, to avoid

(I will not say such a *Judas*,) but a man that creeps into all companies, to
jeer, trepan, and betray them. (312–313)

The last sentence of the Second Part is a bitter observation: "However I
have spit out your dirty Shoon" (327).

In the final analysis, Marvell's speaker stands for moderation and tol-
erance, but, as Marvell must have recognized, his attack upon Parker
was neither moderate nor tolerant. Not only is "Mr. Bayes" revealed as a
fool; he is also, like the clergy who destroyed the peace of the early
Christian community, guilty of "Covetousness, Ambition, Pride, Igno-
rance, Formality, and Contentions" (238). By his wit the speaker defines
himself as a man of good sense who has the unpleasant but necessary
task of muzzling a barking dog. The task is dirty and demeaning, and
witty detachment gives way to personal invective. In the end Marvell
was completely successful: Parker made no response to the second part.
Even Anthony à Wood, who despised Marvell's ideas, had to admit that
Parker was defeated.[8] But anyone who reads these treatises will find an
aspect of Andrew Marvell that even the satirical verses do not reveal—a
deeply felt personal anger that goes beyond wit and playfulness and
comes close to the savage disgust that animates the satires of Swift.

Marvell's other prose treatises can be dealt with briefly. Two were
published either anonymously or under a pseudonym. *Mr. Smirke; Or,
The Divine in Mode* (1676) by Andreas Rivetus, Junior, comes to the res-
cue of Bishop Herbert Croft, a moderate Anglican whose *The Naked
Truth; Or, the True state of the Primitive Church* (1675) incurred a heavy
attack. Marvell responds to the anonymous *Animadversions Upon a Late
Pamphlet* (1676). Although his title is derived from the very popular play
The Man of Mode, or Sir Fopling Flutter, by Sir George Etherege (in which
Mr. Smirke is a pliant parson), Marvell's speaker simply calls his opponent the Animadverter. His method is to quote and refute the Animadverter's words. The work is much shorter than either part of *The
Rehearsal Transpros'd*, but the target is the same: the pride and con-
tentiousness of clergymen who want to force everyone to accept their
religious practices. For the most part the speaker is earnest rather than
witty, and his attitude is best expressed in the final paragraph: "I am
weary of such stuffe, both mine own and his."[9]

Appended to this treatise is *A Short Historical Essay Touching General
Councils, Creeds, and Impositions in Religion*, which was reissued independently in 1680 and 1687. It is a sober exposition of Marvell's belief that
all the troubles that ever racked the Christian Church can be traced to

the ambitions of clergymen who use the power of the state to enforce conformity:

> How came it about that Christianity, which approv'd itself under all Persecutions to the Heathen Emperours, and merited their favour so far, till at last it regularly succeeded to the Monarchy, should, under those of their own profession, be more distressed? But the Answer is now much shorter and certainer; and I will adventure boldly to say, the true and single cause then was the Bishops. (71)

Although this treatise is not formally a defense of the Nonconformists, Marvell contrasts them favorably with the "greater churchmen" (bishops) and ambitious clergymen who still trouble the peace of the Church: "the Moral Hereticks [among the clergy] do the Church more harm then all the Non-conformists can do, or can wish it" (74–75). As in all his prose works, Marvell presents himself as the champion of Christian liberty, the enemy of high-flying churchmen.

An Account of the Growth of Popery, and Arbitrary Government in England (1677) is an altogether different kind of work. As the title indicates, it is a highly detailed, though hardly objective, history of events from November 1675 through July 1677, with a special concern for debates in Parliament.[10] The speaker is essentially a historian, but he frequently takes the liberty of making sarcastic comments. His thesis is that members of the government have engaged in a conspiracy to subvert Parliament and to make England subordinate to Catholic France. Even though the speaker does not name the conspirators, it was a dangerous charge, and the treatise was published anonymously. It begins with an ironically naive celebration of the English system of government: "In short, there is nothing that comes nearer in Government to the Divine Perfection, than where the Monarch, as with us, injoys a capacity of doing all the good imaginable to mankind, under a disability to all that is evil."[11] In contrast, Roman Catholicism and the government it fosters cannot be sufficiently despised: "That Popery is such a thing as cannot, but for want of a word to express it, be called a Religion: nor is it to be mentioned with that civility which is otherwise decent to be used, in speaking of the differences of humane opinion about Divine Matters" (5). There follow several pages in which the speaker warns of all the evils of Popery and concludes that the English church stands "in a direct opposition to all the forementioned errours" (12). England is apparently in no danger: "Nor therefore is there any, whether Prince or Nation, that can with less probability be reduced back to the *Romish* perswasion, than ours of *England*" (12).

But, in fact, there is a great and most insidious danger: "And yet, all this notwithstanding, there are those men among us, who have undertaken, and do make it their businesse, under so Legal and perfect a Government, to introduce a *French* slavery, and instead of so pure a Religion, to establish the *Roman* idolatry" (14). These are Englishmen, "secure men, that are above either Honour or Consciencs [sic]; but obliged by all the most sacred tyes of Malice and Ambition to advance the ruine of the King and Kingdome, and qualified much better then others, under the name of good Protestants, to effect it" (16). The speaker's purpose is to expose the conspiracy, not the conspirators (though Marvell's readers could easily guess whom he referred to), by recalling a series of events that culminated in the meeting of Parliament on 15 February 1676. He presents a narrative with few heroes, many unnamed villains, and a House of Commons made up largely of venal cowards.[12]

The speaker concludes with a warning—"It is now come to the fourth Act, and the next Scene that opens may be *Rome* or *Paris*" (155)—and an explanation of his method:

> If the Relator had extended all these Articles in their particular Instances, with severall other Heads . . . it is evident there was matter sufficient to have further accused his Subjects. And nevertheless, he foresees that he shall . . . be blamed for pursuing this method. Some . . . will expect, that the very Persons should have been named, whereas he onely gives evidence to the Fact, and leaves the malefactors to those who have the power of inquiry. It was his design indeed to give Information, but not to turn informer. . . . But if anyone delight in the Chase, he is an ill Woodman that knows not the size of the Beast by the proportion of his Excrement. (155)

Modern historians find a greater degree of complexity in English politics of the 1670s than Marvell's charge of conspiracy allows. With the benefit of three centuries of hindsight and access to facts that Marvell could not know, they are likely to refer to policy, not conspiracy.[13] But Marvell probably knew more than he could say. The King was certainly trying to favor Roman Catholics, and his policies in effect made England a client of France. To say so, however, would have been a capital crime, and the King's policies had to be blamed on unnamed councillors.[14] Nevertheless, the government offered a reward of £100 for information about the author's identity, and the printer was imprisoned.

Marvell's last prose work was his *Remarks upon a late Disingenuous Discourse* (1678), a defense of the Nonconformist John Howe, who had been attacked by another Nonconformist. The subject is theological: God's foreknowledge (prescience) and the Calvinist doctrine of predestination. The topic may seem dry to a modern reader, but Marvell's speaker (the title page identifies him simply as "a Protestant") reveals some of the same wit and brio which made *The Rehearsal Transpros'd* so popular. His task is to show that Howe's treatise never argues that God's prescience causes human beings to sin. As usual, he mounts a personal attack on Howe's accuser. But, since the accuser published under the initials T. D. (Marvell knew perfectly well who he was), Marvell's speaker chooses to understand T. D. to mean The Discourse, and regularly refers to the author as "It," as if the book had written itself. He argues that "It" distorts Howe's statements and lacks the skill to sustain his attack:

> Now it is indeed fit that a Respondent should gratifie his Opponent as far as may consist with Civility and Safety. But here arises a Case of Conscience: Whether a man may give another leave, that desires it, to speak Non-sense. I say no.[15]

He characterizes "Its" ineptness by a witty analogy:

> Yet how much Powder is spent without doing the least execution! First a Categorical, then an Hypothetical Syllogism fired at him, then forces him to distinguish, which is among Disputants next to crying quarter, but will not give it him; runs him through with three Replies to his Distinction, and leaves him dead upon the place. While the proposition is all this while untoucht, Mr. *Howe* is out of Gun-shot, and his Adversary (if one that only skirmishes with himself, deserves to called so) is afraid to take aim, and starts meerly at the Report of his own Musquet. (54–55)

Two more serious charges are brought against "It":

> Its Dulness, therefore, . . . being so oft attested under *It*'s own hand, and to which, if necessary, *It* might have another Thousand Witnesses, I shall not further pall my Reader on this Subject, but return rather from this digression to my first design of obviating that in the Preface, which hath all the marks upon it of Malice, except the Wit wherewith that vice is more usually accompanied. (137)

With this treatise, Marvell's career as a controversialist in prose comes to an end. His subject, as always, is freedom—in this case the freedom of every human being to choose between good and evil actions. Although he would not have presumed to say so, Marvell will not allow even God to exercise absolute power over human will. While his reputation as a champion of liberty rested largely on his actions in Parliament and his satirical poems, his prose treatises reveal his commitment to freedom and his scorn for every use of power that impinges on the conscience of the individual.

Chapter Nine
Marvell's Reputation

When Andrew Marvell died in 1678, he was known as a member of Parliament, as an author of prose pamphlets, and as the writer of a handful of dedicatory poems and verse satires. At no time in the three centuries since his death has his name been quite forgotten, but the significance of his work has undergone a total reevaluation. For his contemporaries Marvell was a patriot, a satirist, and a champion of liberty. For us he is a poet, the author of a handful of powerful lyrics, and a unique voice in English literature. This chapter will trace the development of these two reputations, concentrating on the gradual recognition of Marvell's lyric verse.

A writer's reputation depends on his work in print. In 1678 Marvell had published several lengthy prose pamphlets, political satires in verse, and a few short poems, none of which forms the basis for his fame in our time. The publication of *Miscellaneous Poems* around 1681 apparently did nothing to change the way his contemporaries thought of him. In fact, his reputation depended to some extent on political satires attributed to him that he may not have written. In his brief notes on Marvell, John Aubrey calls him "an excellent poet in Latin or English" and refers specifically to "The Advice to a Painter" (probably "The last Instructions") and obliquely to "Tom May's Death" (2:53–54). But Anthony à Wood, for whom Aubrey collected biographical data, though he mentions the publication of the folio in 1681 and notes that "persons of [Marvell's] persuasion" cried up the poems as excellent, devotes most of his comments to *The Rehearsal Transpros'd*, which he clearly despises.[1]

Because Marvell was so deeply involved in political controversy, it is hardly to be expected that his contemporaries would have an objective view of his opinions or his writings. Dryden, who had several reasons for disliking Marvell, helped to spread the lie about Marvell's pension of £400 per year (84). The anonymous poem "*On His Excellent Friend* Mr. Anth. Marvell," first published in 1697, describes him as a patriotic guardian of English liberty against the power of Rome (81–82). Both his enemies and his friends responded to Marvell's controversial writings. Often it is not possible to tell whether they are referring to the prose works, the satirical poems, or both. But they do not mention the poems for which he is famous today.

Praise of Marvell's satirical poems is found in several places in the writings of Daniel Defoe (104, 106–108). Thomas Cooke, who in 1726 published the first edition of Marvell's poetry after the 1681 folio, singles out "On Mr. Milton's Paradise lost," "A Dialogue between the two Horses," and "On Blood's stealing the Crown" as examples of his best poems. But Cooke is far more interested in Marvell as an incorruptible patriot, "a Pattern for all free-born *English-men*." In his biographical sketch he proposes to view him "in his Writings": "In all which the same Love, and Hatred, of Right, and Wrong, are as apparent, and the same publick Spirit exerted, as in his other proceedings" (his career as a member of Parliament) (110).

For a long time Marvell was perceived as a champion of liberty in the struggle against monarchy and the Papacy. In his edition of Marvell's complete works in prose and verse (1776), Edward Thompson praises him as "the ardent lover of his country, and the undaunted champion of the common rights of mankind" (121). Some 30 years later, John Aikin calls him "a witty writer and incorruptible patriot," mentions several satirical poems and *The Rehearsal Transpros'd*, but makes only a passing reference to his "early poems" (122–124). In his sonnet "Great men have been among us," William Wordsworth associates Marvell with Milton, James Harrington and other "Moralists" who "knew how genuine glory was put on." The first full biography of Marvell, John Dove's *Life of Andrew Marvell* (1832), introduces him as "one of the most incorruptible patriots that England, or any other country, ever produced" (149). In his review of Dove's biography, Henry Rogers devotes only a few lines to the lyric verse but discusses the prose pamphlets at length, concluding that "admirable as were Marvell's intellectual endowments, it is his moral worth, after all, which constitutes his principal claim on the admiration of posterity" (184).

How is it that the lyric verses upon which Andrew Marvell's modern reputation rests were so lightly regarded for two centuries? One explanation was offered by John Ormsby in 1869:

> If with posterity he has not held his due place among the minor poets of his time, one cause, undoubtedly, is that he already occupies, in another character, a higher position in the eyes of the world. . . . It was Marvell's fate to stand out before the eyes of succeeding generations as an example of purity and integrity in a corrupt age, and the brightness of his virtues has in some degree outshone the lustre of his genius. (221)

It would be hard to disagree with this judgment. If one begins by thinking of Marvell as a patriot and a pattern of incorruptibility, his skill in verse fades into insignificance. Ormsby is correct too in his assertion that "Marvell cannot be said to have been generally recognized as one of the poets until the present century" (222).

But there is another explanation for the undervaluing of Marvell's lyric verse: a radical change in taste that took place during the latter half of the seventeenth century. Marvell's style in the poems we value most highly belongs to the middle years of the century. His wit is like that of Lovelace, Suckling, and Cowley. Only his subjects stand out as different. But Lovelace, Suckling, and Cowley published their poetry in the 1640s and 1650s. By the time the 1681 folio appeared, readers who might have enjoyed Marvell's lyric verse three decades before were looking for other qualities in poetry. An antiquarian with old-fashioned tastes like John Aubrey could admire the English lyrics. No one else seems to have noticed them. Even in 1650 Marvell's topics might have puzzled readers. By 1681 both his topics and his style were out of date.

Later in the eighteenth century when we begin to find responses to the lyrics, they are typically dismissive. Edward Thompson, as editor of Marvell's works, might be expected to speak in praise of the poems. But the praise is hardly enthusiastic. Commenting on Marvell's works in verse and prose, he says, "in general they appear to be the warm effusions of a lively fancy, and are very often thrown off in the *extempore* moment of their conception and birth, whether begotten in satire or humour" (118). Thompson's evaluation of "To his Coy Mistress" (119) as "sweet, natural and easy" must strike us as odd. The fact that he devotes considerably more space to the satirical poems and pamphlets suggests that he has little interest in the lyrics.

Although there may be comments in print concerning Marvell's lyric verse before the nineteenth century, the admirable collection edited by Elizabeth Story Donno does not offer any. Marvell's reputation as a satirist and patriot had begun to fade when English writers started to take an interest in the poetry of the seventeenth century and the first responses to his lyrics appeared. In his essay "The Old Benchers of the Inner Temple" (1821), Charles Lamb quotes from stanzas 5, 6, 7, and 9 of "The Garden" and compliments their "witty delicacy" (132). The critic William Hazlitt, in his *Select Poets of Great Britain* (1825), says of Marvell,

> MARVELL is a writer almost forgotten: but undeservedly so. His poetical reputation seems to have sunk with his political party. His satires were coarse, quaint, and virulent; but his other productions are full of a

lively, tender, and elegant fancy. His verses leave an echo on the ear, and find one in the heart. (134)

Hazlitt was not alone in finding fault with Marvell's satirical verse. Leigh Hunt, who commented frequently on Marvell, saw the humor in the satires but judged that Marvell "wrote a great deal better in prose than verse" and even called Marvell "the inventor of our modern prose style in wit" (139–140, 136). Yet he also commented on "the noble ode on *Cromwell*" ("An Horatian Ode"), "the devout and beautiful" "Bermudas," and "the sweet overflowing fancies" of "The Nymph complaining for the death of her Faun" (139).

The year 1832 was an important landmark in the development of Marvell's reputation. Two biographies published in that year led to a number of reviews that challenged or amplified the biographers' opinions of the poetry. John Dove's *Life of Andrew Marvell* has little to say about his lyric verse, but one reviewer comments specifically on the "quaint and unequal lines" of "To his Coy Mistress" and quotes lines 21–24. The same reviewer mentions several other poems he admires but expresses "strong doubts whether they are justly ascribed to him" (154). Another reviewer finds Marvell's poetry inferior to his prose. A third reviewer, commenting on "Upon Appleton House," sounds a note that is heard with increasing frequency in early nineteenth-century criticism:

> The poem entitled 'Appleton House,' (a seat of Lord Fairfax), . . . displays an intense feeling for the beauties of nature, expressed with a felicity which not infrequently recalls 'L'Allegro' and 'Il Penseroso' of Milton. (156)

The concept of Marvell as a nature poet helped to establish a favorable view of his lyrics.

Hartley Coleridge's brief biography, also published in 1832, expresses another attitude toward Marvell's lyrics that became widespread in the nineteenth century:

> The poems of Marvell are, for the most part, productions of his early youth. They have much of that over-activity of fancy, that remoteness of allusion, which distinguishes the school of Cowley; but they have also a heartfelt tenderness, a childish simplicity of feeling, among all their complication of thought, which would atone for all their conceits. (159)

The praise of tenderness and simple feelings reveals a romantic taste in poetry. Coleridge's response to the political and satirical poems is just as characteristic of romanticism: "As for [the poems] he made to order, for

Fairfax or Cromwell, they are as dull as every true son of the muse would wish these things to be" (159).

In 1836 two journalists expressed genuine praise for Marvell's lyrics. One, Samuel Carter Hall, published his *Book of Gems*, a collection of the best lyric verse in English. He included "The Picture of little T. C.," "Bermudas," "The Nymph," and "To his Coy Mistress." His brief biographical sketch describes Marvell as "an exquisite and tender poet" and "the leading prose wit of England" (160). But Hall's admiration for Marvell's verse was not unbounded:

> As a poet Andrew Marvell was true, and this is the grand point in poetry. He was not of the highest order, not perhaps in even a high order, but what he did was genuine. It is sweetness speaking out in sweetness. In the language there is nothing more exquisitely tender than the 'Nymph complaining for the loss of her Fawn.' Such poems as this and 'the Bermudas' may live, and deserve to live, as long as the longest and the mightiest. Of as real a quality are the majority of the poems of Marvell. In a playful and fantastic expression of tender and voluptuous beauty, they are well nigh unrivalled. (161)

The other journalist, reviewing Hall's *Book of Gems*, is better known to us as a poet and short story writer—Edgar Allan Poe. Though he finds little to admire in most of the poems that Hall collected, Poe singles out what he calls the "Maiden lamenting for her Fawn" for lavish praise:

> How truthful an air of lamentation hangs here upon every syllable! It pervades all. It comes over the sweet melody of the words—over the gentleness and grace which we fancy in the little maiden herself—even over the half-playful, half-petulant air with which she lingers on the beauties and good qualities of her favorite—like the cool shadow of a summer cloud over a bed of lilies and violets, 'and all sweet flowers.' The whole is redolent with poetry of a very lofty order. (164)

Poe sees and admires the pathos of Marvell's poem. Many years passed before critics began to praise its ambiguity and its wit.

Good evidence of the growing reputation of Marvell as a poet is provided by an early history of English literature, Robert and William Chambers's *History of the English Language and Literature* (1835). The brief article on Marvell begins as follows: "After having from upwards of a century been excluded from the ranks of the English poets, ANDREW MARVELL (1620–1678) has recently begun once more to attract attention." But Robert Chambers's enthusiasm is sharply limited. Although he reprints the poem he calls "The Nymph's Description of Her Fawn," he observes that the poem is to be found "amidst much sorry writing" (166). Still, when he published his *Cyclopaedia* in 1844, he included the full text of "Bermudas" and selections from "The Nymph," "The Garden," and "The Character of Holland."

The fullest and most detailed discussion of Marvell's writings in the first half of the nineteenth century is Henry Rogers's tardy review in 1844 of Dove's biography. Rogers comments at length on the prose works, which are for him the most important achievements of Marvell's career. But he recognizes "a rich, though ill-cultivated fancy" in "Bermudas" (which he calls *Emigrants*), the two "Dialogues," and "The Coronet," all of which "contain lines of much elegance and sweetness" (180).

The editor of the first American edition of Marvell's poetry (1857) was the poet James Russell Lowell. Unfortunately, his comments on the poetry take the form of generalizations not associated with particular poems, but they show an appreciation more perceptive than that of any previous critic.

> . . . whenever he surrendered himself to his temperament, his mind sought relief in wit, so sportful and airy, yet at the same time so recondite, that it is hard to find anywhere an instance in which the Court, the Tavern, and the Scholar's Study are blended with such Corinthian justness of measure. Nowhere is there so happy an example of the truth that wit and fancy are different operations of the same principle. The wit is so spontaneous and so interfused with feeling that we can scarce distinguish it from fancy; and the fancy brings together analogies so remote that they give us the pleasurable shock of wit. Now and then, in his poems, he touches a deeper vein, but shuns instinctively the labour of laying it open, and escapes gleefully into the more congenial sunshine. (210)

Here, at last, is a response that acknowledges and praises the elusiveness and the spirit of fun that are so characteristic of Marvell's best verses.

Finally, in 1869, John Ormsby published anonymously in the *Cornhill Magazine* the first detailed and specific study of Marvell's poetry. After a brief sketch of Marvell's life and a discussion of his political writings, Ormsby argues that Marvell's lyric verse belongs to the middle of the century, that "his true place" is with Herrick, William Habington, Suckling, Lovelace, and George Wither, and that "the poet that influenced him most, probably, was Donne" (227). Apparently Ormsby was the first critic to associate Marvell with the "metaphysical school," the chief characteristics of which he describes as "a desire of being distinguished for wit and fancy . . . a nervous dread of being thought trite . . . and a sort of suspicion that the legitimate fields of imagination were already worked out, and that now nothing was left to the poet but to fall back upon ingenuity" (228). Ormsby finds traces of these characteristics in Marvell's earlier verses (he assumes that he can distinguish between earlier and later lyrics), but supposes that "they are not more abundant . . . owing to the fact that he wrote simply to please himself, 'for his own hand,' and not with any ambition of one day claiming a place among the poets" (228).

Omitting a detailed examination of "The Nymph" and "Bermudas" on the grounds that they are "too familiar already to the majority of our readers to justify quotation here," Ormsby proceeds to comment extensively on some of Marvell's "less-known poems." Among these he quotes from and discusses "To his Coy Mistress," "Ametas and Thestylis," "The Fair Singer," "The Mower against Gardens," and "A Poem upon the Death of O. C." In "To his Coy Mistress," he sees and admires the "light, bantering, trivial tone" of the first 20 lines and the "deep feeling" and "solemnity" of those that follow. Of "Ametas and Thestylis" he notes that "Nothing could be more designedly trifling than this, and yet what a finished elegance there is about it" (229). He takes "The Fair Singer" as an example of Marvell's "forcing wit beyond its legitimate bounds," but commends "the graceful turn he gave to a conceit." In several lyrics he finds "a genuine love and reverence for nature," based on "a close observation and study" (230). A 16-line quotation from "A Poem upon the Death of O. C." is used to illustrate Marvell's "graver and loftier verse." Finally he quotes from "The Character of Holland" to establish Marvell's "high place among the poets of wit and humour" (231).

Ormsby's essay is the first extended study of Marvell that takes his lyrics to be more important than his writings in prose. It seems to be the first to make any connection between Marvell and the poetic milieu of the early and middle seventeenth century. No previous discussion exhibited so deep an appreciation both for Marvell's sense of the comic and his gravity. But Ormsby was not a fanatic. His final judgment is moderate:

> Marvell's poetry cannot rank with the very highest in our language, but it unquestionably has high and varied qualities. It makes little pretension to depth or sublimity, but it abounds in wit and humour, true feeling, melody, and a certain scholarly elegance and delicate fancy. (231)

W. D. Christie's 1873 review of Alexander B. Grosart's edition of the verse (1872–1875) indicates how far the reevaluation of Marvell's reputation had come. Christie laments the inclusion of the satires:

> The genuine sweetness and beauty of much of Marvell's serious poetry are enhanced by contrast with the exceeding grossness of language in which his political satires abound, and which must have served as obstacles to the diffusion of his chaste poems. (237)

Again and again Christie refers to the "obscenity," "extreme grossness and unmitigated filth" of the satires, declaring that it "would be better for Marvell's fame if it could be proved that he had written none of the political satires ascribed to him" (238). The Victorian delicacy these comments exhibit is not surprising. What is unexpected is Christie's reference to Marvell's lyrics as his "serious poetry" and his supposition that the political satires inhibited the publishing of the lyrics. He quotes only a few lines from the lyrics because they were available in "a recent cheap edition" (241) and many had appeared in anthologies. In Christie's mind Marvell is "an English classic" (239). The work for which he had been admired and celebrated for the better part of two centuries was a regrettable divergence from his true calling.

In a much fuller and more thoughtful essay, A. C. Benson echoes Christie's assumptions: "It is perhaps to Milton's example, and probably to his advice, that we owe the loss of a great English poet" (249). Benson elaborates a fantasy in which Milton turns the impressionable Marvell toward a life of public service and away from his deepest talent: "The younger and more delicate mind complies; and we lose a great poet, Milton gains an assistant secretary, and the age a somewhat gross satirist." Benson's response to some of Marvell's poetry is rhapsodic:

> The passion for the country which breathes through the earlier poems, the free air which ruffles the page, the summer languors, the formal garden seen through the casements of the cool house, the close scrutiny of woodland sounds, such as the harsh laughter of the woodpecker, the shrill insistence of the grasshopper's dry note, the luscious content of the drowsy, croaking frogs, the musical sweep of the scythe through the falling swathe. (249–250)

This "close observation of Nature" (which is more Benson's than Marvell's) is what makes the early poems "worth all the rest of Marvell's work put together" (251). While the accuracy expected of a botanist or biologist is an odd demand to make of a poet, it is Benson's yard-stick. Applying that standard he gives Marvell high marks, citing only a few instances when he yields to "false tradition and mere literary hearsay" (253).

But, in summing up his opinion of Marvell's lyrics, Benson is less enthusiastic. He finds a certain monotony in Marvell's subjects, "a tendency to diverge and digress," a need to "repress his luxuriance" (256). Balancing these faults, however, is Marvell's originality: "He does not seem to imitate, he does not even follow the lines of other poets." Assuming that the lyrics he admires were all composed between 1650 and 1652, Benson argues that Marvell was "a young man trying his wings." There is only one poem in which "Marvell's undoubted genius burned steadily" throughout—"An Horatian Ode," which "can be classed with no other poem in the language" (257). Benson concludes that "we cannot but grieve when we see a poet over whose feet the stream has flowed, turn back from the brink and make the great denial" (262).

The comments of Ormsby, Christie, and Benson show clearly that by the last decades of the nineteenth century Marvell's reputation depended on his lyric verse. Even a writer like J. Stuart—who describes Marvell as "a man righteous in conduct, with scarce a spark of originality" (264) and judges his poems to have been "often monstrously overrated" ("the work of a young and not too thoroughly equipped writer, who has some fancy at command, and is largely influenced by the fashions of the day" [265])—regards him primarily as a lyric poet.

In his review of G. A. Aitken's two-volume edition (1892), E. K. Chambers concentrates on the lyrics, leaving himself only a brief paragraph to regret the fact that "the greatness of this half-forgotten poet" should have been wasted on "savage invective" (270). He attempts to characterize Marvell's verse by a general description:

> The lyric gift of Herrick he has not, nor Donne's incomparable subtlety and intensity of emotion; but for imaginative power, for decent melody, for that self-restraint of phrase which is the fair half of art, he must certainly hold high rank among his fellows. The *clear* sign of this self-restraint is his mastery over the octosyllable couplet, a metre which in less skilful hands so readily becomes diffuse and wearisome. (268)

Like Benson, Chambers praises Marvell as a nature poet and quotes from "The Garden," "Damon the Mower," and "The Mower to the Glo-Worms." His only objection to Marvell's lyrics involves witty conceits, and he cites "On a Drop of Dew" as a "terrible example" (270).

By the end of the nineteenth century, Marvell was established as a lyric poet whose verses (some of them, at least) were worth quoting and discussing at length. Most critics thought of him as a nature poet, or more pointedly as a garden poet. The response to his wit was almost universally negative, and one critic characterized John Donne as Marvell's "bad angel" (288). A representative statement of these attitudes is found in a lengthy 1913 essay on Marvell's life and work by Francis L. Bickley. Observing that Marvell's place in English literature is not yet established, Bickley argues that at "an Elysian banquet of poets of the Cavalier and Puritan age Herrick and Marvell should be set on either hand of John Milton, their president" (325). Like Samuel Taylor Coleridge and Henry Wadsworth Longfellow, "Marvell is another of the intermittent great." Bickley shares the established opinion of the satires: "Political interests . . . seduced the poet to satire" (329). He writes of Marvell's "almost mystical *rapport* with nature" (330) and dismisses Donne as "a man of daring conceptions which he only marred by his tricksy style" (327), arguing that when Marvell entertained "tortuous conceits" his "natural directness of expression" purified them (327–328).

It is necessary to establish the late-nineteenth- and early-twentieth-century response to Marvell's verse and especially to its affinities with Donne's poetry because, beginning in the late nineteenth century, a revolution in attitudes toward Donne affected Marvell's reputation as well.[2] That this change was already occurring when Bickley published his views is indicated by his waspish comment: "They may have much in them that is admirable, but undue exaltation of such men of their age as Donne and Sir Thomas Browne is sentimental antiquarianism" (327). Nevertheless, the enthusiasts of Donne's verse were to carry not only the day but the rest of this century. For over 50 years Andrew Marvell was to be thought of as a metaphysical poet.

Before examining the twentieth-century reputation of Marvell's verse, it will be useful to look at the availability of his poetry to nineteenth-century readers. Early in the century, when Marvell was still regarded primarily as a satirist and a patriot, Thomas Campbell included a portion of "Bermudas," "The Nymph" (omitting lines 17–24 and everything after line 92), and the complete text of "Young Love" in his *Specimens of the British Poets* (1819). William Hazlitt included eight lyric poems in his *Select Poets of Great Britain* (1825) and recommended "Bermudas," "To his Coy Mistress," and "The Nymph." In 1836 Samuel Carter Hall included "The Picture of little T. C.," "Bermudas," "The

Nymph," and "To his Coy Mistress" in his *Book of Gems*. The most popular anthology of the nineteenth century, Francis T. Palgrave's *Golden Treasury of the Best Songs and Lyrical Poems in the English Language* (first published in 1860), included "An Horatian Ode," "The Garden" (titled "Thoughts in a Garden)," and "Bermudas" (titled "Song of the Emigrants in Bermuda"). By 1905 the *Golden Treasury* also included "The Picture of little T. C." and "The Nymph" (titled "The Girl Describes Her Fawn"). Thomas Humphry Ward's *The English Poets* (1881) reprinted "The Garden," "On a Drop of Dew," "Bermudas," "Young Love," "An Horatian Ode," and "On Mr. Milton's Paradise lost." In the United States, Ralph Waldo Emerson included "On a Drop of Dew," "The Garden," a selection from "An Horatian Ode," "The Nymph," and "Bermudas" in his *Parnassus* anthology (1875). It is no surprise to find that none of these collections includes Marvell's satirical verses, but to a twentieth-century reader the omission of "To his Coy Mistress" from the later anthologies suggests a Victorian squeamishness. The omission of all the Mower poems is harder to explain.

For nineteenth-century readers who wanted a fuller acquaintance with Marvell's verse, there were several editions of the poems. In the United States the publication of *The Poetical Works of Andrew Marvell* in 1857 and its reissues (1858, 1866, 1867, and 1875) provide a clear indication of the growing interest in his verse. The edition by Grosart (four volumes, 1872–1875), published in England, helped to establish Marvell as a writer whose works merited serious consideration. G. A. Aitken's edition of the poems and satires in 1892 made Marvell's poetry available in the highly respected Muses' Library series of English writers.

Two movements that began late in the nineteenth century had an enormous influence on Marvell's reputation. The first, already alluded to, was the rapidly growing interest in the poetry of John Donne and the metaphysical poets, among whom Marvell is often included. The second was the growth of academic criticism and scholarship, which, fairly gradual until the middle of the twentieth century, has since become the dominant force in the publication and analysis of Marvell's verse. There is no need to trace these movements here,[3] but it will be useful to observe their influence on Marvell's reputation.

One of the most important persons in the response to Donne's poetry is H. J. C. Grierson, whose 1912 edition of Donne's poems is widely understood to have stimulated an already existing interest in metaphysical poetry. In his *The First Half of the Seventeenth Century* (1906) Grierson discusses the term *metaphysical* in connection with Donne's verse. In his one-page treatment of Andrew Marvell, he associates Marvell with Waller, Vaughan, and Jonson, not with Donne, nor does he use the term *metaphysical* in connection with Marvell. But in his *Metaphysical Lyrics & Poems of the Seventeenth Century* (1921), Grierson not only includes 10 of Marvell's poems but also argues that Marvell's "few love poems and his few devotional pieces are perfect exponents of all the 'metaphysical' qualities—passionate, paradoxical argument, touched with humour and learned imagery . . . and above all the sudden soar of passion in bold and felicitous image."[4] Quoting lines 21 through 32 of "To his Coy Mistress," Grierson observes, "These lines seem to me the very roof and crown of the metaphysical love lyric, at once fantastic and passionate" (xxxviii).

Another publication in 1921 had a great impact on Marvell's reputation. T. S. Eliot wrote a brief assessment of the poet's achievement and significance. Having acknowledged that "Marvell has stood high for some years," Eliot argues that it is the combination of wit and imagination, "this alliance of levity and seriousness," that produces the best of Marvell's lyrics. Eliot contends that such a combination existed in English verse only in the late sixteenth and the seventeenth centuries. In an attempt to define wit, Eliot makes a statement that was to be repeated often by the enthusiasts of metaphysical poetry:

> [Wit] involves, probably, a recognition, implicit in the expression of every experience, of other kinds of experience which are possible, which we find as clearly in the greatest as in poets like Marvell. Such a general statement may seem to take us a long way from *The Nymph and the Fawn*, or even from the *Horatian Ode*; but it is perhaps justified by the desire to account for that precise taste of Marvell's which finds for him the proper degree of seriousness for every subject he treats.

Eliot's approach to his topic is an odd combination of magisterial pronouncement undermined by verbal gestures of tentativeness (e.g., the words *probably*, *seem*, and *perhaps*). Nevertheless, his opinion carried great authority, and when (in his review of Grierson's *Metaphysical Lyrics*) he coined the phrase "dissociation of sensibility" to describe a separation of thought and feeling that in Eliot's opinion happened to English verse in the later seventeenth century, Eliot made it possible to regard metaphysical poetry as the product of a unique moment in English literature. To the extent that Marvell's poetry was a reflection of that moment it acquired a special value.

The resulting search for an exact definition of the term *metaphysical* generated even more interest in Marvell's verse. And while no single definition ever received universal acceptance, it was generally agreed that metaphysical poetry involved a strenuous exertion of the intellect. It became impossible to think of Marvell as the composer of sweet meditations and serene responses to nature. Furthermore, the emphasis on wit as a defining character of metaphysical poetry fostered an appreciation of Marvell's highly original analogies, which had been, for nineteenth-century critics, the most objectionable aspect of his lyric verse.

An emphasis on intellectual content could only add to the reputation of Marvell's verse; however, his status as a metaphysical poet had the less desirable effect of obscuring his individuality. A considerable amount of heavy-going analysis sought to find the essential characteristics of the poetry of Donne and his "school." Although Marvell's verse is unique, the attempt to place him among the followers of Donne drew the attention of critics away from the poems that hardly resemble Donne's. Moreover, the attempt to define metaphysical poetry and to link it with a privileged moment in English literature was carried out with a degree of solemnity ill-equipped to appreciate the spirit of fun that pervades most of Marvell's verse. Eliot had noted Marvell's combination of levity and seriousness. Scholars concentrated so much on the latter quality that several critics felt it necessary to warn their colleagues against taking the poems too seriously.[5]

By the middle of the twentieth century the study of Marvell's poetry had become almost exclusively the province of academic critics. Between 1900 and 1949 over 150 books and articles devoted at least in part to the study of Marvell were published. Between 1950 and 1969 the number jumped to 360. In 1978 alone (the 300th anniversary of his death), there were over 50 books and articles devoted exclusively to Marvell's works.[6] Similarly, the number of editions of some or all of Marvell's verse increased rapidly. Between 1904 and 1948 there were six editions; between 1952 and 1991 there were 20. Most of these publications were the work of academics who tended to assume that the reader was either an academic specialist in seventeenth-century literature or a college student.

A survey of these works[7] indicates that between 1900 and 1979 the most frequently studied poem was "To his Coy Mistress" (examined in at least 175 books and articles). "The Garden" is second (136), followed by "Upon Appleton House" (122) and "An Horatian Ode" (97). There is then a sharp drop to "The Nymph" (60), "The Definition of Love" (60), and "Bermudas" (54). A survey of 20 anthologies of seventeenth-century poetry published in the last 70 years shows a somewhat different order: "To his Coy Mistress" (20), "Bermudas" (19), "The Garden" (18), "The Definition of Love" (16), and "An Horatian Ode" (15).

Recently there has been a revival of interest in Marvell's political satires and in his prose pamphlets. The result has undermined the concept of Marvell as detached and elusive and produced striking new interpretations of poems that, on their face, give little evidence of a political orientation. It has also affected the interpretation of poems that obviously impinge upon politics by attributing to Marvell a political *purpose*, a deliberate manipulation of historical facts to advance the interests of a faction. When, in a famous controversy, Cleanth Brooks and Douglas Bush put forth opposing interpretations of "An Horatian Ode," they agreed that Marvell maintained a critical detachment that allowed him to see the admirable qualities of both Charles I and Cromwell.[8] But recent studies argue that Marvell's focus on these two men disguises the complexity of the situation in 1650. By reducing the possibilities to a choice between a dead king and a living general, Marvell, whether he intended to or not, was in effect writing propaganda for Cromwell.[9]

As to what will happen to Marvell's reputation in the years to come, the only certain conclusion is that it will change, probably in the direction of increased complexity. Michael Wilding's view in 1969 is already undergoing a challenge:

> Fortunately Marvell seems as well able to survive the weight of commentary as his earlier neglect. His elusiveness, his obliqueness, his ironic, wry detachment save him from any firm critical categorisation. After the most formidable of critical accounts, we can turn again to his poetry and find it as untouched, as evasive, as enigmatic as ever.[10]

There will be no return to the eighteenth-century Marvell, the incorruptible patriot, or the nineteenth-century Marvell, the sweet singer of nature's beauties. But the twentieth-century Marvell described by Wilding may be replaced by a writer who is conceived of as far more committed and partisan than he had been thought to be.[11]

The interest in Marvell's writings shows no signs of slowing down. Clearly he is regarded as a poet whose work merits a close examination and a prose writer of considerable skill. Although it is small in bulk and uneven in quality, at its best Marvell's poetry is the equal of any verse in the English language. In 1964 Hugh Kenner called Marvell "the great-

est minor poet in the English language."[12] Twenty-five years later
Harold Bloom described Marvell as "the most enigmatic, unclassifiable,
and unaffiliated major poet in the language."[13] Philip Larkin, himself a
citizen of Hull and an accomplished poet, praised "the ease with which
[Marvell] manages the fundamental paradox of verse—the conflict of
natural word usage with meter and rhyme—and marries it either to hal-
lucinatory images within his own unique conventions or to sudden sin-
cerities that are as convincing in our age as in his."[14] Whether he is a
major poet or not, Marvell speaks to modern readers with a wit and
grace that make his voice unique. There is no reason to suppose that
readers will ever tire of it.

Notes and References

Chapter One

1. John Kenyon, "Andrew Marvell: Life and Times," *Andrew Marvell: Essays on the Tercentenary of His Death*, ed. R. L. Brett (Oxford: Oxford University Press for the University of Hull, 1979), 6. This volume is hereafter cited in notes as "Brett."

2. Allan Pritchard in "Marvell's 'The Garden': A Restoration Poem?" *Studies in English Literature 1500–1900* 23 (1983): 371–88, considers evidence of composition or revision in the late 1660s.

3. Michael Craze, in *The Life and Lyrics of Andrew Marvell* (London: Macmillan, 1979), studies the lyrics in a conjectured order of composition.

4. For a useful discussion of the development of parties during Marvell's Parliamentary career, see K. H. D. Haley's *Politics in the Reign of Charles II* (Oxford: Blackwell, 1985), 23–38.

5. For a fuller analysis of the constituency letters, see N. H. Keeble, "'I would not tell you any tales': Marvell's Constituency Letters" in *The Political Identity of Andrew Marvell*, ed. Conal Condren and A. D. Cousins (Aldershot, England: Scolar Press, 1990), 111–34. This volume is hereafter cited in notes as "Condren and Cousins."

6. *The Diary of John Milward*, ed. Caroline Robbins (Cambridge, England: Cambridge University Press, 1938); Anchitel Grey, *Debates in the House of Commons from the Year 1667 to the Year 1694*, 4 vols. (London, 1783).

7. H. M. Margoliouth, ed., *The Poems and Letters of Andrew Marvell*, 3d ed., rev. by Pierre Legouis and E. E. Duncan-Jones, 2 vols. (Oxford: Clarendon Press, 1971), 2:342; hereafter cited in the text as "Margoliouth."

8. *Puritanism and Revolution: Studies in the Interpretation of the English Revolution of the 17th Century* (London: Secker & Warburg, 1958), 351. See also J. M. Newton, "What Do We Know about Andrew Marvell?" *Cambridge Quarterly* 6 (1973): 125–43.

9. For an example of a political reading of the Mower poems and an excellent bibliography of such readings, see Rosemary Kegl, "'Joyning my Labour to my Pain': The Politics of Labor in Marvell's Mower Poems," in *Soliciting Interpretation: Literary Theory and Seventeenth-Century English Poetry*, ed. Elizabeth D. Harvey and Katharine Eisaman Maus (Chicago: University of Chicago Press, 1990), 89–118. This volume is hereafter cited in notes as "Harvey and Maus."

10. Pierre Legouis, *Andrew Marvell: Poet, Puritan, Patriot*, 2d ed. (Oxford: Clarendon Press, 1968), 220–23.

11.   Frank Kermode and Keith Walker, *Andrew Marvell* (Oxford: Oxford University Press, 1990), xii; hereafter cited in the text as "Kermode and Walker." But for evidence that Marvell was a Nonconformist, see William Lamont, "The Religion of Andrew Marvell: Locating the 'Bloody Horse,' " in Condren and Cousins, 135–56.

12.   For a quirky but wonderfully entertaining narrative of Marvell's life, see William Empson's "Natural Magic and Populism in Marvell's Poetry," in Brett, 36–61.

13.   See K. H. D. Haley, *William of Orange and the English Opposition, 1672–74* (Oxford: Clarendon Press, 1953), 57–59, for the possibility of Marvell's involvement in espionage.

14.   This study omits the Latin poems and the following poems in English: "Upon the Death of Lord Hastings," "To His worthy Friend Doctor Witty," "Two Songs at the Marriage of the Lord Fauconberg and the Lady Mary Cromwell," and a translation of some lines from Seneca. It includes two of the fourteen satires attributed to Marvell.

15.   For a detailed textual analysis of the 1681 folio, see Margoliouth's edition. The Popple manuscript is discussed at length by Warren L. Chernaik, *The Poet's Time: Politics and Religion in the Work of Andrew Marvell* (Cambridge, England: Cambridge University Press, 1983), 206–14. *Andrew Marvell: Poet & Politician, 1621–1678. An exhibition to commemorate the tercentenary of his death*, ed. Hilton Kelliher (London: Published for the British Library by British Museum Publications Ltd., 1978) provides photographic reproductions of several manuscript copies of Marvell's lyrics.

16.   *Andrew Marvell* (Plymouth, England: Northcote House, 1994), 1–6.

17.   Kelliher reproduces portraits of Marvell on pages 81, 122, and as a frontispiece. For the comments of Marvell's enemies, see M. C. Bradbrook and M. G. Lloyd Thomas, *Andrew Marvell* (Cambridge, England: Cambridge University Press, 1940), 16–21; hereafter cited in the text and notes as "Bradbrook and Thomas." See also Elizabeth Story Donno, "The Unhoopable Marvell," *Tercentenary Essays in Honor of Andrew Marvell*, ed. Kenneth Friedenreich (Hamden, Conn.: Archon Books, 1977), 21–45. This volume is hereafter cited in notes as "Friedenreich."

18.   *Brief Lives*, ed. Andrew Clarke, 2 vols. (Oxford: Clarendon Press, 1898), 2:53–54.

19.   Grey, *Debates*, 4:328–31; Annabel M. Patterson, *Marvell and the Civic Crown* (Princeton: Princeton University Press, 1978), 31, 44; John Dixon Hunt, *Andrew Marvell: His Life and Writings* (London: Elek Books, 1978), 181.

Chapter Two

1.   The best discussion of Marvell's acquaintance with and use of other poets' work is J. B. Leishman's *The Art of Marvell's Poetry*, ed. John Butt (Lon-

don: Hutchinson, 1966, 2d ed. 1968). Bradbrook and Thomas also make perceptive comments, as does Joseph H. Summers, *The Heirs of Donne and Jonson*
(New York: Oxford University Press, 1970), 130–33.
    2.   All quotations from Marvell's poetry are taken from Margoliouth,
vol. 1.
    3.   A. J. Smith examines the special character of Marvell's wit in *Meta-
physical Wit* (Cambridge, England: Cambridge University Press, 1991),
212–35. In " 'To Make His Saying True': Deceit in *Appleton House*," *Studies in
Philology* 77 (1980): 84–104, Peter Schwenger argues that Marvell's wit
depends upon a specific seventeenth-century theory of metaphor.
    4.   The only reference to bleeding in ancient accounts occurs in Diony-
sius of Halicarnassus, *Roman Antiquities*, 4:59–61.
    5.   In "Jonson, Marvell, and Miscellaneity?" (in *Poems in Their Place:
The Intertextuality and Order of Poetic Collections*, ed. Neil Fraistat [Chapel Hill:
University of North Carolina Press, 1986], 95–118), Annabel M. Patterson dis-
cerns a pattern of organization culminating in active republicanism and concludes that "the original order of the volume *was* its meaning in 1681" (115).
    6.   Barbara Everett's "The Shooting of the Bears: Poetry and Politics in
Andrew Marvell," in Brett, 62–103, presents a different concept of *public* and
private in Marvell's poems, as well as a perceptive and challenging view of the
"strikingly original sensibility" which they convey. For another concept of *public*
and *private* poems, see Summers, *Heirs*, 156–81.
    7.   Andor Gomme, in "The Teasingness of Andrew Marvell—I," *The
Oxford Review*, no. 8 (1968): 13–33, states the point this way: "the safer as well
as more modest way is to treat every poem as a new beginning and to maintain
a degree of humility in the face of new possibilities of organization and experience" (17).

Chapter Three

    1.   An 80-line companion piece, "Upon the Hill and Grove at Bill-
borow," uses many of the devices and techniques that receive a fuller development in "Upon Appleton House."
    2.   G. R. Hibbard, in "The Country House Poem of the Seventeenth
Century," *Journal of the Warburg and Courtauld Institutes* 19 (1956): 159–74,
argues that "Upon Appleton House" fulfills all the traditions of the genre.
William Alexander McClung, however, finds it significantly different in several
respects, especially in its concentration on the estate instead of the house (*The
Country House in English Renaissance Poetry* [Berkeley: University of California
Press, 1977], 147–74). Don Cameron Allen traces the lineage of the country
house poem and analyzes this poem in detail in *Image and Meaning: Metaphoric
Traditions in Renaissance Poetry* (Baltimore, Md.: Johns Hopkins Press, 1960),
115–53. In *"My Ecchoing Song": Andrew Marvell's Poetry of Criticism* (Princeton:
Princeton University Press, 1970), 196, Rosalie L. Colie identifies "Upon
Appleton House" as a "gallery-poem."

3. A "verbal prankster," according to Harold Skulsky, "*Upon Appleton House*: Marvell's Comedy of Discourse," *ELH* 52 (1985): 591–620. Skulsky views the poem as a "comic study of the cooperative efforts of talkers and listeners" (591), a game that depends on the "intellectual corruptness" of the guide (609).

4. For different views of the order of the poem see Louis L. Martz, "Marvell and Herrick: The Masks of Mannerism," in *Approaches to Marvell: The York Tercentenary Lectures*, ed. C. A. Patrides (London: Routledge & Kegan Paul, 1978), 194–215. This volume is hereafter cited in notes as "Patrides." See also James G. Turner, *The Politics of Landscape: Rural Scenery and Society in English Poetry 1630–1660* (Cambridge, Mass.: Harvard University Press, 1979), 61–84; and Maren-Sofie Røstvig, "Andrew Marvell and the Caroline Poets," in *English Poetry and Prose 1540–1674*, ed. Christopher Ricks (New York: Peter Bedrick Books, 1987), 201–44.

5. Frank J. Warnke discusses the playfulness of "Upon Appleton House" on pages 460–63 of "Sacred Play: Baroque Poetic Style," *Journal of Aesthetics and Art Criticism* 22 (1964): 455–64.

6. This point is disputed by John Newman, "Marvell's Appleton House," *Times Literary Supplement*, 28 January 1972, 99, and J. G. Turner, "Upon Appleton House," *Notes & Queries* 222 (December 1977): 547–48.

7. Graham Parry reads the poem as providential history in *Seventeenth Century Poetry: The Social Context* (London: Hutchinson, 1985), 234–40.

8. Robert Wilcher, *Andrew Marvell* (Cambridge, England: Cambridge University Press, 1985), 25–31, presents an excellent brief analysis of this phenomenon and its origin in pastoral poetry.

9. In "High Summer at Nun Appleton, 1651: Andrew Marvell and Lord Fairfax's Occasions," *The Historical Journal* 36 (1993): 247–69, Derek Hirst and Stephen Zwicker discuss the patron-client relationship between Fairfax and Marvell on 266–69.

10. Isabel G. MacCaffrey, "The Scope of Imagination in *Upon Appleton House*," in Friedenreich, 224–44.

11. For a totally different approach arguing that every aspect of the poem is related to the political situation in 1651 as it affected Fairfax, see Hirst and Zwicker, "High Summer."

12. Muriel C. Bradbrook, "Marvell and the Masque," in Friedenreich, 204–23.

13. Leah S. Marcus develops a political interpretation of this episode in *The Politics of Mirth: Jonson, Herrick, Milton, Marvell, and the Defense of Old Holiday Pastimes* (Chicago: University of Chicago Press, 1986), 256–57.

14. Lee Erickson, "Marvell's *Upon Appleton House* and the Fairfax Family," *English Literary Renaissance* 9 (1979): 158–68, argues that Marvell's invention of the convent episode is connected with the family's attempt to break off an engagement between Mary and Philip Stanhope.

15. For a highly detailed analysis of "Upon Appleton House," see Colie, *Ecchoing*, 181–294. See also Kitty W. Scoular, *Natural Magic: Studies in the Presentation of Nature in English Poetry from Spenser to Marvell* (Oxford: Clarendon Press, 1965), 119–90, for a discussion of Marvell's skillful adaptation of conventional themes and images.

16. For an analysis of the poem as a political statement, the elusiveness interpreted as a strategy made necessary by the still unsettled situation of the kingdom, see Michael Wilding, *Dragons Teeth: Literature in the English Revolution* (Oxford: Clarendon Press, 1987), 138–72.

Chapter Four

1. For a detailed treatment of this poem, see the analyses of Barbara Kiefer Lewalski, 261–65, and Donald M. Friedman, 313–20, in Patrides.

2. Christine Rees, *The Judgment of Marvell* (London: Pinter Publishers, 1989), 170–78, sketches the intellectual background and identifies the "gentler Conqueror" as Thomas Fairfax.

3. Colie, *Ecchoing*, 36–40, interprets the poem as a game Marvell is playing with traditional pastoral conventions. But Bruce King, reading the poem as an allegory, regards the mower as a Leveller, "'The Mower against Gardens' and the Levellers," *Huntington Library Quarterly* 33 (1970): 237–42. For a lengthy bibliography of the Mower poems, see Linda Anderson, "The Nature of Marvell's Mower," *Studies in English Literature, 1500–1900* 31 (1991): 131–46.

4. Rees, *Judgment*, 151–58, considers Damon complex and ambiguous, not simply naive, not simply wise.

5. Colie, *Ecchoing*, 40, finds him silly and "a dear." But Kegl, "Joyning my Labour," in Harvey and Maus, 91–102, charges Marvell with eliding the economic exploitation of seventeenth-century laborers by utilizing a speaker who does not understand his true situation.

6. Philip Brockbank discusses the historical background in "The Politics of Paradise: 'Bermudas,'" in Patrides, 174–93.

7. In "The Difficulty of Marvell's 'Bermudas,'" *Modern Philology* 67 (1970): 331–40, R. M. Cummings argues that the poem is far from a simple idealization.

8. See, for example, J. Max Patrick, *The Unfortunate Lover*, Explicator 20 (April 1962), item 65, and Colie, *Ecchoing*, 109–13.

9. Ruth Nevo, "Marvell's 'Songs of Innocence and Experience,'" *Studies in English Literature, 1500–1900* 5 (1965): 1–21, calls it "a miniature comedy of manners."

10. Colie, *Ecchoing*, 46–48, and Rees, *Judgment*, 123–27, call attention to the antipastoral nature of this poem, whose characters bear the names of famous pastoral lovers. Both scholars condemn Daphnis as unfeeling and irresponsible.

11. Barbara Kiefer Lewalski in Patrides, 268–71, reads the poem as a "resolution of the dichotomy between nature and grace," associating it with pastoral conventions illustrated frequently in Spenser.

12. See the textual notes in Margoliouth, 1:247–49. Kermode and Walker omit the poem.

13. Rees, *Judgment*, 165, reads it as "a rare, perhaps a unique, moment of unshadowed sexual pleasure in Marvell's poetry."

14. Frank Kermode, "The Banquet of Sense," *Bulletin of the John Rylands Library* 44 (1961): 68–99, argues for a Christian interpretation; Harold E. Toliver, "The Strategy of Marvell's Resolve against Created Pleasure," *Studies in English Literature, 1500–1900* 4 (1964): 57–69, reads the poem as Platonic.

15. In "Marvell's 'Soul' Poetry" (in Friedenreich, 76–104), Joseph Pequigney analyzes the poem as an academic disputation won by the Body.

16. Peter Berek, "The Voices of Marvell's Lyrics," *Modern Language Quarterly* 32 (1971): 143–57, calls them a "comic duo" (144).

17. Discussed in detail in Leishman, *Art of Marvell's Poetry*, 209–14. Michel-André Bossy, "Medieval Debates of Body and Soul," *Comparative Literature* 28 (1976): 144–63, judges this poem to be "the subtlest of all debates between sinful Soul and Body" (160).

18. In the Popple manuscript the last four lines are crossed out.

Chapter Five

1. Allegorical interpretations are offered by Bradbrook and Thomas, 47–50; Everett H. Emerson, "Andrew Marvell's *The Nymph Complaining for the Death of Her Faun*," *Études Anglaises* 8 (1955): 107–10; Bruce King, *Marvell's Allegorical Poetry* (New York: Oleander Press, 1977), 47–65; Yvonne L. Sandstroem, "Marvell's 'Nymph Complaining' as Historical Allegory," *Studies in English Literature, 1500–1900* 30 (1990): 93–114.

2. The theme of loss of innocence is discussed by Don Cameron Allen, "Marvell's 'Nymph,' " *ELH* 23 (1956): 91–111; Jack E. Reese, "Marvell's 'Nymph' in a New Light," *Études Anglaises* 18 (1965): 398–401; and Earl Miner, "The Death of Innocence in Marvell's *Nymph Complaining for the Death of Her Faun*," *Modern Philology* 65 (1967): 9–16. Ruth Nevo, "Marvell's 'Songs of Innocence and Experience,' " and Phoebe S. Spinrad, "Death, Loss, and Marvell's Nymph," *PMLA* 97 (1982): 50–59, read the poem as a record of the death of innocence and as a psychological journey through the nymph's mind.

3. The Mower poems are discussed as a group in John Creaser, "Marvell's Effortless Superiority," *Essays in Criticism* 20 (1970): 403–23; Patrick Cullen, *Spenser, Marvell, and Renaissance Pastoral* (Cambridge, Mass.: Harvard University Press, 1970), 191–98; King, *Allegorical*, 110–44; and Rees, *Judgment*, 147–64.

4. Creaser, "Marvell's Effortless Superiority," 409–12, analyzes the "complexity of suggestion" and the "confidence and gaiety with which the suggestions are handled."

5.   David Kalstone, "Marvell and the Fictions of Pastoral," *English Literary Renaissance* 4 (1974): 174–88, discusses the poem as an autobiographical statement and an illustration of Marvell's inability to find a satisfying stance or role in the pastoral mode.

6.   Annabel M. Patterson, "*Bermudas* and *The Coronet*: Marvell's Protestant Poetics," *ELH* 44 (1977): 478–99, reads "The Coronet" as a devotional poem that is rather darker than Herbert's or Donne's lyrics.

7.   For a detailed analysis, see Joan Hartwig, "Tears as a Way of Seeing," *On the Celebrated and Neglected Poems of Andrew Marvell*, ed. Claude J. Summers and Ted-Larry Pebworth (Columbia: University of Missouri Press, 1992), 70–85. This volume is hereafter cited in notes as "Summers and Pebworth." See also Wilcher, *Andrew Marvell*, 13–19.

8.   Charles H. Hinnant, "Marvell's Gallery of Art," *Renaissance Quarterly* 24 (1971): 26–37, discusses the resemblance of the portraits in the poem to paintings in the Whitehall Collection of Charles I.

9.   Colie, *Ecchoing*, 108, notes the "curiously aseptic quality" of the poem. But Frank J. Warnke, "Play and Metamorphosis in Marvell's Poetry," *Studies in English Literature, 1500–1900* 5 (1965): 23–30 calls it "a serious attempt to participate in the realities of Nature and Love" (25).

10.   H. M. Margoliouth, "Andrew Marvell: Some Biographical Points," *Modern Language Review* 17 (1922): 351–61.

11.   Patrick Cullen, "Imitation and Metamorphosis: The Golden Age Eclogue in Spenser, Milton, and Marvell," *PMLA* 84 (1969): 1559–1570, asserts that the poem uses the conventions of the "golden age eclogue" in imitation of Virgil; Anne Ferry, *All in War with Time: Love Poetry of Shakespeare, Donne, Jonson, Marvell* (Cambridge, Mass.: Harvard University Press, 1975), 200–10, compares it to several of Jonson's lyrics.

12.   E. B. Greenwood, "Marvell's Impossible Love," *Essays in Criticism* 27 (1977): 100–109, argues that what Marvell's speaker really wants is penetrability, "the occupation by two bodies of precisely the same region of space at the same moment of time" (101).

13.   Angela G. Dorenkamp, "Marvell's Geometry of Love," *English Language Notes* 9 (1971): 111–15, analyzes the geometrical and astronomical terminology. Ferry, *All in War*, 249, reads the poem as "a criticism of Donne's kind of poetry."

Chapter Six

1.   For a useful review of modern criticism, see French Fogle, "Marvell's 'Tough Reasonableness' and the Coy Mistress," in Friedenreich, 121–39.

2.   Bruce King, "Irony in Marvell's 'To His Coy Mistress,' " *Southern Review* n.s. 5 (1969): 689–703, argues that the poem is "bordering upon the comic in tone, and satiric in purpose" (690). For Stanley Stewart, "Marvell and the *Ars Moriendi*," *Seventeenth Century Images*, ed. Earl Miner (Berkeley: University of California Press, 1971), 133–50, the poem belongs to another genre.

Robert Daniel, "Marvell's *To His Coy Mistress*," *Explicator*, 1 (March 1943), item 37, notes that the lack of a lament for the brevity of youth makes this "unique among mutability-poems."

3. Jeffrey W. Karon, "Cohesion as Logic: The Possible Worlds of Marvell's 'To His Coy Mistress,' " *Style* 27 (1993): 91–105, argues that a linguistic analysis affirms the poem's logical cohesiveness; but Clarence H. Miller, "Sophistry and Truth in 'To His Coy Mistress,' " *College Literature* 2 (1975): 97–104, points to the logical fallacy on which the lover's argument is based.

4. In "The Changing Face of Andrew Marvell," *English Literary Renaissance* 9 (1979): 149–57, Philip Larkin points out that because this is the "only one of the major poems where matter approximates to manner . . . no one so far has propounded a political or theological explanation of it" (153).

5. The phrase "vast eternity" is borrowed from Cowley's "My Diet."

6. In "Love and Death in 'To His Coy Mistress' " (in *Post-structuralist Readings of English Poetry*, ed. Richard Machin and Christopher Norris [Cambridge, England: Cambridge University Press, 1987], 105–21), Catherine Belsey argues that the poem conveys a medieval attitude of contempt for death in conflict with a developing fear of death that is the dominant attitude of modern culture.

7. In "The Voices of Seduction in 'To His Coy Mistress': A Rhetorical Analysis," *Texas Studies in Language and Literature* 10 (1968): 189–206, Joseph J. Moldenhauer observes that "[t]he argument is so framed as to allow no reasonable alternative but erotic union" (206). For a contrasting view see Bernard Duyfhuizen, "Textual Harassment of Marvell's Coy Mistress: The Institutionalization of Masculine Criticism," *College English* 50 (1988): 411–23.

8. Cleanth Brooks, "Andrew Marvell: Puritan Austerity with Classical Grace," *Poetic Traditions of the English Renaissance*, ed. Maynard Mack and George deForest Lord (New Haven, Conn.: Yale University Press, 1982), 219–28, maintains that both poems are the product of "a mind of the late Renaissance at its best" (228).

9. Colie, *Ecchoing*, 303–5, characterizes Marvell as "[m]ercurial, unsystematic, irreverent, fantastic" and comments on his playfulness and experimentation.

10. For the gardening background, see Nicholas A. Salerno, "Andrew Marvell and the *Furor Hortensis*," *Studies in English Literature, 1500–1900* 8 (1968): 103–20, and John Dixon Hunt, " 'Loose Nature' and the 'Garden Square': The Gardenist Background for Marvell's Poetry," in Patrides, 331–51.

11. Summers, *Heirs*, 143, sees extravagance as a crucial element in the poem.

12. Colie, *Ecchoing*, 167, refers to the "silliness" of this stanza.

13. Summers, *Heirs*, 159, says that "[Marvell] conceived of himself neither as a professional nor as a dedicated poet."

14. There are useful discussions of the problems of interpretation in Frank Kermode, "The Argument of Marvell's 'Garden,'" *Essays in Criticism* 2 (1952): 225–41, and in Colie, *Ecchoing*, 141–77.

15. Roger Sharrock, "Marvell's Poetry of Evasion and Marvell's Times," *English* 28 (1979): 3–40 (26). Summers, *Heirs*, 143, argues that the poem makes fun of extravagant claims for the retired life.

16. In her highly detailed and perceptive analysis of "The Garden," Colie, *Ecchoing*, 157, characterizes the speaker as a *faux-naïf*, like the shepherds in pastoral poetry. Carol Marks Sicherman, "The Mocking Voices of Donne and Marvell," *Bucknell Review* 17, no. 2 (1969): 32–46, refers to him as "an amusing fanatic" (45).

17. Blair Worden, "Andrew Marvell, Cromwell, and the Horatian Ode," *Politics of Discourse: The Literature and History of Seventeenth-Century England*, ed. Kevin Sharpe and Steven W. Zwicker (Berkeley: University of California Press, 1987), 147–80, calls the ode "the most private of public poems" (150).

18. For the Roman background, see John S. Coolidge, "Marvell and Horace," *Modern Philology* 63 (1965): 111–20; A. J. N. Wilson, "Andrew Marvell, *An Horatian Ode upon Cromwel's Return from Ireland*: The Thread of the Poem and Its Use of Classical Allusion," *Critical Quarterly* 11 (1969): 325–41; Franklin G. Burroughs Jr., "Marvell's Cromwell and May's Caesar: 'An Horatian Ode' and the *Continuation of the Pharsalia*," *English Language Notes* 13 (1975): 115–22; and Nicholas Guild, "The Context of Marvell's Allusion to Lucan in 'An Horatian Ode,'" *Papers on Language and Literature* 14 (1978): 406–13.

19. For a detailed survey of criticism, see Judith Richards, "Literary Criticism and the Historian: Towards Reconstructing Marvell's Meaning in 'An Horatian Ode,'" *Literature & History* 7 (1981): 25–47.

20. The Machiavellian connection is discussed by Brian Vickers, "Machiavelli and Marvell's *Horatian Ode*," *Notes & Queries* 234 (March 1989): 32–38.

21. Michael McKeon, "Pastoralism, Pluralism, Imperialism, Scientism: Andrew Marvell and the Problem of Mediation," *Yearbook of English Studies* 13 (1983): 46–65, argues that Marvell sees Cromwell as "only the instrument of a higher authority that is implicitly divine and explicitly republican" (53). But Thomas M. Greene, "The Balance of Power in Marvell's 'Horatian Ode,'" *ELH* 60 (1993): 379–96, contends that Marvell is baffled by Cromwell, who embodies "the inscrutable in human affairs" (385).

22. In "Marvell's 'Horatian Ode' and the Politics of Genre" (in *Literature and the English Civil War*, ed. Thomas Healy and Jonathan Sawday [Cambridge, England: Cambridge University Press, 1990], 147–69), David Norbrook notes, "Marvell's ode . . . sees immense possibilities in the revolution, but is also aware of the deep-seated irony in the fact that its greatest defender

and its destroyer might be one and the same man" (164). Norbrook argues that Marvell is founding "a new and more innovative genre of poetry" (156).

   23. For a dissenting opinion, see Wilding, *Dragons Teeth*, 114–37.

Chapter Seven

   1. For a succinct account of the publication history of the satirical poems, see John M. Wallace, *Destiny His Choice: The Loyalism of Andrew Marvell* (Cambridge, England: Cambridge University Press, 1968), 146–47.

   2. R. I. V. Hodge, *Foreshortened Time: Andrew Marvell and Seventeenth Century Revolutions* (Cambridge, England: D. S. Brewer, 1978), 106–13, argues that "The First Anniversary" "as a whole does not hang together" (112). For a review of scholarship, see Gerald M. MacLean, *Time's Witness: Historical Representation in English Poetry, 1603–1660* (Madison: University of Wisconsin Press, 1990), 242–43.

   3. Joseph Anthony Wittreich Jr., "Perplexing the Explanation: Marvell's 'On Mr. Milton's *Paradise Lost*,' " in Patrides, 280–305, reads the poem as a complex amalgam of praise, criticism, and self-assertion. See also Kenneth Gross, " 'Pardon Me, Mighty Poet': Versions of the Bard in Marvell's 'On Mr. Milton's *Paradise Lost*,' " *Milton Studies* 16 (1982): 77–96.

   4. Richard Todd's "Equilibrium and National Stereotyping in 'The Character of Holland,' " in Summers and Pebworth, 169–91, presents a detailed analysis.

   5. For details see George deForest Lord, gen. ed., *Poems on Affairs of State: Augustan Satirical Verse, 1660–1714*, 7 vols. (New Haven, Conn.: Yale University Press, 1963–1975), 1:xxxii–xlii.

   6. Wallace, *Destiny*, 145–83, analyzes the poem as a statement of Marvell's loyalism. Patterson, *Civic Crown*, 111–67, discusses the background of "advice to a painter" poems. Both works supply useful bibliographies.

   7. Steven N. Zwicker, "Virgins and Whores: The Politics of Sexual Misconduct in the 1660s," in Condren and Cousins, 102–4.

   8. David Farley-Hills, *The Benevolence of Laughter: Comic Poetry of the Commonwealth and Restoration* (London: Macmillan, 1974), 72–98, argues that the poem has a well-defined structure and is "Marvell's finest poetic achievement" (76). Patterson, *Civic Crown*, considers it "a major foray into heroic satire" (113).

Chapter Eight

   1. *The Complete Works in Verse and Prose of Andrew Marvell*, ed. Alexander B. Grosart, 4 vols. (Blackburn, England: Privately Printed, 1872–1875). Reprint, New York: AMS Press, 1966.

   2. *The Rehearsal Transpros'd and The Rehearsal Transpros'd, the Second Part*, ed. D. I. B. Smith (Oxford: Clarendon Press, 1971), 45. All quoted passages from both parts are taken from this edition. Page numbers are cited parenthetically in the text.

3. D. I. B. Smith, "Editing Marvell's Prose," in *Editing Seventeenth Century Prose*, ed. D. I. B. Smith (Toronto: The Committee of the Conference on Editorial Problems, 1972), 51–69.

4. George Villiers, Duke of Buckingham, was the husband of Mary Fairfax, the Maria of "Upon Appleton House."

5. Jennifer Chibnall, "Something to the Purpose: Marvell's Rhetorical Strategy in *The Rehearsal Transpros'd* (1672)," *Prose Studies* 9 (1983): 80–104, presents a different view of Marvell's speaker and Marvell's aims in this treatise.

6. For detailed discussions of the prose treatises, their context, and their style, see Legouis, *Andrew Marvell*, 193–223 and Patterson, *Civic Crown*, 175–252. See also Raymond A. Anselment, *"Betwixt Jest and Earnest": Marprelate, Milton, Swift & The Decorum of Religious Ridicule* (Toronto: University of Toronto Press, 1979), 94–125; Chernaik, *The Poet's Time*, 102–50; and Jon Thomas Rowland, *Faint Praise and Civil Leer: The "Decline" of Eighteenth-Century Panegyric* (Newark: University of Delaware Press, 1994), 85–106.

7. Gilbert Burnet, *Bishop Burnet's History of His Own Time*, 6 vols. (Oxford: Oxford University Press, 1833), 1:477–78.

8. *Athenae Oxonienses*, 2 vols. (London, 1691) 2:619.

9. *Mr. Smirke: Or, The Divine in Mode* (London, 1676), 43. Subsequent references to this volume are given parenthetically.

10. Dean Morgan Schmitter, "The Occasion for Marvell's *Growth of Popery*," *Journal of the History of Ideas* 21 (1960): 568–70, argues that the occasion for the publication of *An Account* was the marriage of James's daughter Mary to William of Orange.

11. *An Account of the Growth of Popery, and Arbitrary Government in England* (Amsterdam [false imprint], 1677), 5. Subsequent references to this work are given parenthetically.

12. See Marvell's letter to his nephew, in Margoliouth, 2:317.

13. In *England in the Reign of Charles II* (Oxford: Clarendon Press, 1934), 2:359–60, David Ogg discusses the propensity of Marvell's contemporaries to find plots everywhere.

14. For a detailed summary of this treatise and a useful analysis of Marvell's rhetorical strategy, see Conal Condren's "Andrew Marvell as Polemicist: His Account of the Growth of Popery, and Arbitrary Government," in Condren and Cousins, 157–87.

15. *Remarks upon a late Disingenuous Discourse* (London, 1678), 31–32. Subsequent references to this work are given parenthetically.

Chapter Nine

1. Elizabeth Story Donno, ed., *Andrew Marvell: The Critical Heritage* (London: Routledge & Kegan Paul, 1978), 53–54. All subsequent page references are cited parenthetically in the text.

2. For excellent brief treatments of Marvell's reputation, see *Andrew Marvell*, ed. John Carey (Baltimore, Md.: Penguin Books, 1969), 22–33, and

Michael Wilding, *Marvell: Modern Judgements* (London: Macmillan, 1969), 10–39.

   3.   See Theodore Spencer and Mark Van Doren, *Studies in Metaphysical Poetry* (New York: Columbia University Press, 1939), and Joseph E. Duncan, "The Revival of Metaphysical Poetry, 1872–1912," *PMLA* 68 (1953): 658–71.

   4.   H. J. C. Grierson, *Metaphysical Lyrics & Poems of the Seventeenth Century* (Oxford: Clarendon Press, 1921), xxxvii.

   5.   Frank Kermode, ed., *Andrew Marvell: Selected Poetry* (New York: New American Library, 1967), vii–xxx; Creaser, "Marvell's Effortless Superiority," 403–4; Warnke, "Play and Metamorphosis," 30.

   6.   These figures are based on Dan S. Collins's *Andrew Marvell: A Reference Guide* (Boston: G. K. Hall, 1981) and the annual bibliographies of the Modern Language Association.

   7.   Based exclusively on Collins's *Reference Guide*.

   8.   Cleanth Brooks, "Literary Criticism," *English Institute Essays 1946* (1947): 127–58; Douglas Bush, "Marvell's 'Horatian Ode,' " *Sewanee Review* 60 (1952): 363–76.

   9.   Thomas N. Corns, *Uncloistered Virtue: English Political Literature, 1640–1660* (Oxford: Clarendon Press, 1992), 227–31. See also Wilding, *Dragons Teeth*, 114–37.

   10.   *Marvell: Modern Judgements* (London: Macmillan, 1969), 39.

   11.   Thomas N. Corns, *Uncloistered Virtue: English Political Literature, 1640–1660* (Oxford: Clarendon Press, 1992), 310, having examined the attempts of scholars to find a unified core of being in Marvell's works, concludes pessimistically, "Marvell does not hold together."

   12.   *Seventeenth Century Poetry: The Schools of Donne and Jonson*, ed. Hugh Kenner (New York: Holt, Rinehart and Winston, 1964), 444.

   13.   *Andrew Marvell: Modern Critical Views*, ed. Harold Bloom (New York: Chelsea House, 1989), 1.

   14.   Philip Larkin, "The Changing Face of Andrew Marvell," *English Literary Renaissance* 9 (1979): 149–57 (156).

Selected Bibliography

PRIMARY SOURCES

Collected Works

Grosart, Alexander B., ed. *The Complete Works in Verse and Prose of Andrew Marvell*. 4 vols. The Fuller Worthies' Library. Privately printed. Blackburn, England: 1872–1875. Reprint. New York: AMS Press, 1966. The only complete edition in the last two centuries and still the only source since the eighteenth century for *Mr. Smirke, An Account of the Growth of Popery*, and *Remarks upon a late Disingenuous Discourse*.

Guffey, George R. *A Concordance to the English Poems of Andrew Marvell*. Chapel Hill: University of North Carolina Press, 1974. An alphabetical list of all significant words, the context lines, and a list of words in order of frequency, based on Margoliouth's 1952 edition.

Kermode, Frank and Keith Walker, eds. *Andrew Marvell*. The Oxford Authors. Oxford: Oxford University Press, 1990. Excellent one-volume modern-spelling edition of the poems in the 1681 order and *The Rehearsal Transpros'd: Part One*.

Margoliouth, H. M., ed. *The Poems and Letters of Andrew Marvell*. 2 vols. Oxford: Clarendon Press, 1927. 2d ed., 1952. 3d ed., revised by Pierre Legouis and E. E. Duncan-Jones, 1971. The standard modern edition of the poems (vol. 1) and letters (vol. 2). Includes many satires of disputed authorship and rearranges the 1681 order of the poems. Each volume fully annotated.

McQueen, William A. and Kiffin A. Rockwell, eds. *The Latin Poetry of Andrew Marvell*. Chapel Hill: University of North Carolina Press, 1964. Prints the text of each poem, with a brief introduction, an English translation on the facing page, and a following commentary. Includes the Latin epitaphs on John and Edmund Trott and on Jane Oxenbridge.

Smith, D. I. B., ed. *The Rehearsal Transpros'd and The Rehearsal Transpros'd, the Second Part*. Oxford: Clarendon Press, 1971. An old-spelling edition, with an introduction and 78 pages of textual and explanatory notes.

SECONDARY SOURCES

1. Books and Parts of Books

Andrew Marvell: Poet & Politician, 1621–1678. An exhibition to commemorate the tercentenary of his death. Catalogue compiled by Hilton Kelliher. Published for the British Library by British Museum Publications Ltd., 1978. A catalog of 115 exhibits, including life records, manuscripts, portraits, maps and drawings, letters, seal rings, pages (especially title pages) from early editions of Marvell's works, each exhibit accompanied by a brief commentary, each of the nine sections preceded by a biographical sketch. Well over 100 photographs.

Bradbrook, M. C. and M. G. Lloyd Thomas. *Andrew Marvell*. Cambridge, England: Cambridge University Press, 1940. Reprint 1961. Still an excellent brief biographical and critical study, sensitive to Marvell's various styles.

Brett, R. L., ed. *Andrew Marvell: Essays on the Tercentenary of His Death*. Oxford: Oxford University Press for the University of Hull, 1979. Four perceptive essays on Marvell's life, his sensibility, and the major trends in criticism of his verse.

Chernaik, Warren L. *The Poet's Time: Politics and Religion in the Work of Andrew Marvell*. Cambridge, England: Cambridge University Press, 1983. Detailed analysis of Marvell's satires and prose treatises maintains that they defend the liberty of individual conscience against absolutism, espousing ideas and attitudes associated with Milton and "libertarian Puritanism."

Colie, Rosalie L. *"My Ecchoing Song": Andrew Marvell's Poetry of Criticism*. Princeton: Princeton University Press, 1970. Devoted almost entirely to the lyrics, especially to "The Garden" and "Upon Appleton House," this study argues that Marvell's poetry constitutes a summing up and a criticism of all the traditions within which he worked.

Collins, Dan S. *Andrew Marvell: A Reference Guide*. Boston: G. K. Hall, 1981. Lists and summarizes accurately over 1000 writings on Marvell from 1640 to 1980.

Condren, Conal and A. D. Cousins, eds. *The Political Identity of Andrew Marvell*. Aldershot, England: Scolar Press, 1990. Seven essays which apply the methods of new historicism in an attempt to establish Marvell's political identity and religious affiliation.

Craze, Michael. *The Life and Lyrics of Andrew Marvell*. London: Macmillan, 1979. Although it is not an academic study and has no central thesis, this work is full of original insights and is sensitive to poetic form and to classical and biblical allusions.

Cuthbert, Denise. *The Poetry of Andrew Marvell*. Sydney: Sydney University Press, 1993. Excellent brief treatment of Marvell's lyrics, concerned less with explication than with raising questions based on a combination of formalist, new historicist, and feminist perspectives.

Donno, Elizabeth Story, ed. *Andrew Marvell: The Critical Heritage*. London: Routledge & Kegan Paul, 1978. Reprints entire or in part over 100 critical responses to Marvell's work from 1673 to 1923.

Empson, William. *Some Versions of Pastoral*. London: Chatto & Windus, 1934. This detailed analysis of "The Garden" is among the first studies in the twentieth century to recognize the intellectual complexity of Marvell's verse.

Estrin, Barbara L. *Laura: Uncovering Gender and Genre in Wyatt, Donne, and Marvell.*
    Durham: Duke University Press, 1994. Feminist readings of "Damon,"
    "The Gallery," "The Nymph," and "Upon Appleton House."
Friedenreich, Kenneth, ed. *Tercentenary Essays in Honor of Andrew Marvell.* Ham-
    den, Conn.: Archon Books, 1977. Fourteen essays on various aspects of
    Marvell's poetry.
Friedman, Donald M. *Marvell's Pastoral Art.* Berkeley: University of California
    Press, 1970. Taking the term *pastoral* in a broad sense, provides detailed
    discussions of most of the lyrics and the Cromwell poems.
Hunt, John Dixon. *Andrew Marvell: His Life and Writings.* London: Elek Books,
    1978. Biography designed to associate Marvell's life and writings with
    his times. Noteworthy for its many illustrations (66 plates).
Legouis, Pierre. *André Marvell: Poète, Puritain, Patriote, 1621–1678.* Paris:
    Didier, 1928. Translated and abridged by the author as *Andrew Marvell:
    Poet, Puritan, Patriot.* Oxford: Clarendon Press, 1965. 2d ed., 1968. Still
    the standard biography even in abridged form. More valuable as a record
    of Marvell's life than as a criticism of his works.
Leishman, J. B. *The Art of Marvell's Poetry.* Edited by John Butt. London:
    Hutchinson, 1966. 2d ed. 1968. Best single source for Marvell's acquain-
    tance with and borrowings from the lyric poetry of the ancients and of
    the seventeenth century. Argues that Marvell transmuted his borrow-
    ings, making them into something unmistakably his own.
Norbrook, David. "Marvell's 'Horatian Ode' and the Politics of Genre." In *Liter-
    ature and the English Civil War*, edited by Thomas Healy and Jonathan Saw-
    day. Cambridge, England: Cambridge University Press, 1990, 147–69.
    Reads the poem as a response to the political situation in 1650 and a cel-
    ebration of republican virtues.
Patrides, C. A., ed. *Approaches to Marvell: The York Tercentenary Lectures.* London:
    Routledge & Kegan Paul, 1978. Reprints 15 lectures delivered at the
    University of York covering many aspects of Marvell's poetry.
Patterson, Annabel M. *Andrew Marvell.* Writers and Their Work. Plymouth,
    England: Northcote House, 1994. A strikingly original, sometimes cryp-
    tic introduction to the man and his writings. Especially good on biogra-
    phy and the peculiar ways in which editors have treated Marvell's poetry.
———. *Marvell and the Civic Crown.* Princeton: Princeton University Press,
    1978. Argues that the political and satirical works reveal the same
    artistry and innovative skill as the lyric poetry. Provides detailed analysis
    of the "Painter" poems and *The Rehearsal Transpros'd.*
Rees, Christine. *The Judgment of Marvell.* London: Pinter Publishers, 1989.
    Thoughtful discussions of the lyric poems, incorporating a wide range of
    scholarly views and very full bibliographic notes.
Summers, Claude J. and Ted-Larry Pebworth, eds. *On the Celebrated and
    Neglected Poems of Andrew Marvell.* Columbia: University of Missouri
    Press, 1992. Twelve essays dealing with Marvell's lyric and political

verse, and a panel discussion on the special nature of Marvell's achievement.

Summers, Joseph. *The Heirs of Donne and Jonson*. London: Oxford University Press, 1970. Perceptive analyses (especially of "The Garden") based on an appreciation of the unique qualities of Marvell's lyric and satirical poems.

Wallace, John M. *Destiny His Choice: The Loyalism of Andrew Marvell*. Cambridge, England: Cambridge University Press, 1968. Argues that Marvell consistently viewed English history in providential terms and traces his devotion to decorum, modesty, and moderation in the Cromwell poems, "The last Instructions," and the prose works.

Wilcher, Robert. *Andrew Marvell*. Cambridge, England: Cambridge University Press, 1985. Perceptive discussions of the lyric poems, especially in relation to themes and images common to seventeenth-century poetry.

Wilding, Michael. *Dragons Teeth: Literature in the English Revolution*. Oxford: Oxford University Press, 1987. Contains essays on the political significance of "An Horatian Ode" and "Upon Appleton House," as well as useful footnote citations of relevant scholarship.

2. Articles

Berek, Peter. "The Voices of Marvell's Lyrics." *Modern Language Quarterly* 32 (1971): 143–57. Argues that because Marvell's speakers are limited and inadequate to their experiences, the poems present not a systematic philosophy but a set of unresolved conflicts.

Brooks, Cleanth. "Literary Criticism." *English Institute Essays 1946* (1947): 127–58. Argues that "An Horatian Ode" shows a tension between the speaker's admiration for Cromwell's virtues that have won him power and his disturbing realization that such power can be maintained only by unrelenting exertion.

Bush, Douglas. "Marvell's 'Horatian Ode.' " *Sewanee Review* 60 (1952): 363–76. Responding to Brooks, contends that the speaker's attitude toward Cromwell is an unambiguous admiration for the man who has become an instrument of God.

Campbell, Heather. "Burlesque in Marvell's *The Rehearsal Transpros'd*." *English Studies in Canada* 6 (1980): 263–76. Discusses Marvell's skillful use of techniques based on Buckingham's *The Rehearsal*.

Creaser, John. "Marvell's Effortless Superiority." *Essays in Criticism* 20 (1970): 403–23. Argues persuasively that readers must recognize the balance of levity and seriousness to appreciate the delicate poise and the joy of Marvell's lyrics.

Eliot, T. S. "Andrew Marvell." *Times Literary Supplement*, 31 March 1921, 201–2. An enormously influential statement that defines Marvell's wit as a blend of levity and seriousness, "a tough reasonableness beneath the slight lyric grace," a combination found in English literature only in the seventeenth century.

Herz, Judith Scherer. "Milton and Marvell: The Poet as Fit Reader." *Modern Language Quarterly* 39 (1978): 239–63. The argument—that each poet influenced the other—is broadly focused, not always convincing, but full of interesting verbal, thematic, and structural parallels.

Hirst, Derek and Steven Zwicker. "High Summer at Nun Appleton, 1651: Andrew Marvell and Lord Fairfax's Occasions." *The Historical Journal* 36 (1993): 247–69. Contends that every detail in "Upon Appleton House" is a response to the dilemmas facing Fairfax in 1651; the speaker is a character developed to allow Marvell to teach his patron tactfully.

Kermode, Frank. "The Argument of Marvell's 'Garden.'" *Essays in Criticism* 2 (1952): 225–41. Argues that the poem offers no difficulties if one understands the traditions of the genre to which it belongs.

Parker, G. F. "Marvell on Milton: Why the Poem Rhymes Not." *Cambridge Quarterly* 20 (1991): 183–209. In addition to a perceptive reading of "On Mr. Milton's Paradise lost," provides an analysis of the peculiar character of Marvell's verse in its combination of seriousness and levity.

Richards, Judith. "Literary Criticism and the Historian: Towards Reconstructing Marvell's Meaning in 'An Horatian Ode.'" *Literature & History* 7 (1981): 25–47. Contends that interpretation of the poem requires an understanding of seventeenth-century ways of viewing the world and of the language in which these views were expressed.

Spinrad, Phoebe S. "Marvell and the Mystic Laughter." *Papers on Language and Literature* 20 (1984): 259–72. Argues that Marvell was able to convey the serious and comic sides of things simultaneously, allowing the reader to perceive his own absurdity in the foolishness of the speakers.

Thieme, J. A. "The Metaphysicality of Andrew Marvell." *Language & Literature* 2 (1974): 69–77. Contends that Marvell's wit involves a self-conscious extravagance; unlike Donne, he laughs at the metaphysical approach.

Warnke, Frank J. "Play and Metamorphosis in Marvell's Poetry." *Studies in English Literature, 1500–1900* 5 (1965): 23–30. Argues that a full response to Marvell's art requires an awareness of his playfulness.

Young, R. V. "Andrew Marvell and the Devotional Tradition." *Renascence: Essays on Value in Literature* 38 (1986): 204–27. Useful discussion of the "religious" poems, arguing that Marvell stands outside the devotional tradition and implicitly criticizes its aims and methods.

Index

Aikin, John, 151
Aitken, G. A., 158, 160
Allen, Don Cameron, 167n2, 170n2
Anderson, Linda, 169n3
Anselment, Raymond, 175n6
Aubrey, John, 1, 11, 150, 152

Bacon, Sir Francis, 22, 95, 97
Belsey, Catherine, 172n6
Benson, A. C., 157–58
Berek, Peter, 170n16
biblical references, 41–42, 61, 93, 100, 113
Bickley, Francis L., 159
Bloom, Harold, 164, 176n13
Bossy, Michel-André, 170n17
Bradbrook, Muriel C., 12, 166n1, 166n7, 168n12, 170n1
Brett, R. L., 165n1, 166n12, 167n6
Brockbank, Philip, 169n6
Brooks, Cleanth, 163, 172n8, 176n8
Browne, Sir Thomas, 22, 159
Burnet, Gilbert, (bishop of Salisbury), 175n7
Burroughs, Franklin G. Jr., 173n18
Burton, Robert, 22
Bush, Douglas, 163, 176n8
Butt, John, 166n1

Caesar, Julius, 107, 108, 173n18
Campbell, Thomas, 159
Carew, Thomas, 22, 31, 33, 90, 101
Carey, John, 175n2
Chambers, E. K., 158
Chambers, Robert, 154–55
Chambers, William, 154
Charles I, king of England, 6, 24–28, 37, 41, 105, 107–8, 110, 139–41, 163, 171n8
Charles II, king of England, 4, 6–8, 111, 121–22, 125–26, 131–33, 136, 138, 140–42, 147
Chernaik, Warren, 166n15, 175n6
Chibnall, Jennifer, 175n5

Christie, W. D., 157–58
Clarke, Andrew, 166n18
Cleveland, John, 13, 22, 101, 121
Clifford, Thomas, 12
Coleridge, Hartley, 153–54
Coleridge, Samuel Taylor, 159
Colie, Rosalie L., 167n2, 169n3, 169n5, 169n8, 169n10, 169n15, 171n9, 172n9, 172n12, 173n14, 173n16
Collins, Dan S., 176n6, 176n7
Condren, Conal, 165n5, 175n14
Cooke, Thomas, 151
Coolidge, John S., 173n18
Cornewall, Theophila, 85
Corns, Thomas N., 176n9, 176n11
Cousins, A. D., 165n5
Cowley, Abraham, 13, 20, 22, 101, 152, 153, 172n5
Crashaw, Richard, 22, 80
Craze, Michael, 165n3
Creaser, John, 170n3, 170n4, 176n5
Croft, Herbert, (bishop of Hereford), 145
Cromwell, Elizabeth, 4
Cromwell, Mary, 20, 166n14
Cromwell, Oliver, 2, 4, 5, 7, 10, 28, 40, 48, 105–10, 111–13, 115, 127, 130, 131, 138, 141, 154, 163, 173n17, 173n18, 173n21
Cromwell, Richard, 4
Cullen, Patrick, 170n3, 171n11
Cummings, R. M., 169n7

Daniel, Robert, 172n2
Daniel, Sir Thomas, 124
Davenant, William, 14
Defoe, Daniel, 151
Denham, John, 116
Dionysius of Halicarnassus, 167n4
Donne, John, 13, 14, 20, 21, 22, 48, 79, 80, 84, 87, 88, 90, 102, 116, 155, 158, 159, 160, 161, 162, 167n1, 171n6, 171n11, 171n13, 173n16, 176n12

183